Tickbox

Tickbox

How it is taking control of

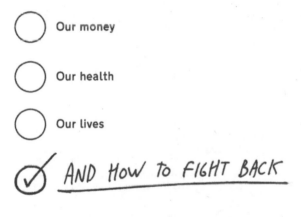

○ Our money

○ Our health

○ Our lives

✓ AND HOW TO FIGHT BACK

David Boyle

Little, Brown

LITTLE, BROWN

First published in Great Britain in 2020 by Little, Brown

1 3 5 7 9 10 8 6 4 2

Copyright © David Boyle 2020

A CIP catalogue record for this book
is available from the British Library.

ISBN 978-1-4087-1187-3

Typeset in Caslon by M Rules
Printed and bound in Great Britain by
Clays Ltd, Elcograf S.p.A.

Papers used by Little, Brown are from well-managed forests
and other responsible sources.

Little, Brown
An imprint of
Little, Brown Book Group
Carmelite House
50 Victoria Embankment
London EC4Y 0DZ

An Hachette UK Company
www.hachette.co.uk

www.littlebrown.co.uk

For Ursula, with love

Contents

When you try to grab a fish, it slips right out of your grasp; so how do you get a hold of it? You use a net. In the same way, we use nets to hold on to the wiggly world. If you want to control a wiggle, you've got to throw some kind of net over it. That's our foundation for measuring the world – nets with so many holes across and so many holes up and down to help us determine where each wiggle is in terms of holes in the net and this is how we break up wiggles into bits. ... But in nature, wiggles don't come 'pre-bitted.' That's just our way of measuring and controlling patterns and processes. If you want to eat a chicken, you have to cut it up in order to take a bite – it doesn't come already bitten. In the same way, the world doesn't come thinged.

Alan Watts, *Out of Your Mind*, 2004

There are dead zones that riddle our lives, areas so devoid of any possibility of interpretive depth that they seem to repel any attempt to give them value or meaning. They are spaces, as I discovered, where interpretive labour no longer works. It's hardly surprising that we don't like to talk about them. They repel the imagination. But if we ignore them entirely, we risk becoming complicit in the very violence that creates them.

David Graeber, 'Dead zones of the imagination', London School of Economics, 2012

1

Little Boxes

There's a pink one and a green one,
And a blue one and a yellow one,
And they're all made out of ticky-tacky
And they all look just the same.

'Little Boxes', Malvina Reynolds, 1962

It was on 27 February 2013, when Anthony Bryan applied for his first British passport at the age of fifty-nine – to visit his mother in Jamaica – that the trouble started.

There were reasons, or at least explanations, why this simple application caused as much trouble as it did. The coalition government still had two years to run, but the Home Office was firmly under the control of the immigration 'hawks', including Theresa May. The anti-immigration UKIP had won an unprecedented 150 council seats. Something had to be done, and the immigration department of the Home Office was about to do it. This was, after all, the period when the Home Office had been preparing its controversial 'GO HOME OR FACE ARREST' posters. The issue was becoming overheated.

And so it was that immigration officials saw Mr Bryan's non-standard application. Since arriving in the UK in 1965 (or thereabouts), he had never gone abroad again, so he had never needed a passport. Even so, he was surprised and concerned when they told him he was 'illegal', and made a note to that effect on his electronic file.

It was the first inkling of what was to happen to him over the next four years, caught in a nightmarish Kafkaesque world presided over by those same officials, which left him drained and nearly bankrupt. They were operating various different kinds of software, all based on the same 'tickbox' system designed to simplify the immigration process and make it easier and faster to administer – for the officials, not necessarily for the applicants. Over the following months and years, the system simply refused to believe him, putting him through hoops requiring evidence that he consistently provided but which it refused to accept – leaving him finally battered, penniless and unemployed.

It is the way we increasingly automate decisions about people's lives by ticking boxes that this book is about. It is a peculiar business, this 'tickbox' which was blamed – along with a great deal else – for Anthony Bryan's ordeal. It is partly a description of how people use software, partly a metaphor for the gulf between those taking decisions based on inflexible rules and those on the receiving end, and partly a new way of understanding the phrase 'square peg in a round hole', which was the old way in which we communicated the same bundle of ideas, particularly in previous generations subject to boneheaded military bureaucracy – a characteristic defined beautifully by the military historian Richard Adams as 'oppressive attention to marginal detail'.[1] This covered everything from dressing tall recruits in short trousers (and vice versa) because that was what they were given, right through to Catch-22, and all the rest – deliberately designed, in the USA at least, to prevent soldiers from thinking too much.

'When you think of the long and gloomy history of man, you will find more hideous crimes have been committed in the name of obedience than have ever been committed in the name of rebellion,' wrote the novelist C. P. Snow. He was referring to the Nazis, but this is dangerous stuff for anyone, as we will see.[2]

Yet tickbox is also something new, it seems to me. It is the word we have given to the algorithm-driven world we now live in, where so many decisions have been taken out of human hands and devolved to apps using information derived from the boxes we have ticked – or where people behave *as if* that were the case, surrendering their human judgement. This book is my attempt to pin down the meaning and to understand the implications.

For me, *tickbox* is a noun as well as an adjective. It has a mind of its own and seems determined to take every decision. This would clearly be nonsense, were it not for the fact that those who run the world appear to be determined to automate decisions along the rules they have set. Those who believe in this post-bureaucratic vision are in power across the world, leading in my view to the kind of widespread disaffection that is currently turning the world inside out (though not yet upside down). The greatest advocates of tickbox live in the best-paid management consultancies. The greatest believers run government departments – especially, for some reason, in the UK. The greatest tickbox gurus are those who own the vast IT companies of Silicon Valley.

They also believe, as data experts, that measuring things is more important than doing things. There is a Scottish proverb: You don't make sheep any fatter by weighing them. This is what a friend of mine, the director of a volunteering charity, told the Home Office official responsible for their grant for the following year. He told me later about the look of rage and horror that spread over the official's face in response.

It is certainly true that I am peddling a heresy that is profoundly shocking to those who run the world. In fact, that is one of my main motivations for writing this book. What I believe

I am doing, however, is naming a modern scourge, one we are supposed to accept as part of modernity, but is actually something else – a phenomenon that is taking slow control over our money, our health and our lives, stealing away our influence as customers, making public services ruinously expensive and, most of all perhaps, undermining our ability – even our desire – to act on the world.

Tickbox is a close relative of something a little more familiar: the numbers, targets and key performance indicators (KPIs) which underpin it, and which so infuriatingly tend to miss the point. For example, it leads services to concentrate on ticking the boxes rather than helping their customers, wasting vast sums of money producing inaccurate figures. Some years ago, there was a revealing fly-on-the-wall documentary about the security staff at Heathrow Airport, which demonstrated that by far their greatest concern was not catching potential terrorists. It was identifying the fake travellers sent by their managers to test their adherence to protocols.

Perhaps that amounts to the same thing, but I am not convinced that they use the same kind of intuition to sniff out the former that they would do to detect the latter. Imagine that state of affairs prevailing in every service, public or private, when the attention of staff shifts to meeting their batteries of targets and KPIs, because their bonuses depend on them doing so. Imagine their frustration as they go through the approved motions to tick the boxes, rather than meeting the needs of their clients. There is the impetus of the iron rule-of-thumb which has become known as Goodhart's Law, of which more in Chapter 4.

These kinds of KPIs and targets have a particularly ludicrous effect on policing. There was the child arrested for throwing a slice of cucumber and the man cautioned for 'possession of an egg with intent to throw'.[3] Would he have been arrested had it not been for the targets that encouraged arrests? Small changes in definition also have dramatic effects. Bag-snatching used to be defined as lost property until the 1930s, while minor vandalism became defined as criminal only in 1977 – doubling the crime rate overnight, and fuelling some of the angst about rising crime that followed.[4] The point is not whether these definitions are right or wrong – the criminalisation of bag-snatching definitely seems like progress – but that these feed through into statistics which seem entirely objective, but are actually tweaked as much by definitions as they are by real crime trends.

This kind of centralised control, public and private, tends to suck in everyone else's time. In Dickens' Circumlocution Office (the dismal bureaucratic morass where Arthur Clennam is forced to discuss the debtors' prison in *Little Dorrit*), those running this circularising office – armed with batteries of Victorian statistics (the Victorians loved their figures) – regarded themselves as defending the integrity of the system. They did not mind, as tickbox doesn't mind, that it is a nightmare for anyone who has to deal with them. It is the system that matters.

And so it is that if you are a fully qualified teacher, applying to be a teaching assistant, you will find you have to go through the whole disclosure procedure for criminal records again, even though you are up to date in your previous role. This kind of absurdity is part of a wider problem – it is what happens when generic HR departments take over from local or specialised personnel staff, perhaps also covering more than one local authority area, and probably lacking any understanding of or interest in education. It is one of the hidden ways that shared services – the current buzzword in administrative circles – tend to add to costs. In a tickbox world, where boxes replace human bureaucrats, then all the effort and responsibility falls on us.

Tickbox subsumes all these examples. It includes the peculiar way in which the numbers miss the point, which I first discovered listening to Alan Milburn, as Labour Health Secretary, congratulating the NHS on the rising number of prescriptions they issue, without asking whether that figure was related to health. In the same way, it meant Victorian statisticians trying to measure the morality of children by counting the number of hymns they knew by heart. But then previous ages were more alive to the way that numbers or data were used to manipulate. During the First World War, according to David Lloyd George, the War Office used to keep three sets of figures – one to delude the cabinet, one to delude the public and one to delude itself.

It also means, not so much the process of ticking boxes, which may sometimes be the right response – but the belief that you can replicate the world in this way, can take effective decisions, that the data represents reality. What I mean is not so much the algorithm itself; I mean the attitude that lies behind that algorithm among those who manage the world. That is why I personalise it by using the term 'tickbox', as if I was describing something alive – because I regard myself as facing down an attitude which, taken together, has some monstrous elements.

So when people complain about tickboxing, as they increasingly seem to do, what do they mean? The answer is that they mean something more informal than the phrase means in its strict dictionary definition. In other words, tickbox has taken on layers of meaning that were never quite intended by the people who write the forms, the programs and algorithms designed to manage us.

When we use the phrase 'tickbox solution', we refer normally to the fact that it isn't actually a solution at all. That is why I humbly define tickbox as an automated solution that is at one remove from reality. That gap between appearance and reality turns out to be very important, as it was for Anthony Bryan.

Tyranny by KPI

Tickbox pretends the whole world is a computer program. So you need to be absolutely precise to communicate with it, and this was the danger faced by people in Anthony Bryan's situation. They were being asked about details of their lives decades before, when they were children, and they could not be precise. On the face of it, Bryan had as much right to live in the UK as anyone else. It was just that, because he had arrived in the mid-1960s, on his brother's passport, he had no proof of actually entering the country. The old landing cards had been destroyed by officials back in 2010, at the beginning of the period when Theresa May was formulating her 'hostile environment' for illegal immigrants.

Mr Bryan's problem was shared with a number of others in the so-called Windrush Generation, broadly those who came to the UK from the Caribbean between the first arrival of the *Empire Windrush* at London docks in 1948 and Enoch Powell's inflammatory 'rivers of blood' speech in 1968: his papers were not in order. Like them, he had arrived unrecorded as a baby or child, and had needed no passport since. Yet, under the Immigration Act 1973, he not only had the right to citizenship, but he could apply for an indefinite delay before applying for it. He knew that, and so did his family and friends. The difficulty was to persuade the Home Office system of this.

From there, the pressure began to mount. Capita, agents of the Home Office, began to phone him and ask him for evidence to support his claim. He was a painter and decorator and self-employed, so for a time this seemed difficult to provide. But Mr Bryan did the sensible thing and consulted a solicitor. The solicitor told him that, when you have lived in a nation since the age of nine – especially when that was five decades ago – you are bound to leave some documentary traces, whether at school or via your bank account or what you pay in tax. Sure enough, he had.

There were thirteen years of National Insurance contributions, a letter from a former partner describing the three children she'd had with him, and a letter from his son confirming the story. There were birth certificates to confirm it further, plus payslips and photos. But then came the real bombshell. None of this evidence seemed to make any difference. The immigration services' tickbox system rolled inexorably on. By August 2015, the Home Office decided that, if Mr Bryan could not provide precisely what the system demanded at the right moment, that meant there was no evidence and that he had no 'leave to remain'.

MPs on the Human Rights Select Committee decided later that the 'hostile environment' policy, in practice, meant 'failing to treat individuals as deserving of respect and basic dignity'. The hostility had by then been extended from illegal migrants to anyone who might just possibly have entered the UK illegally. 'We found the Home Office's approach to, and handling of, Windrush immigration detention cases dehumanising and deeply problematic,' the committee said in its report on Bryan and another migrant. 'In both cases, multiple opportunities to resolve [their] cases and to confirm their status were missed. They were seemingly treated with suspicion and incredulity despite consistent information and evidence, supported by multiple witnesses confirming their life stories.'

In fact, it was worse than that. The experience of dealing with the system was itself alienating in the extreme. 'No support was offered to individuals navigating such a complex immigration system,' said the report, 'in which it seems even the officials did not know which laws and rules to be applying and instead presented an obstructive attitude of simply asking individuals for more and more impossible historic evidence and resorting too readily to detention if this was not satisfied. Indeed, there seemed to be a lack of a basic culture of humanity, care and respect in dealing with people.'

The difficulty is that tickbox encourages people to believe that any job can be organised on the basis of a production line and split up into its constituent parts. This makes it hard for the next person to understand the missing informal knowledge – maybe something a patient said during the night, or other nuanced peculiarities such as those from tax cases. It also takes no account of the kind of attention to detail staff will give cases when they are doing the whole thing, which is why mistakes have rocketed since HM Revenue and Customs took an assembly-line approach.[5] It did this in the mid-2000s in a programme called PaceSetter when, with the help of the tickbox consultancy McKinsey, it imposed on its procedures the whole business of assembly-line management, as thought up by Frederick Winslow Taylor (whose role in the development of tickbox we will explore in Chapter 2). It was by all accounts a demoralising period of data and stopwatches. One staff member told researchers: 'We never see the finished product. Senior management use statistics to lie to us to pretend things have improved. We are treated like imbeciles …'[6]

Since then, the number of tax inspectors who deal with each return has increased from two to six – even though staff numbers have been cut – and every one of those handovers is an opportunity for confusion, misunderstandings and mistakes (perhaps that is why a million people now pay the wrong amount of tax every year).[7] The more work gets sorted, batched, handed over and queued, the more it has to be done again. It is the same in offices, where nobody sees the whole job, except – theoretically at least – the distant manager, poring over the misleading statistics on the screen.

Whether it was an honest mistake or not, by the end of summer

2015, Mr Bryan's application for leave to remain, which he had been told to submit, was marked 'REJECTED' and he was told he had been turned down because of 'insufficient evidence'.

What on earth had been going on? You don't expect this kind of behaviour from all-powerful officials in the UK – in Soviet Russia or a Middle Eastern dictatorship, perhaps. Which is why MPs gave so much attention to Bryan's story.

But putting the story in the context of the 'hostile environment' was not enough of an explanation. It implied malevolence, which did not really seem to be there. The system was operated by otherwise sane people, many of them recent asylum seekers or immigrants themselves. Treating people in this way while going through the process goes far beyond creating a hostile environment, and – if you have the resources – it could be challenged in the courts, quite apart from anything else. Something else was happening, and it went back some time before Theresa May's period in office.

Lunar House in Croydon, Ground Zero of the UK immigration system, has always had a terrifying reputation for inefficiency and inhumanity. But I found myself, as I researched this book, increasingly sympathetic with immigration staff, caught between their sense of humanity and a system that seems to take no account of individual cases or shades of grey, operating 'in a constant state of crisis', according to one rare whistleblower, when often they have only recently arrived in the country themselves.

It is one peculiarity of the Home Office worker bees that so many have recently survived the system themselves. That may be one reason why so few whistleblowers come forward. Most of those working there want to support their beleaguered colleagues under pressure, but they are also aware that speaking out may undermine their own leave to remain in the UK.

Part of the problem of tickbox, like old-fashioned bureaucracy, is that it can encourage groupthink. It shifts the attention of organisations away from what the public want, what their users need or what their customers might like – and fixes their attention almost exclusively on what their managers want. And what their managers want is often to make the best impact on the company hierarchy. Then the argument shifts, almost imperceptibly, away from 'Is this launch safe?' (I'm thinking of the space shuttle *Challenger*), or 'Is this cladding the best thing for the tenants of this tower block?', or 'Can we do better for this patient?' – to 'Are we meeting our KPIs?'

Look at the most disastrous public service failures, like that at Mid Staffs Hospital, and you find that staff often turn on the handful of courageous whistleblowers for letting the side down – never mind how many patients have been allowed to die of neglect. Take, for example, primary care in north-west London, where there are 379 surgeries and 750 contracts; there are also a terrifying 30,000 key performance indicators for the clinical commissioning groups (the so-called CCGs) to meet.[8]

Few of these KPIs are silly by themselves, but they are ridiculously detailed – and there are so many of them Here is ND1, for example:

> Proportion of babies registered within the CCG both at birth and on the last day of the reporting period who are eligible for newborn blood spot (NBS) screening and have a conclusive result recorded on the child health information system (CHIS) at less than or equal to 17 days of age.

And here is NH1:

> The proportion of babies with a no clear response result in one or both ears or other result that require an immediate onward

referral for audiological assessment who receive audiological assessment within the required timescale.

These are both Public Health England KPIs, but they certainly impact on CCGs.

Perhaps the silliest is the target for ambulance and A&E services to get more than a 15 per cent response rate to the Friends and Family Test question: 'How likely are you to recommend our service to friends and family?' As if most people would be *recommending* their situation to anyone in those circumstances. My understanding is that the response rate is hardly ever reached. A friend of mine was told by an A&E receptionist that they had to hide the feedback box, especially at weekends. The problem was that a few drunk patients got into the habit of throwing up in the feedback boxes, so that they could say: 'That's how likely I'll be to recommend it!' Mental health and Prison Service NHS staff have mainly refused to collect data about recommendations, for the sake of their own safety when they ask the question.

The effect of all this numerical detail is to strangle any other conversation about the NHS in north London – like, for example, caring for patients. It gives us a fake, simplified and mechanistic view of what is undoubtedly a complex system – but complex in a different way. Anyone who thinks differently looks as if they are missing the point, but it is actually the system that misses the point.

As this book will show, this is part of what might be described as the simplification – not to say vulgarisation – of the official mind. And it is already having consequences. Because, in immigration for example, simply importing a hostile environment policy fails to explain the sheer incompetence of the system, and its staggering ability to lose precious documents and then demand more. In 2017, the *Guardian* investigated cases of lost birth certificates, children's passports going missing, education certificates disappearing and the misplacing of appeal bundles. The most serious was the case of a woman who had lived in the UK for twenty-one years, who was refused leave to remain and whose documents were never returned. She found herself in a fearsome international limbo. 'The situation has left her suffering significant financial losses,' the newspaper wrote.[9] Recently, at least four examples have come to light of people waiting for more than two decades for a decision. It puts Dickens' Circumlocution Office to shame.

The former borders and immigration inspector, John Vine, told MPs that the issue of lost documents features 'in every inspection'. During one of his inspections, 150 boxes of post, including correspondence from applicants, MPs and their legal representatives, were discovered in a room in the immigration office in Liverpool. To put this into some kind of context, a friend of mine, originally from North Africa but working in south London, sent his passport to the Home Office to apply to visit his family. The office then promptly lost it, which meant he could not make the journey, even though his mother was dying. When he asked his MP to take up the case, he was told that two years was, in comparison to other similar cases, not nearly serious enough. 'Come back in a year's time,' he was told.

There was no suggestion that the case workers at the immigration service responsible for Anthony Bryan's documents had lost any of them. The problem was not that they had lost them; it was that they had failed to look at them. Whether this failure to look applies to everyone from Russian oligarchs to refugees, I don't know, but I fear the worst.

Part of Mr Bryan's problem was that he could not remember whether he had arrived in 1957, 1965 or 1966. Nor could he – and this was the crucial bit – provide the four items of proof that he had been in the UK for every year since 1973, which was what tickbox required. Which may be why he was taken into custody, although only in September 2016 – the wheels of the Home Office grind slowly. But at this point, his partner of five years, Janet, intervened and the evidence began to mount. She provided photographs of five of his children, and his solicitor found evidence of NI contributions going back to 1972. The Home Office response: his request for temporary release was refused.

That was how Mr Bryan found himself behind bars in his own country. His son was dying in hospital and he could not visit him. His mental state was such that he was now prepared to capitulate.

'They gave me plane tickets to send me back to Jamaica, a country where I didn't know no street,' he said, describing how his time in detention had broken him. 'I was ready to go back to a country that I didn't know because I didn't see any other choice. I just wanted to get out of the cell.'[10]

Luckily for Bryan, his MP Kate Osamor intervened and asked the Home Office to investigate. It released him pending an investigation, but refused to discuss his case with her on the grounds of data protection and privacy.

But at this point, the Bryan story just gets crazier. Having released him from custody, the IT system began to flag up the fact that his boxes had still not been ticked. It seemed obvious to the tickbox mind that he should be arrested again – where, after all, were the four items of proof for every year of residence that he had been asked for? Since events move at snail's pace at the Home Office, it was not until a year later that it arrested him again pending deportation. Then in November 2017, his solicitors secured a stay on his removal from the UK through the courts, and received a letter from his primary school confirming when he had started. Bryan was released again. Even so, it was not until February 2018 that the Home Office finally accepted he had every right to be here.

No simple malevolence could manage something like that. It is a bit like people who drive obediently into a river, or the path of an oncoming train, because their sat-nav system tells them to. For some reason, the immigration system has developed a kind of boneheaded stupidity. And there are now projects to research the fates of all the other 850 cases similar to Anthony Bryan's, and which seem to have resulted in at least some wholly unjust and unwarranted deportations. A similar tickbox system is employed to manage the lives of claimants of all kinds, though the requirement for four items of proof has now been relaxed.[11]

The Home Office defended itself to MPs, claiming that the detentions were the result of 'a series of mistakes over a period of time', but officials were unable to give the committee details of any action that had been taken to stop such mistakes happening again. 'We did not find that explanation credible or sufficient. We take the view that there was in all likelihood a systemic failure,' its report concluded. Instead, the Home Office blamed the system.

The system. It is a catch-all phrase, but taken literally, it does actually get to the nub of things.

A non-straightforward case

The release was a little brutal as well. Paulette Wilson was another example, along with Anthony Bryan, taken up by the select committee of MPs in its investigation. Her daughter had been banned from the reporting centre when her mother became confused during her immigration interview. This was Wilson's evidence to MPs about the day the immigration officials finally accepted she had no case to answer.

The day I was released, they put me outside the airport. The man who let me out said, 'A cab is going to pick you up and take you to the station.' I was outside the airport. I was in tears, crying, because the planes were just taking off over my head. I had to stand and squeeze my head. I was praying for this taxi man to come and pick me up. They shoved me out. No one stayed with me. I waited for the cab. The cab man came. He said, 'Are you Paulette Wilson?' I said, 'Yes.' He put me in the cab and took me to the station. From the station, they gave me a travel warrant to get from here back to Wolverhampton, and that was it. I was on the Underground. Then I got to Euston and I was put on the fastest train back to Wolverhampton. They have not said anything to me ever since.[12]

Anthony Bryan had also been abandoned by his tormentors, so to speak. He told MPs that he had been facing bailiffs because of the legal debts he had run up trying to make his case. It was, for both of them, an unpleasant end to an appalling experience.

Meanwhile, the Home Office is under new leadership, having officially rid itself of the targets for removing people. It might be a good moment to consider in a little more detail what went wrong, and how it could treat long-standing, law-abiding people with such cruel and deaf disdain.

Parts of the answer are obvious. The Home Office has lost almost a quarter of its budget during the austerity years. Yes, there was also a deliberate policy to make life uncomfortable for illegal migrants – which, in practice, meant making life uncomfortable for legal ones too. Then there was the business of shredding landing cards from the 1960s, before demanding proof that people were unable to produce. Especially when, like Anthony Bryan, they had arrived as children travelling on their family passport.

We should not perhaps condemn the destruction of the cards in itself. Back in 1837, the government took a similar decision to clear the old wooden tally sticks representing government debt back to the Middle Ages. An enthusiastic functionary put them all in the parliamentary boiler, which overheated as a result and burned the place to the ground. You can't, in other words, leave these things to mount up. What was a problem was demanding that people should prove their arrival when the evidence had been destroyed.

Neither was the real problem targets in themselves. Yes, there were tough targets for excluding people, just as there were targets for the processing of applications. But it was the way those processes were organised that we need to look at more closely.

It may have been no coincidence that Anthony Bryan ran into real difficulties in 2015, because that was when the immigration service took the decision to reorganise its IT system, and to make savings by removing some of the human teams that roved around seeking out potential injustices and putting them right. The Home Office are the truest believers in IT solutions in a civil service of true believers. It is one of the reasons so much money is made from central government by IT consultants for systems that work fitfully at best.

I should say at this point that – during a brief period working at the Cabinet Office in 2012–13 – I had a government computer that took ten minutes to turn on every morning, requiring ten password stages, four of which were never available. I could have bought a computer which turned on within seconds at any supermarket, but somehow the government had trussed itself up in a support agreement with its IT supplier (Fujitsu, in this case) which really benefited nobody but Fujitsu.

This is not a book written to spread scepticism about technology. Quite the reverse. But there are two problems with the Home Office approach to technology which go to the heart of the tickbox problem.

The first is that, as we shall see later in this book, if you try to make decisions about complicated people – and everyone is pretty complicated, let's face it – using automated, IT or tickbox systems, then you find they don't do it very well. Complicated, non-standard people – potentially most of us – get bounced around the system until officials manage to find a way of ducking the case and sending it on to somebody else.

Asylum case workers are anyway under pressure to label their cases as 'non-straightforward'. This means those cases can simply be put aside so that staff have time to process visa applications, which earn money for the department – and for which, of course, there are targets too. In fact, in this simple example, we can begin to see how tickbox systems start to interact with money flows until it is difficult to disentangle them.

As a result of this, by March 2017 about half of all immigration applications had been designated as non-straightforward. This meant, for example, that even pregnant women were routinely expected to wait two years before their decisions were made. By then, only a quarter of non-straightforward cases had been reviewed. 'Sometimes, they don't even have time to read the applications properly,' one whistleblower told the *Guardian* by the end of the year.[13]

The second problem is that human beings, at the moment – and they may always do – provide the very best way of dealing with complexity, especially when fine judgements or a whiff of humanity is required. Which is a problem when your managers don't believe this and are under financial pressure to believe otherwise. One of the reasons the truest believers in IT solutions can be found at the Home Office is because it seems to provide a way out which will let them escape the other twin options – either failure, or confrontation with their political masters, neither of which are very attractive things with which to decorate your CV.

Another whistleblower emerged from the Family and Human Rights Unit, which decides visa applications for the husbands, wives and parents of British and European nationals. In a chronically understaffed department, with case workers expected to decide complicated applications after just a few weeks of training, it was hardly surprising that the whistleblower revealed that cases were being delayed by eighteen months by the end of 2017. There was a backlog of 49,000 cases – each one representing a family in agonies of indecision, their lives on hold, sometimes with illness or worse hanging over them.

But at least there was still a human being who was supposed to view them. The problem was that this was a period when eighty-five different immigration databases were in the process of being put onto the Cloud – where information is held on the internet, rather than on banks of computers in the Home Office – by Cap Gemini and Amazon Data Services. This project appears to have been delivered successfully enough for the consultants to win an IT award for it, stressing that it was about 'allowing the department to take a more person-centric view of immigration applications'.[14]

This is rather a giveaway, and is clearly an attractive dream. But of course, decision-making software can only ever be as good as the system you embed in it. So don't let us blame the IT system: the real problem – and there is a clue here about the treatment of Anthony Bryan and the other 850 Windrush Generation applicants threatened with deportation – is the tickbox system at the heart of it.

In fact, it is easy to imagine – since the two events coincided – that the Cloud project award reassured the department enough to abolish their fail-safe roving human teams. Either way, that is what happened. The teams would no longer be needed, or so they thought. And so it was that immigration officials came to believe you could automate humanity, when in fact their tickbox system of decision-making had already removed it. If you use a tickbox system to try to make a series of complex decisions about human beings in a consistent or objective manner, or to remove the human element, then in the end it hollows out your institution.

Fine to tick a box to order a pizza, or vote, or pay your council tax, or do anything simple and measurable – we do it every day. But if the element of human oversight is removed, or if complexity is replaced by a kind of fake simplicity, then common sense and a sense of humanity are both removed. If you add in targets – another critical element of tickbox – then that process will happen even faster.

That is how immigration officials came to persecute Anthony Bryan and others. The ubiquitous tickbox had replaced their brains: they paid attention to the over-simplified descriptions for each tickable box, and only that. If there was no box that said 'exercise a little common sense, why don't you' (and there wasn't), then they didn't. They had only wanted to do good as individuals, but they reckoned without the tickbox process that hollowed them out as well.

By 2018, the immigration service was already forking out another £10 million to replace their 1995 Casework Information Database (CID) with a new tickbox system called Immigration Case Work, which would bring together their different databases.

This was just the latest attempt. The previous one, dating back to 2014 and called the Immigration Platform Technologies, had cost over £200 million by the end of 2017. Then there was the 2008 Immigration Case Work system, written off in 2014 at the cost of £347 million.[15] By April 2018, 'digital change managers' were being recruited on a day rate of £1000. By this time, the old system was having outages as often as once an hour. We ought to feel a little for the human beings at the heart of this dysfunctional machine – applicants and staff alike.

Among the problems they found was that the CID had never been designed for immigration and so had no boxes for recording actual or potential legal challenges – which surely would have flagged up Anthony Bryan's case as problematic. But instead of a human team, they organised a parallel database called Jira that would record anything with legal implications. It went live in 2016. Jira is used also by the Ministry of Justice and HMRC and is a definite improvement. It is made by the software provider Atlassian and is designed to encourage teams to work together and check each other's work. The difficulty is that, when the first inspection took place in 2017, only the immediate team had access to Jira, which rather defeated the purpose.[16]

Still, it was immediately clear to Home Office managers that some kind of extra human intervention was going to be needed. They set up 'virtual litigation teams', which met every two months or so to review any cases that seemed likely to land them in the courts. In the following year, they also set up 'detention review teams' to oversee Jira.

The Home Office has never come up with a detailed explanation about why it detained Anthony Bryan and others like him, so we don't know if he reached Jira at all. But we do know that one of the patterns that the review teams began to recognise was that the courts were backing entrepreneurs who had been refused indefinite leave to remain because of 'discrepancies in the applicants' financial returns to the Home Office and to HM Revenue and Customs'.

And here we find ourselves encountering another characteristic feature of tickbox systems. They don't ask *why* there are discrepancies, or whose mistake it might be, because that would require human intervention and nobody has time for that. The mere fact that there is a disagreement is enough: in fact, the tickbox system adapts so that discrepancies indicate lies on behalf of the applicant. So, if the tax system or your bank makes a mistake, the Home Office assumes it was yours. They reduce the possibilities for multiple meanings. They reduce and curtail language. Soon, if you disagree with the bank or the taxman, it means *you* must be wrong. Off with his head – chuck him out!

Again, this goes some way towards explaining why a group of human beings, individually intelligent and humane, can still behave with such cruel stupidity. When things have the sheen of hyper-organisation, people are more likely to believe the rules that are in place are justified.

At least the victims of sat-navs have only themselves or their driver to blame; the immigration service ruins lives all around it. And you need have no doubts about its basic purpose – we clearly need restrictions on entry to the UK – to see that.

Tickbox does the job it is actually designed for very well indeed. It is intended to force staff to make no judgements of their own and to leave their consciences outside the door. It wasn't me, they might have said – I just ticked the boxes. And when human beings turn themselves into machines – perhaps the strain would otherwise become impossible – well, that is what happens.

The all-seeing eye

It was the philosopher Jeremy Bentham's brother Samuel who designed the notorious Panopticon. He had the idea of a circular factory where one overseer could watch, and therefore control, the whole workforce just by sitting at the centre. Jeremy imagined instead the same design working as a prison, where one warder could watch a whole floor just by sitting in the middle. Or, as he described it in 1798:

The prisoners in their cells, occupying the circumference – The officers in the centre. By *blinds* and other contrivances, the inspectors concealed … from the observation of the prisoners: hence the sentiment of a sort of omnipresence – The whole circuit reviewable with little, or if necessary without any, change of place. *One* station in the inspection part affording the most perfect view of every cell.[17]

Bentham himself persuaded the government to buy the site for a prison like this; it was located on the northern embankment of the Thames where Tate Britain now stands. But the Duke of Grosvenor objected to the presence of a penal institution so near his property and it was never built, much to Bentham's rage. Even so, the idea is horribly modern: we don't need the manager to sit at the heart of an organisation any more – all they need to do is look at the target data to get that slightly delusory feeling of omnipresence.

Delusory because, just as Bentham would not actually be able to see into the minds of the prisoners, the roomful of target data about schools at the Department for Education in Whitehall can really tell them nothing of what is actually going on in classrooms. Yet Bentham's Panopticon has become a symbol of the apotheosis of tickbox. It is too simple to say that this is simply a strange philosophy that renders human beings, with all their intuition and judgement, into heartless machines. Nor is it just the way that our great institutions and hierarchies operate these days: by breaking skills, considerations or questions into their constituent parts and, by ticking boxes, providing the basic data needed to take decisions. Nor is it the way that IT now allows tickbox to take on a more sophisticated role, whereby the boxes provide the basic data that computers and cloud systems need to drive the machinery.

No, tickbox goes further than that. It represents the philosophy that human life would be better if all services, all government and all businesses could be run in this way, designed by a handful of programmers and maintained by a tinier elite who mind the machines of state – while the rest of us go shopping, lie on the beach or scrabble around for the next meal.

Tickbox is, in short, the great technocratic dream in which those who rule us have believed, at least until recently, but which they never debate in public. It is a dream of the huge IT behemoths, Google, Amazon and Facebook, who aspire to rule us.

Let's start with the positive side. It is a dream that we might opt out of those flawed decisions, which carry so much bias or racism or sexism when human beings make them, and hand them over to the batteries of algorithms and apps which run the world – while we relax in the knowledge that the job will be done. You can see why they like the idea – and you can see also why the Home Office in particular buys into it – encouraged by the IT consultancies which can smell the potential profits.

The trouble is that it doesn't work. Why doesn't it work? Well, for lots of reasons, but three in particular.

First, because – as we have seen – tickbox systems don't deal with variety very well. When you manage a range of people, then every other case will find you wishing there was another box to tick – for example, for the kinds of pretty conclusive evidence that Anthony Bryan was able to provide. Everyone has their particular issues and peculiarities, which a tickbox system will miss unless there are an infinite number of boxes to tick. Any tickbox system designed to manage people or human life in any way, or to process them, tends either to be ruinously expensive or to cost so much to run that it really isn't worth it.

Think of tickbox decisions like trying to sum up a court case – a complex human story that is eventually summed up by a judge – all boiled down and reduced to one tick in a series of boxes. Court cases are too complex to be treated in this way.

The second reason follows on from this: most of life, and especially human life, is not actually black or white, tickable or not tickable, on or off, dead or alive. There are acres of grey space in between which we navigate using language.

For me that is the best explanation for what the immigration service did to Anthony Bryan, and why the Home Office managed to get itself tied into such knots that it detains a staggering 30,000 people a year in immigration detention centres, at huge cost (about £34,000 a year per detainee) – mainly, according to the Bar Council, for administrative convenience.[18] In June 2017, about eighty of these people had been there for more than a year (the UK was the only EU country that imposed no limit on how long people could be held in this way). Because, when people are regarded as either illegal or legal, there is no room for shades of grey.

The third reason is linked to the way that language slips through the boxes, so to speak. The fluidity of language is exactly why Home Office managers want to run a less ambiguous system, which is perfectly understandable. So, like bureaucrats before and since, they choose numbers over words. They choose targets or key performance indicators, because these feel objective and hard-nosed.

But when it comes to anything that needs to be described using words, things get much more difficult. The back ends of tickboxes are descriptions. Those hard-nosed numbers are chained to words, and this makes them endlessly malleable. They are not objective at all – or at least, no more objective than the dictionary is. This has some peculiar side-effects, including a narrowing of the language until we forget that we don't know.

The final lines of the film *It's a Wonderful Life* see the characters giving a toast to 'George Bailey, the richest man in town!' Now, we know that 'rich' in this case doesn't refer to money. But there may come a time when only data on money is recognised by the term.

If we stop using this informal knowledge completely, we start to forget it is there, along with all the poetic ambiguity that goes with it. At that point, *It's a Wonderful Life* becomes completely incoherent. Or imagine we selectively breed human beings who are skilled at maths, because that is how we measure intelligence. The meaning of the word 'intelligence' would then have shrunk to the boundaries of the data, and the world of reality would follow suit. Or imagine that only our data denoted by Facebook emoticons counted as real emotions. How quickly would we forget about ambiguity or contradictory feelings once the language had shrunk?

For me, that particular problem is by far the most important. If we allow this peculiarity to change the way we understand words, it will represent the final victory of tickbox over life – the reduction of the breadth of the human mind to the limitations of data. It will be a victory for those who believe we can diminish human beings to blips on silicon – not because our skills at artificial intelligence have increased, but because we have started to regard human emotions as increasingly limited. 'On the one hand, they seduce us, we want them to contain, include and involve us,' wrote Bryan Appleyard about smart machines in *The Brain is Wider than the Sky*.[19] 'On the other hand, they demand that we become more "machine readable". We pay for inclusion and involvement by becoming more like machines.'

Nor can we escape this conundrum by measuring more objectively. The sad fact is that the data we collect reflects our own bias in subtle but fundamental ways, because of what data we choose to feed into the system. Virtual policing systems may note the higher level of arrests of black people and build that into their data banks. Virtual bank lending systems may note the postcodes of poorer areas and blacklist them without realising this will lead to biased lending patterns.[20]

This realisation emerged, as it usually does, the hard way, after the demise in 2016 of Microsoft's chat-bot Tay, a friendlier version of Amazon's Alexa or Microsoft's Cortana, which had been programmed to talk like a sassy teenage girl. The safeguards included a few obvious words which she was designed to ignore. But nobody appears to have realised what would happen once she started learning from her users. During her first day, the online world had trained Tay to compare President Obama to a monkey and to deny the Holocaust. Microsoft took her down, and some of the world's best-paid AI experts began to realise not so much that other AI systems could be subverted, but that they would only be as good as the data they learned from. Hence the worries about insurance data that goes back to redlining certain neighbourhoods, or beauty contests – like the AI version organised shortly after Tay by the Russians – that appeared automatically to sideline black faces.

Then again, one of the fundamental problems about boxes is that they appear to have boundaries. Something is either in or out, and the demand of top management or ministers is that we should usually fit neatly inside. I hesitate to use the management cliché of all clichés, but that does make it difficult – and increasingly so – to 'think outside the box'.

These days management writers urge us to leave any meeting at which we hear this particular piece of jargon.[21] It emerged partly out of the psychologist J. B. Guilford's famous nine-dot test. You were supposed to come up with a way of linking every one of nine dots arranged in the shape of a box using four straight lines, and without taking your pen off the paper. The solution (I'm giving it away here!) is that the lines need to go outside the area defined by the box.

For a long time in the 1970s, the phrase became a metaphor for creative thinking. Until another study found that, even when you tell people the answer, it hardly helps them solve it. Creativity has nothing actually to do with being either in or out of any box. What the old cliché did provide us with was an idea that you are unlikely to be very creative if you think too obsessively about whether an idea fits within the existing neat, intellectual framework.

A political insult

Most of the time, for most of us, tickbox just represents an irritation, one of many in modern life. Have you had trouble getting your address changed on your mobile phone bill? Or tried explaining via Gov.uk that you can't tax your new car without getting an MOT – but getting an MOT requires a tax disc? Or have you ever been asked to rate your bank's indifferent service on a five-point scale, or pressed the alarm button on the Underground, and found that nobody came?

If so, you have been tickboxed. You have been treated as a one-dimensional problem, in order to process you more *efficiently*, and you will have found that – although it is sometimes more efficient for the giant, faceless bureaucracies, public and private, that manage our lives – it isn't always very *effective*. Certainly not if you're on the receiving end.

But you must realise that tickbox is only marginally interested in the receiving end. It is obsessed with the *process* of delivery. Even when it sends you more tickbox surveys about what you think of the service, there is a certain sleight of hand: as I will explain.

There is, in any case, a much more serious worry about the tickbox world. It is irritating but it is also rendering the services we use pointlessly and expensively ineffective. And if our culture becomes unable to act on the world, we are much more seriously at risk – especially when the bundle of ideas around tickbox (that systems – including political ones – are delivered better auto-matically and without human intervention), then the global elite has seriously disempowered us all. And begun to invite a terri-ble backlash.

In short, we are all the recipients of advertisements and market-ing decided by tickbox. Data about our purchasing, our financial activities, our health and our viewing habits pours into the data-banks, to be diced and packaged like money (which is itself just data, mainly about borrowing and spending). We are drowning in the stuff, and it leads to an important paradox.

We are drowning in data from tickbox systems, but we seem to be losing our ability to make things happen. I believe these two facts are connected. The danger is that, just as junk mortgage bonds got mixed up with reliable mortgage bonds, rendering the whole bundle toxic, so junk data gets mixed up with the truth. Because tickbox finds the multi-dimensional human world diffi-cult, tickbox systems can produce streams of sometimes toxic data which we are expected to rely on because it is 'evidence-based', when it has actually veered a long way from the essential truth of the situation.

When I worked briefly in the Cabinet Office, the main and most prestigious task was drawing graphs for the Prime Minister. I've seen first hand how tickbox-generated data is a dangerous commodity. I am also only too aware that the tickbox phenom-enon isn't new – it's just a particularly new and virulent strain of an old virus. Previous generations have condemned bureaucratic systems, and bureaucracy made similar attempts to reproduce the real world, a phenomenon described by the pioneer sociologist Max Weber as an 'iron cage'. It certainly isn't new.

But there is a sense in which tickbox is the central story of our time, unremarked and largely untold, and is one of the most im-portant challenges – politically, economically and socially – before us. Yes, we may need to accept it and humanise elements of it. But we may also need to fight back. Because tickbox is not just a modern irritant; there is also a compelling argument that it is a block on human progress which goes to the heart of our economic problems.

Why, I ask myself, has the cynical meaning of the term 'tickbox' yet to bed down in the USA? I can't say I really understand this. Is it because of a serious lack of irony in American life? Is it that they trust software more than we cynical Europeans do? They did write most if it, after all. I might propose the latter, were it not that other European languages seem to lack a more sceptical meaning to the terms *case à cocher*, *kontrollkästchen* or *casilla de verificación*.

I don't know whether the reason we ascribe our own meaning to the term tickbox in the UK is that we are more cynical than our neighbouring cultures – or whether, perhaps more likely, we have had to face down a particularly virulent attack of tickbox here. Either way, the new, more negative meaning of the word 'tickbox' seems to have appeared in the early years of this century, just as IT was increasingly used as a model – or even a metaphor – for government as government regulation embraced the New Public Management wave from the USA. It referred to the new targets and key performance indicators even before these were actually connected to boxes one might tick online. Officials were ticking them, even if the rest of us were not yet doing so.

In the past ten years, the term tickbox has also become part of the language of political abuse, except that its full meaning – as set out above – still seems to slip through the fingers of the lexicographers, and is anyway usually also connected to other words. *Tickbox exercise* seems to imply that the system of control used by regulators or ministers has an emptiness or a pointlessness about it – a special kind of vacuity that is damaging because the tick does not refer to reality on the ground. Sometimes, I think, it implies that the tick has been put here *instead* of taking real action.

It is via phrases like these that the word has entered the political lexicon. As in, for example, 'Labour's unhealthy obsession with a tick-box culture has often been at the expense of competence and efficiency ...'[22] That was in an editorial in *The Times* in 2009, complaining about Labour's deputy leader Harriet Harman's plans to outlaw and tackle discrimination against northerners.

This is, of course, the kind of language that political oppositions tend to use against governments. The government changed in 2010, so soon Harriet Harman was using it herself. In government, she had been accused year in, year out by the website Conservative Home of being a kind of queen of tickbox – but, by 2018, she was using the term on radio to describe the immigration regime that so failed Anthony Bryan.

The only party which seems to use the term both in and out of government appears to be the Liberal Democrats. There was Steve Webb, pensions minister in 2011, talking about avoiding 'demoralising ... tickbox schemes'.[23] Then there was Vince Cable as Lib Dem leader in 2018 condemning Ofsted's inspection regime for turning education into a 'tickbox exercise'.[24]

The phrase seems to pop up more than most in schools or diversity monitoring, again normally in a context of action without action, of empty gesture politics. Here is the London primary school teacher Tricia Bracher:[25]

> No rise in pay or reduction in workload can compensate for the pain of an adult-driven, spreadsheet-ready objective replacing a child's joy in sharing what they actually know or what interests them. Only those who can harmonise – that is, those who can convince themselves that children would talk about targets even if they had not been specifically trained to do so – thrive in a system that fetishises the tickbox ...

Perhaps this is because there was a time when the UK Department for Education sold itself hook, line and sinker on tickbox, as it regards itself as the dashboard of the great British Education Machine. But since a friend of mine was employed as a learning assistant in a school where her teacher hid during most of the lessons in the stationery cupboard, abandoning the children – without apparently affecting the school's status in the league tables – I found this a little peculiar. More on the knotty issue of tickbox in schools later.

The other phrase you find occasionally, mainly in the *Daily Telegraph*, is 'tickbox society' – as in 'Britain's tick box society has forced a generation of police officers into playing the role of "jobsworths" too frightened to use their initiative for fear of fall-ing foul of procedures and targets ...'[26] This is from a Conservative newspaper complaining about the moral purpose behind the questions being asked. Or from doctors, complaining about the Care Quality Commission, under the headline: 'Never mind the patient, tick the box'.[27] This is from a more centrist political posi-tion, complaining about the inspection system.

The emerging theme appears to imply a meaning something along the lines of 'empty' or 'pointless'. Yet there is something else here. Perhaps it is the implication that the same gap between ap-pearance and reality can be glimpsed in other attempts to let the world run itself by numbers. It is rather like handing over govern-ment to the market to manage; you might believe in the impor-tance of market power, but it is another leap of faith entirely to say that every decision should be outsourced in this way. In the same way, you might have a few tickable lists to help with professional services, but it would be another matter to hand over every single decision to a giant tickable algorithm.

Maybe it is also implied that the gap between appearance and reality represented by tickbox is part of an explanation why so many people are so disaffected at the moment. They live with systems run by people who believe the tickbox numbers – who run the trains and hospitals and schools as if they referred to something in the real world. Those closest to these systems, who have to deal with them every day, are more aware of that gap than anyone else. Just as they are aware of the same gap in the economy – while billionaires in 2018 had their best year ever, the food banks in Birmingham ministering to the poor were running out of supplies. And despite all the vastly expensive regeneration programmes directed at the poorest areas in the UK over the past forty years, they appear to be as poor as ever.

Is that the fault of tickbox? In a sense, it is. Because it has led to a vigorous push against measurable symptoms rather than unmeasurable causes, and those taking the decisions are in the grip of the fog of delusion that I am calling 'tickbox'.

We are not talking about a mere irritation, a mere fleabite (*ticbox* perhaps). We are talking about a threat to the way we live. This book will tell some stories from the front lines of the tickbox wars – and will finally suggest a way out.

The checklist culture

It so happened that, as I sat down to write this book, I ran across its mirror image – a 2009 book apparently praising the same phenomenon, written by the surgeon and *New Yorker* essayist Atul Gawande, also chief executive of the new Amazon healthcare project. It was called *The Checklist Manifesto*.

There was a difference, of course, and you can see this running through what passes for a debate on these issues, at least a tendency to choose different kinds of language. If you disapprove, you call it tickbox. If you approve of it, you tend to call it a *checklist*.

And because I am genuinely in search of knowledge here, I immediately sat down and devoured *The Checklist Manifesto* to see why – on the face of it at least – we have been thinking so differently.[28] As Gawande sees it – and he is right – tickboxes and checklists emerged for the same reason: as ways of managing the increasing complexity of the world.

It certainly is ferociously complicated. I remember Vince Cable stomping around in a rage, early in his period as business secretary, complaining that he had done what he promised and changed the funding formula for further education, only to find he had inadvertently undermined funding for women in their fifties. He had not intended to do that. Nobody had warned him because nobody really understood the fiendishly complex funding formula, which is – like most of UK government policy – the sum total of every tweak, fudge and stitch-up going back a couple of centuries or so. In the same way, after I had laboriously persuaded Transport for London, back in 2001, to alter their Oyster card (a means of paying for travel) so that you could buy sweets and newspapers with it, nothing happened. Why? It turned out that the Oyster operator dared not make changes to another complex system, in case the underground gates failed to open the next morning. It wasn't worth the risk.

The World Health Organization now lists 13,000 different diseases, while we still expect doctors to somehow remember the whole lot. It is hardly surprising that negligence actions are rising so fast against them. The conventional solution hardly works very well either – we divide the knowledge into different specialisms. Then you find these new boundaries are defended with professional zeal: the specialists don't speak to each other much, and when you find, for example, links between back pain and depression or depression and inflammation, all you can do is employ two specialists rather than one.

Something else is required. Gawande hails the checklist.

He describes its invention following the fatal test crash of a B-17 Flying Fortress four-engined bomber at Wrights Airfield, Ohio, in October 1935.[29] It was already known that the separate checks necessary on each of the four engines made it a complicated monster to fly. It transpired that the test pilot – Major Ployer Hill, who was killed – had forgotten to release a brand new locking mechanism on the controls.

The committee of experts and pilots convened to make proposals for the future could have dodged the challenge and just called for better training. But they were honest with themselves, realising that Major Hill probably had more experience than anyone else in the air force. He could not have been better trained, but he could perhaps have been better prepared. So instead, they designed a checklist for all the processes that pilots had to go through, before, during and after take-off. And vice versa when it came to landing.

This is still how flying is done safely to this day. If you saw the film *Sully*, about the strange story of the Airbus 320 which landed in the Hudson River in 2009, you would see the co-pilot reaching for the checklists telling him what to do if both engines failed. It is a good system, and it has been extended to other situations, notably in medicine and building control.

Building control is an important case, because the building inspectors are not using their checklist to personally verify – for example – that the building teams have built the foundations or installed the damp proof course properly. It is to help them remember and to liaise with the professionals about what they should do. They can hardly dig the foundations up to check, after all. In other words, it shifts the responsibility downwards. 'Just ticking boxes is not the ultimate goal here,' writes Gawande. 'Embracing a culture of teamwork and discipline is.'[30]

In fact, as Gawande explains it, the purpose of a checklist is very different from tickbox. Checklists put the power back into the hands of professionals. The checklist is for them – and for all of us – to use; as many as thirteen million are said to use the website todoist.com.[31] Tickboxes are designed to achieve the opposite: to look over the shoulder of professionals from central headquarters, to remove their power and responsibility in the name of transparency or central control.

That is a huge difference. Checklists are designed to empower; tickboxes to disempower. Checklists have a belief in human judgement at their heart; tickboxes want it replaced by algorithms designed by the elite. They may look alike. They may derive from a similar process. But there is actually all the difference in the world between them.

Little boxes

It occurred to me at this point that the song 'Little Boxes', popularised by the American folk singer Pete Seeger, and quoted at the top of this chapter, might have some parallels with the tickable boxes I am writing about here.

Not on the face of it. The song was written by Malvina Reynolds after a journey through the suburbs of Daly City, California – like Los Angeles, immortalised by Gertrude Stein who said, after one visit, that there was 'no there there'. 'Stop the car!' Malvina said to her husband. 'I feel a song coming on!'[32]

But the little boxes made of ticky-tacky in the song were repositories for the identikit people and identikit suburban families who lived there, who – apart from the different colours – all went to university, where 'they all get put in boxes / and they come out just the same'. Perhaps, I wondered to myself, these boxes were the same as the little tickboxes, which also indicate – quite mistakenly in fact – that every example ticked, every human in that category, thinks, needs and wants 'just the same' too.

As such, the song is a little like this book. Both are, in their very different ways, complaints about the human spirit categorised by tickboxes, or stashed away in identikit boxes made of ticky-tacky. We are not all just the same, we both say. Nor do the tickboxes, connected as they are to the machinery of services, which require us to be identical to make us easier to process, describe the world very well.

We are not all made of ticky-tacky. We are not processable by tickbox or any other kind of box. We are, after all, what we are.

2

Towards a History
of Tickbox

The most entrepreneurial, innovative people behave like the worst time-serving bureaucrat or power-hungry politician six months after they have taken over the management of a public service institution.

Peter Drucker, *Innovation and Entrepreneurship*, 1985

Frederick Winslow Taylor rose to speak on the evening of 23 June 1903 at the United States Hotel in Saratoga, in upstate New York. He was a small, dapper, intense man, and his impact on the audience – if any – was not noted. But by the time he had finished speaking, he had in effect changed the world. He had laid the groundwork for the phenomenon I have called tickbox. Nor was it just tickbox; Taylor opened the way for the full range of management by numbers, targets, key performance indicators, and all the panoply of obsessive measurement which is so familiar to us a century or so later. Taylor's talk was the critical development of the idea that you can sum up a working task completely in terms of numbers, and reward the effort people might make along those lines.

Taylor was never known as one of the world's most inspirational speakers and his talk reads now as somewhat leaden. This was also one of the few times he spoke in public about his ideas. But then 1903 was an eventful year for management theory. Some months earlier, the pioneer car manufacturer Henry Ford had finished his experiments with assembly lines, which were also to play an influential role in the splitting up of jobs between different people, specialists or functions. The way Ford's assembly line spread out of the factory to society as a whole was described as 'Fordism' by the Italian Marxist thinker Antonio Gramsci.

The ideas that became 'scientific management' meant breaking every task down into units, measuring how long they took and setting targets for workers to meet. They have also been hugely influential. That is why a cultural historian like Martha Banta could describe Taylor's 1903 lecture as 'one of the key documents shaping ... modern industrialisation',[33] and leading management writer Peter Drucker call it 'the most powerful as well as the most lasting contribution America has made to Western thought since the Federalist Papers'.[34]

But it was Taylor who provided the numbers and the power of the stopwatch. This was at first an American phenomenon; though 1903 also marked the year the Oxford bicycle dealer William Morris decided to build cars, it took some years before the combination of 'scientific efficiency' and time–and–motion study crossed the Atlantic.

Taylor was addressing a meeting of the American Society of Mechanical Engineers on the subject of 'Shop Management'. By 'shop', Taylor meant the 'shop floor' of a factory. As far as he was already known to the meeting, it was as a controversial industrial manager who was supposed to have worked miracles of productivity at the giant Bethlehem Steel plant in Bethlehem, Pennsylvania, churning out steel plating for the world's battleships.

According to the historian E. P. Thompson in his classic 1967 essay on 'Time, Work-Discipline and Industrial Capitalism' watches have always been symbols of industrial servitude.[35] But there is also no doubt about Taylor's influence.

Forced by failing eyesight to leave Harvard in 1878, Taylor went to work at the Midvale steel plant in Philadelphia. Philadelphia was then one of the biggest industrial centres on the planet, the second biggest city in the USA, with a population of nearly 850,000, and responsible for more than 5 per cent of the nation's exports. In the six years before Taylor started work, three thousand miles of steel rail had been laid across America. The city's working population could be seen streaming off the dirty black ferries of the Delaware in the early mornings, or onto the horse-drawn trams, bound for the great smelters, locomotive works and carpet factories that were the source of the city's wealth.

When Taylor went to work at Midvale, the skilled craftsman, direct heir to the medieval craft or guild system, was the respected heart of any factory. Taylor was quickly promoted to sub-foreman, but he was determined to force former shop-floor colleagues into more productive methods. This earned him death threats. 'In all such cases, however, a display of timidity is apt to increase rather than diminish the risk,' wrote Taylor later. 'So the writer told these men to say to the other men in the shop that he proposed to walk home every night right up that railway track; that he never had carried and never would carry any weapon of any kind, and that they could shoot and be damned.'[36] They never did.

He laboriously analysed which tools were most effective and what kinds of steel were most productive to calculate how much work each employee should do each day. 'Scientific management' meant regimented experimentation and Taylor's experiments went like this:

1. Break down any job into its component parts – as far as possible, to the basic movements.

2. Next, time each of those parts with a stopwatch to find out just how quickly they can be achieved by the quickest and most efficient workers.
3. Get rid of any unnecessary parts of the job.
4. Add in about 40 per cent to the time, for unavoidable delays and rest.
5. Organise pay scales so that the most efficient people can earn considerably more by meeting the optimum times, while the average have to struggle to keep up.

This was the formula for efficiency that led to job cards, time clocks, inventory control and all the other paraphernalia of twentieth-century manufacturing. (You can see it to this day in the way Amazon manages the workers in its warehouses.) It was the system that made him famous at Bethlehem, where he put his ideas fully into practice. Bethlehem at the time boasted the largest machine shop in the world and a 90ft steam hammer – also the world's largest. But the American steel industry was reeling from a price-fixing scandal relating to the sale of armour plating, and desperately needed to find some way of cutting costs. Bethlehem's hopes rested on Taylor.

His big experiment started in earnest in March 1899, with his ten 'best' men, who immediately refused to carry pig iron on the basis of his formula and were sacked. Taylor then tried Dutch and Irish workers. They wouldn't budge either. By offering higher wages there and then, Taylor and his assistants managed to attract volunteers but, by the end of May, he reckoned he could only really describe a miserable three out of his team of forty as 'first class men'.

It soon became clear that even the three strongest men could only manage to carry weight for exactly 42 per cent of the day. Any more, and they got exhausted. All except one. He was called

Henry Noll – or Knolle, according to which account you read – although Taylor named him 'Schmidt' in almost everything he wrote, describing him as an ox and 'stupid and phlegmatic'. Noll was Taylor's great example: he was what he really wanted working men to be – focused, uncomplicated and compliant.

'If you are a high priced man, you will do exactly as this man tells you tomorrow, from morning to night. When he tells you to pick up a pig, and walk, you pick it up and walk,' Taylor told Noll. 'And when he tells you to sit down and rest you sit down. You do that straight through the day. And what's more, no back talk.'[37]

Noll was Taylor's breakthrough. His contention was that workers generally kept their employers in the dark about how hard they could work. Once he had identified what was humanly possible, he could fix day rates so that the workforce could earn more – if they worked more efficiently. By 1901, the workforce at Bethlehem was handling three times as much material as before and their wages were 60 per cent higher. He reduced the number of shovellers in their two-mile goods yard from 500 to 140.

But it wasn't enough. Taylor fell foul of management infighting, and they were already angry with him for all his sackings. As well as running the plant, Bethlehem needed workers to rent their homes, and it sometimes seemed as if Taylor was intent on emptying the company villages of tenants.

After his surprise dismissal in 1901, Taylor never worked as an employee again. Despite being the father of mass production, he was also the first of a breed of workers that would eventually displace the whole concept. He was the first of the new knowledge workers whose activities would undermine his own legacy – the first management consultant.

After his 1903 lecture, Taylor came to national prominence thanks to the future Supreme Court justice Louis Brandeis, who realised 'scientific management' could win a case he had undertaken against the railroad companies for raising fares. In fact, it was Brandeis who coined the term.

But Taylor's methods were extremely controversial. A series of strikes followed the introduction of his ideas in the vital American armaments factories, which in turn led to a series of gruelling congressional hearings. During one of these Taylor was subjected to eight hours of continuous questioning, after which he lost his temper so uncontrollably that his answers were struck from the record. He left immediately afterwards to take his wife – who was suffering from serious depression – on a Mediterranean cruise.

Three years later, he was dead. He died of influenza in hospital in 1915, in the early hours of the morning after his fifty-ninth birthday, immediately after winding his precious stopwatch.

There is no doubt that Taylor was a brilliant innovator. When he died, he held forty lucrative patents of his own inventions: a bobsled brake, a special tennis racket with a spoon-shaped head – and a gadget that stopped him rolling onto his back in his sleep. Sleeping on his back caused him to dream what he called 'disturbing thoughts'. Had he encountered his great contemporary Sigmund Freud – which unfortunately he never did – we might have a better insight into the 'disturbing thoughts' that led to such regimentation. And although Ford always claimed never to have read him – but then Ford claimed that he didn't read books at all ('They muss up my mind,' he said)[38] – the establishment of the first assembly line, at Ford's Dearborn plant in 1913, would probably have been impossible without Taylor and his endless measuring.

The two men had things in common. They both disliked financiers, and both claimed to be on the side of the workers. 'What really happens is that, with the aid of the science ... and through the instructions of the teachers (the experts) each workman ... is enabled to do a much higher, more interesting and finally more developing and more profitable kind of work than he was before able to do,' said Taylor.[39] But the workforces didn't see it that way. And they won: Congress banned time-and-motion study methods from government factories in 1915.

The trouble was that Taylor's ideal worker wasn't really human at all. He was a cog – an automaton who did what he was told. 'Every day, year in and year out, each man should ask himself over and over again two questions,' said Taylor in one lecture:[40]

> First, 'What is the name of the man I am now working for?' And having answered this definitely then 'What does this man want me to do, right now?' Not, 'What ought I to do in the interests of the company I am working for? Not, 'What are the duties of the position I am filling?' Not, 'What did I agree to do when I came here?' Not, 'What should I do for my own best interest?' but plainly and simply, 'What does this man want me to do?'

Hand in hand with this assumption – that the workforce had nothing to offer but brawn – was an enthusiasm for standardisation. 'My dream is that the time will come when every drill press will be speeded just so,' his assistant Carl Barth told the congressional hearings in 1914, 'and every planer, every lathe the world over will be harmonised just like musical pitches are the same all over the world … so that we can standardise and say that for drilling a one-inch hole the world over will be done with the same speed.'[41]

This caught the totalitarian spirit of the decade. Mussolini set up a propaganda arm of his government to promote Taylorism. Taylor's ideas inspired Lenin's director of the Central Institute of Labour, poet Andrei Gastev, to write 'Factory Whistles, Rails and Tower', based on the ideal of 'subordinating people to mechanisms and the mechanisation of man'. Lenin wrote in *Pravda* in 1919 that Taylor combined the refined cruelty of bourgeois exploitation with a number of the most valuable scientific attainments. 'We must introduce in Russia the study and the teaching of the Taylor system, and its systematic trial and adaption.'[42]

During the Cold War, the industry behind both American consumerism and Stalin's grandiose planning had Taylorism at its heart. 'The First Five Year Plan was written largely by American Taylorists and directly or indirectly they built some two-thirds of Soviet industry,' said the cultural historian and Canadian governor-general John Ralston Saul in his 1995 Massey Lectures. 'The collapse of the Soviet Union was thus in many ways the collapse of Scientific Management.'[43]

American historians tended to pay more attention to Taylor than did the British, with their traditional emphasis on the first Industrial Revolution (Mr Gradgrind was an obsessive measurer). They argue about his relative importance compared to the other time-and-motion pioneers, Frank and Lilian Gilbreth – who had the benefit of a 1950 Hollywood film about them, *Cheaper by the Dozen* (they had twelve children, which may have been why they needed to save time).[44]

But by then, with experience of how mass production could be misused – in the mechanical destruction of the Western Front and the concentration camps – Taylor's reputation had begun to suffer. If Aldous Huxley's novel *Brave New World* held up Fordism to ridicule, Yevgeny Zamyatin's dystopia *We* (1921) – which depicts a society where every mouthful of food has to be chewed exactly fifty times – was hitting back at Taylor.[45]

By 1973, a study by Harvard economic historian Keith Aufhauser was arguing that Taylor had simply borrowed his methods from the slave plantations. The idea that Taylor was actively de-skilling his workers – by refusing to let them think – was first put forward the following year by the Marxist historian Harry Braverman.[46] It is now the standard criticism.

Since then, though, there have been suspicions that Braverman's pre-Taylor idyll never really existed. Peter Drucker, probably the most influential management writer since Taylor, argues that Taylor shares the honour of having as much influence on the twentieth century as Freud and Darwin – more even than Marx. The rehabilitators say that, whatever his faults, Taylor was responsible – maybe more than anyone else – for the unprecedented wealth created by twentieth-century industry. Between 1907 and his death, manufacturing efficiency per employee went up by a staggering 33 per cent every year. In some ways, the modern industrial world has been basking in his success ever since.

But in another sense, this argument about his legacy has been taking place in an academic bubble. In the real world, you can see Taylorism everywhere: in call centres, fast food systems, targets and key performance indicators in exam results, even in the NHS. All owe their existence to Taylor's questionable but potent legacy. It was Taylor who coined the phrase 'the one best way'; Taylorism which peddled the idea that there is only one good way of doing any task – and that it can be scientifically measured – which is at the very heart of tickbox.

His bundle of ideas and practices influenced Morris Motors, as it did Ford, but generally speaking it was not until the emergence of the new industrial revolution of the 1930s – toothpaste factories, cereal factories, tinned fruit, tinned meat, tinned milk, tinned beans (to borrow from John Betjeman's poem 'Slough') – that Taylorism came to the UK, just as it was making the leap from industry to offices. Catalogue orders, sales invoices, information processing all began to come under Taylor's influence, from the blue-collar workforce to the white collars.

From there, it took only half a century or so – pushed forward by the increasing power of computing – for it to move from white-collar workers and begin to regulate the way that professionals work. Giving the impression of transparency, it shifted power from the professionals to their technocratic managers, just as Taylor intended it to do.

The birth of bureaucracy

To understand where the whole thing began, we have to go back to the Babylonian empire, and to the emperor Nebuchadnezzar II, who made it all possible. Why was it the Babylonians who invented such a sophisticated counting system, based on the number 60? Because they needed numbers to render the complexity of their vast empire, stretching from Cyprus to modern Iran, into something simple enough to govern from Babylon.

I have no idea of Nebuchadnezzar's personal capacity for nuance, but it simply did not cut the mustard when it came to governing so complicated an empire. Numbers were invented as tools of empire; they remain the way that centralised structures – imperial cities or corporate headquarters – maintain their control. And with the numbers that are reported into the heart of the machine come the need for all those tasks of empire: inspectors (to verify), counters (to do what they are told), collaters (to turn the numbers into reports for the emperor's aides), bureaucrats (to run the system). The Egyptian empire used to keep a record of every Egyptian and what they were paid. The Inca empire managed to maintain itself with accountants but no written alphabet. These systems pre-dated the huge increase in trade in Europe in the twelfth century, where numbers became an essential arm of business.

There is a well-reported tendency for the bureaucrat class to breed excessively (as a group, I mean, rather than as couples). The Roman empire under Augustus managed to run itself with just two thousand officials in Rome. The tens of thousands of bureaucrats employed by Rome four centuries later have been blamed by the archaeologist Joseph Tainter for providing the dead weight which brought the empire crashing down.[47] According to Tainter, there comes a point when societies need all the energy they have just to maintain their complex systems, at which point they are so overstretched that climate crises or barbarians at the gate are enough to finish them off. Organisations tend to serve themselves; absolute organisations tend to serve themselves absolutely. They serve the hierarchy, which adds layers of management, each layer making it more difficult for people to be effective, tougher for them to work their magic and harder for them to make change happen. It also makes the needs of the internal system far too important, and often turns the outside world – the clients and customers – into an irritating distraction.

The humorist C. Northcote Parkinson, whose management classic *Parkinson's Law*, published in 1958, explains that work expands to fill the time available, looked at the British Admiralty, and discovered that there were two thousand civil servants working there at the outbreak of the First World War in 1914 to administer a navy of 146,000 seamen. By 1928, just fourteen years later, that figure had grown to 3569 civil servants to manage 100,000 seamen. There are now only 33,450 personnel in the navy, and they and the other two services are managed by nearly 57,000 civil servants.[48]

But these are historians. The phenomenon of bureaucracy was barely noticed by contemporary writers until the second half of the eighteenth century. Only in 1764 did the French philosopher Friedrich Melchior, Baron von Grimm note that bureaucracies tend, first and foremost, to look after their own interests. 'Here the offices, clerks, secretaries, inspectors and intendants are not appointed to benefit the public interest,' he wrote. 'Indeed the public interest appears to have been established so that offices might exist.'[49]

It was no coincidence that it was pre- and post-Napoleonic France, highly centralised and authoritarian, where the word 'bureaucracy' emerged. The novelist Honoré de Balzac popularised the word in his novel *Les Employés*, defining it rudely as 'the giant power wielded by pygmies'. Thomas Carlyle called bureaucracy 'the continental nuisance'. In 1792 came the first expression of the idea at the heart of this book, when Prussian philosopher Wilhelm von Humboldt said he was afraid that people were being transformed into machines because the affairs of state were becoming mechanical.[50]

But it was the great liberal philosopher and Liberal MP John Stuart Mill who really got to grips with the idea, afraid that the more efficient the machinery of administration, the more it would monopolise the talent of the nation. Worse, it would monopolise the action too: 'Where everything is done through bureaucracy, nothing to which the bureaucracy is really adverse can be done at all.'[51] Then emerged probably the greatest theorist of bureaucracy, a young lawyer from Saxony called Max Weber. Weber's main intellectual wrestling was with the rise of a secular society and disenchantment with the modern world. Weber argued that every religion led to political and economic beliefs, and that the work ethic of Protestantism had led to the bundle of ideas that we know as capitalism.

Weber was able to see, as Taylor could not, that inflexible bureaucracies dehumanise and that big organisations tend to underestimate their employees and waste their abilities – because rules, procedures and regulations tend to suppress their creativity and problem-solving abilities. Weber identified the main replacement for the authority of the church in the modern world as what he called the 'rational-legal'. He was not clear, or not sure, whether this was a good thing or not. On the one hand, the bureaucratic mind is responsible for a series of improvements in the human condition. On the other hand, it tends to treat people as interchangeable cogs in a vast machine, and to trap us all in his famous 'iron cage'.[52] This phrase is all most people remember about Weber, but – although he coined it in 1904 – it wasn't translated to reach the English-speaking world until 1930. Nor is it quite clear what he meant.

Over the past century or so, the two minds of Weber have expanded into a political divide about bureaucracy. Broadly speaking, conservatives hate the idea as a symbol of state power, which they want to argue is inevitably inefficient; socialists want to argue the opposite.

In practice, it isn't quite as simple as that. Fascists liked bureaucracy as an elite group prepared to assist them taking power. And recent decades in the UK have seen social democrats like the Blair and Brown administrations developing targets, while conservatives like the Thatcher and Major administrations centralised power and both laid the foundations for tickbox as a result.

'One cannot visualise, in the conditions of modern society, the socialist organisation in any form other than that of a huge and all embracing bureaucratic apparatus,' wrote the economist Joseph Schumpeter.[53] 'Every other possibility I can conceive would spell failure and breakdown.' The problem is that this applies to any government that centralises power – not just socialist ones.

It was the emergence of the counterculture in the 1950s and 60s – equally hostile to bureaucracy – which tipped the balance against it. 'In saying that our system is bureaucratic, I mean primarily that decisions tend to be taken by the pressure of various organisations acting in the interests of their own apparatus,' said the Liberal leader Jo Grimond, speaking for a new approach.[54] A decade later, there were black leaders in the USA attacking the Department of Labor for assuming it was black lower-class families which needed restructuring, rather than the administrative system which was supposed to help them.

It was this assault on state institutions, led by maverick priests like Ivan Illich or renegade economists like Fritz Schumacher, or – all too soon – the whole weight of voluntary sector campaigners, which shifted our attitudes to bureaucracy. Were hospitals making people ill? Were industrial schools purveyors of stupidity and narrow-mindedness? Was the mental health system driving people mad? The answer seemed to be yes, at least enough for us to demand change.

Ironically, the solution has been to chop processes up into bits to make these institutions more transparent, so that we can look inside without mystery and see what is happening – or at least count it. This has to be one reason why the bureaucracy has renewed itself as tickbox.

You can get a whiff of this argument, which goes around and around, from the House of Commons debate in 1968 on a Conservative motion condemning the continued growth of bureaucracy. Speeches deplored the government's failure to reduce the numbers employed by public services. Then one MP said bureaucracy was only being measured in numbers. Quite right too. It is fascinating, in retrospect, that the only method our representatives could imagine, even then, to estimate the impact of bureaucracy was to count the heads of the bureaucrats.

Two years later, in his book *In Praise of Bureaucracy*, the sociologist Paul du Gay mounted an all-out defence of bureaucrats – and especially the idea that bureaucrats needed to think more like problem-solving entrepreneurs. 'We should not expect the bureaucrats to express morality,' he wrote. 'That is not their job. Their task is to be able to divorce administration from private morality ... The citizen who scoffs at the elaborate record-keeping undertaken by government offices might well be equally annoyed should an official lose track of their affairs through relying on memory and telephone conversations.'[55]

Du Gay particularly took issue with management writers like Peter Drucker and Tom Peters. 'Each and every one of you should develop a passionate and public hatred of bureaucracy,' said Peters in one of his inspirational, not to say visionary performances.

Du Gay responded with a quotation from Weber in his more rationalist mood: 'He who yearns for visions should go to the cinema,' the great thinker had said.[56]

As we will see, paradoxically, both du Gay and Peters turned out to be on the winning side. We don't have bureaucrats any more – at least not nearly so many of them – but we do have tickbox software instead. The bureaucrats have been pensioned off, leaving behind a concreted system which takes decisions automatically when boxes are ticked. It is worse than bureaucracy in that there is now nobody at the controls.

That is why you get these constant muddles. Like the ecstasy of categorisation involved in NHS mental health services, initially between 'depression' and 'anxiety', which is now the all-embracing divide in the NHS – and then to show how ill you are using the PHQ9 scale (for depression) or the GAD7 scale (for anxiety). These are self-scored, which means that professionals have to tweak the answers to avoid highs like falling in love or lows like losing one's job, which make them obviously less than objective. The only trump card is what they call, in the Pfizer instruction manual used by the NHS to manage these scorecards, 'suicide ideation' – which means, in humanspeak, wanting to kill yourself.

Even so, all too many do take that desperate step. An anonymous article appeared in 2017 in the *Guardian* by a children's physiotherapist-turned-NHS manager, whose friend took his own life after he had been unable ever to see a qualified mental health nurse, and when his final five NHS appointments had been with different people. The anonymous manager resigned after being asked to spend his time scrutinising his staff's travel claims and counting hand-washing training completions. 'I know hand washing is important. However, the focus was on hitting a percentage to prove compliance with training to senior managers,' he wrote. 'It was a tick box exercise, not one aimed at reducing infection.'[57]

Or when you start connecting your boxes, as the Japanese rail company Keikyu did in 2009, when they began using a computerised scanner to check the facial expressions of their staff to make sure they were displaying sufficient cheeriness. As many as 45 per cent of American companies now say they monitor employees' keystrokes – as if that will tell them anything useful.[58] The number of software systems that monitor employee computers has made monitoring a $200 million industry. One company found that eighty hours a month of employee time were spent watching cat videos.[59] But then some people work better with a few cats around, and you won't find that out by looking at their keystrokes.

Once you start to think about it, you can suddenly see it everywhere. Even the most mundane example is on the railway wifi website in front of me as I write: 'Tick the box that you are over 18'. I can think of few more pointless boxes to tick, though it might provide some legal cover for the company if I was a child and I strayed innocently into the dark web. It also reminds me of the early tickbox on the back of the US Immigration Department's entry form, which used to ask travellers to confirm that they were 'not planning terrorist action during your stay'.

The management consultant

If the first knowledge worker was Frederick Winslow Taylor, the man who applied his stopwatch to American factories, then the first management consultant was James Oscar McKinsey, a US army logistics officer who became a professor of accounting at Chicago University after the First World War. A copy of his text-book on accountancy – an exhausting read – is still available in the British Library.[60]

Taylor may have lost his head under cross-examination by a Congressional committee, but his followers were in great demand during the 1920s boom, to show how factories could work at the peak of efficiency by breaking down jobs into a few rational move-ments and measuring, measuring, measuring.

McKinsey shared some of Taylor's famous workaholism and puritanism, especially when it came to his children – he was in-clined to tell them that toys were non-essentials. He also believed that a similar approach could be applied to all businesses, not just factories. He thought that rigorous measurement could even help successful and efficient companies when it came to developing new strategies. A man with great charisma and huge confidence, he took the risk of launching himself on his own to apply his ideas to other companies. He set up McKinsey & Co. in Chicago in 1926.

It was one of those thrilling periods of economic expansion, and accountancy was busily transforming itself from an art into a science. The very first accountant in America, James Anyon, gave a valedic-tory speech in 1912 urging his successors to 'use figures as little as you can'. 'Remember your client doesn't like or want them,' he said, 'he wants brains.'[61] But Mac, as he was called, didn't see it that way.

It has never been clear quite who coined the McKinsey slogan 'everything can be measured and what can be measured can be managed', but that was certainly what McKinsey believed. The huge global influence of the company he founded is now clearly apparent, after more than nine decades, not only in most of the biggest companies in the world but in many of the most powerful governments too.

The impact of his slogan is also everywhere, and that goes some way to explaining why our contemporaries have been chopping up aspects of work into measurable chunks and exercising increasing control over the people who put them into effect. It explains a little about why, despite all the vast investment in IT, human capacity seems to have become so seriously constrained. Because the McKinsey slogan is a fallacy: everything *can't* be measured. In fact, the more important it is – love, learning, wisdom, imagination – the less it can be measured at all, and the more disastrous the attempt to do so tends to be. To the extent that McKinsey follows the dictates of its own fallacy, it is responsible for a great deal that doesn't work in the world we live in.

McKinsey himself didn't live to see his company become the elite in a new cadre of consultants worldwide. He made the mistake of getting too close to one client, the troubled Chicago department store Marshall Field, and – always infuriated when his advice was ignored – the further mistake of becoming the company's chief executive in order to put it into practice.

This was a stress-inducing error. He received death threats when he closed the wholesale division; the staff laughed at him when he expected them to sell lower-quality goods. He made bad buying decisions when prices were dropping. The company carried on losing money. By the beginning of 1937, owner Marshall Field III ran out of patience. He told McKinsey he would have to change his abrasive management style or go by the end of the year. McKinsey was shocked; he caught a cold, it turned into pneumonia and he died. He was only forty-seven.

The work of building the business that bore his name fell eventually to a former debt collector and lawyer, the editor of the *Harvard Business Review*, called Marvin Bower, who had risen to manage McKinsey's New York office. There were tensions with the Chicago office and eventually the two halves of the company split. The Chicago manager called his half A. T. Kearney after himself, and Bower kept the McKinsey name because it was more convenient.

Bower was formidable. He died as recently as 2003, aged ninety-nine, by which time McKinsey employed over nine thousand consultants in fifty-one countries, working for two-thirds of the Fortune 500 index and for thirty-five governments, and earning somewhere around $5.3bn a year. Bower was not only the author of McKinsey's success, he also the originator of some of its more peculiar quirks, especially those which contribute to its aura of mystique. One was obsessive client confidentiality, which Bower adopted in imitation of law firms; it means that McKinsey consultants never speak publicly, perhaps especially when everything goes wrong. We merely glimpse them in the distance, as the authors of learned articles in the *Harvard Business Review* or on their own blogs.

The other quirk is the extraordinary old boy network that extends across the globe. Once inculcated into the McKinsey way, and steeped in the McKinsey Fallacy (that everything can be measured, and so on), former consultants find their way into the highest echelons of government and corporate positions, and then employ their old colleagues for support in boardroom battles or when making strategic leaps of faith. What their customers seek is a whiff of this unworldly, monkish objectivity. They like the atmosphere where the consultants seem to measure everything, then emerge with their clipboards from technocratic purdah – the very heirs of Taylor and McKinsey himself – to reveal their solutions.

Let's pause for a moment and give rigorous measurement its due. It can take situations by surprise, so to speak, and grasp some insights that are waiting under the very noses of the existing management. That is the justification for management consultancy. But equally, there can be something akin to autism about this use of numbers to escape human relationships, in this case based on innocence of the world as it really is, and of the possibilities of human beings – especially service staff. The figures can blind even the superhuman to broader truths.

That might explain some of McKinsey's more famous disasters, in situations which required more understanding of the world than provided simply by a facility with measurement and analysis. Like recommending to AT&T that mobile phones were only going to be a niche market. Or urging Railtrack to sweat their assets – to cut back on track maintenance – immediately before the string of rail disasters caused by faulty track which forced the company into bankruptcy.[62] Or the collapse of its client Enron in 2001, the biggest bankruptcy in American corporate history.

Enron had a deliberately obscure business model, mainly based on energy trading, but was in many ways a creation of McKinsey's. Enron's CEO Jeff Skilling – later given a twenty-four-year jail sentence – was a former McKinsey consultant. There were usually between five and fifteen McKinsey consultants based at Enron's Houston headquarters, and senior McKinsey partner Richard Foster advised the board meetings in Enron's final year. McKinsey used Enron's apparent success as good marketing, praising its water investment in 1999 in *McKinsey Quarterly*, before Enron finally wrote off $300 million and escaped from the water business altogether. But when Enron went into administration, it took down its accountants Arthur Andersen with it, while McKinsey escaped apparently unscathed.

But then, of course, McKinsey consultants are actually like the rest of us. They don't, as the mythology suggests, measure the solution. They have a sense of what the problem is, they test that idea against the figures, then they modify it and test again. 'Figure out the solution to the problem before you start,' wrote former McKinsey consultant Ethan Rasiel in *The McKinsey Way*. 'This sounds counter-intuitive, but you do it all the time.'[63]

There they were in the years that followed, increasing their hold on the British government. By the end of the Tony Blair era, his Downing Street policy unit was stuffed with former McKinsey consultants, and former BBC director-general Lord Birt – in charge of Blair's 'blue skies thinking' – was also being paid a £100,000 retainer by McKinsey. He was offered the job after challenging Blair to a game of tennis, but the prime minister managed to block any leaks about the thinking that took place, and it never has emerged. Even so, McKinsey's fingerprints – their slogans and graphs – were everywhere, from Cabinet Office presentations to the handbooks of NHS managers. They're still there.

Under the hammer

To explain why bureaucracy is still with us, when the bureaucrats have pretty much gone, we have to go back a quarter of a century to the night that Al Gore developed the idea of his National Performance Review, which he used as a weapon of reform while he was vice-president. Among those who met Gore that snowy evening early in 1993, and persuaded him to back the idea of a review to reinvent government, was Bob Stone. Formerly the Pentagon's Deputy Assistant Secretary for Defense Installations, Stone worked out that about a third of the entire defence budget – probably amounting to $100 billion a year – was wasted because of poorly drafted regulations. He experimented by cutting the regulation book for forces housing from eight hundred pages to forty. One commander asked permission to let craftsmen decide for themselves which spray paint cans could be thrown away, rather than having each one certified by the base chemist. It was Stone who put together the original principles that would dominate the National Performance Review.

The review was partly a political response to the scandal of wasteful Pentagon spending, which had emerged in the months before. The cost of numerous simple items had ballooned by the time they had gone through armed forces bureaucracy – a serious lesson about centralised procurement. The coffee percolator bought by the air force for $7622 was the most spectacular, but the one that really caught the public imagination was a $436 hammer, or – as the Pentagon called it – a 'uni-directional impact generator', bought for the navy.

One of the first schemes launched under the review was an annual Hammer Award for public-sector employees who had made huge efforts to work more effectively. And that was the point. The review set out a series of principles for saving money by scrapping rules and bureaucracy and giving power back to staff. Then it urged them to go to it and told stories about their progress. It wasn't like the usual exercises along these lines in the UK, whereby huge bureaucracy regulates people's efforts even further. The staff were given the principles and asked to get on with it, and the results were publicised.

Regular newsletters were packed with suggestions. Abandon sign-in sheets and clocking-in machines. Buy equipment locally if you think you can get a good price. Waive the need for travel expense receipts for sums under $75. One of the key stories was about the Occupational Safety and Health Administration (OSHA) office in Maine, the equivalent of the UK's Health and Safety Executive. It consistently came top of the league for how much its employees were doing, for the most citations and fines, yet workplace safety in the state was still the worst in the country.[64]

When they realised this, the Maine office created a small revolution. They tackled the most difficult factories first, creating employee teams to solve the problems. If the companies agreed to support the teams, their inspections and punishments would be suspended. This too worked: the accident injury rate went down by two-thirds. It is a brilliant example of how you can humanise a service by dodging tickbox and starting with the human energy below. Why does it work? Because it is the inflexibilities in the system that ultimately waste money.

By 1995, OSHA's Maine office had pioneered a number of flexibilities, including reduced fines for small companies and anyone they believed had been acting in good faith – precisely the kind of flexibility that tickbox has been designed to root out.[65] The Federal Reports Elimination and Sunset Act 1995 ended hundreds of reporting requirements, with the rest to be wound down after five years unless they were specifically renewed. The 10,000-page Federal Personnel Manual was junked. Public organisations were allowed to recruit people however they wanted.[66]

The findings of Gore's Performance Review fed into a debate about how entrepreneurial cities should be. Since 1978, and the Proposition 13 vote in California – which cut tax receipts to local government in half and spread rapidly across other states – US cities had seen a catastrophic collapse in their tax income. They had been forced to become seriously entrepreneurial whether they wanted to or not. It was the only way to survive.

This was the height of the privatisation boom on both sides of the Atlantic, and the argument went that public institutions were more effective, responsive and flexible when they were run by the private sector. The same argument was repeated in the emergence of the so-called New Public Management movement, the idea that services should be set free from political control, to be managed remotely by a set of targets or indicators. This was before anyone grasped that targets were just as fatal as a way of centralising power, and they certainly never set anyone free.

As it turned out, New Public Management emerged in the UK rather differently from the way it had in the USA. American targets were about 'outputs'; they were about what you did. British targets were about process – they were more controlling because they tended to be about the way you did it. They also dovetailed with a very important shift indeed.

The tail end of Margaret Thatcher's government saw a flurry of activity around improving the way governments manage services. Thatcher had brought in Derek Rayner, the flamboyant chief executive of Marks & Spencer, who proposed that swathes of government would be better run like businesses. In 1988, her government set up the Next Steps Unit, run by a former Treasury permanent secretary, to establish a series of semi-autonomous units, each with its own chief executive. The Prison Service was one of the first, and they are now ubiquitous in nearly every area of administrative life. They had their own contracts and targets, as they still do: NHS England, the Environment Agency and all the other arm's-length agencies which manage our lives.

You can see why the politicians succumbed to the temptation. It appeared to give clarity to what they were responsible for and what they were not. What they did not see – nor, really, did anyone else – was how it would usher in the basis for tickbox: it would narrow down what we expect from the professionals who serve us to a series of measurable deliverables. Everything else then gets cut out – all the personal care and personal touches – because it is too expensive and can't be measured. It is the McKinsey Fallacy extended into every area of life.

But at the time, it seemed like a solution to the politicisation of our battered civil servants, after a decade in which Margaret Thatcher had been in charge, noting critically whether they were 'one of us' or not. 'I sometimes think that the advice going to ministers is suppressing arguments because it is known that ministers will not want them,' wrote one senior civil servant at the time, 'and that for me is a betrayal of the civil service.'

To solve the problem of this narrowing of focus, advocates of New Public Management in the UK began to pay more attention to customer satisfaction. It was a way of measuring broad so-called 'outcomes'. So when John Major's government came to put these ideas into practice in the 1990s, they came along with other initiatives – like the much-maligned Citizen's Charters – designed to persuade people to demand more from their services.

So from Frederick Winslow Taylor, via James Oscar McKinsey, it is possible to see a somewhat winding route towards the dream that was now taking shape – the idea that, with guidance from contracts and performance indicators, and with one eye on customer satisfaction ratings, services could run themselves. Without decisions from politicians, or from any human beings at all.

All that was now required was to remove the bureaucrats and the dream would be complete.

The cost of compliance

Cast your mind back to the year 2001. I stood for Parliament that year (Regent's Park and Kensington North; I came third) in the general election which marked the end of Tony Blair's first term in office. It had been a tumultuous four years in public services too – Gordon Brown had not stinted with the resources but, in return, he had constructed his own iron cage of targets to guarantee that managers would be accountable for the extra money. John Major's framework of outsourced administrations were suddenly outsourcing their own operations, attaching their former functions umbilically by contract. It was not privatisation, but it might as well have been.

To keep the managers to the straight and narrow (quite literally the narrow), as many as ten thousand numerical targets had been imposed, on everything from A&E waiting times to the state of sailors' teeth in the navy. It was done in the name of localisation and empowerment, but in practice it was absolutely the reverse.

What worried critics at the time was that the new regime was extremely expensive. The Treasury assumed that in order to restrain spending, iron central control was required. They had not grasped then – and may not have grasped even now – that iron central control is actually rather wasteful. Because someone has to pay for the whole edifice of targets, standards, inspections and audits which drive the centralised state.

How much do they have to pay? Well, by 2001, the cost of the various standards and auditing agencies was already £600 million a year. At the time they had barely begun to create the system which now so frustrates the effectiveness of public services. Five years later, the amount had doubled.[67] Every local authority also spent an average of £1.8 million simply on preparing for an inspection and showing that they were complying with targets – the cost of the effort of collecting figures and reporting back. That was just local authorities. We never knew the equivalent costs for health authorities, primary care trusts and police authorities, hospital trusts and other local quangos. But add that amount to the cost of the auditors themselves, and you might reach a figure somewhere around £4–5 billion a year by the end of the Blair–Brown years to pay for the basic infrastructure of target compliance.

To that, you would have to add in the cost of the time spent on compliance by front-line staff and the extra staff in local authorities or primary care trusts assigned to enforcing each target. Like the trading standards officers who had to subdivide all their visits into thirty different categories, on each of which they had to report. Or the child protection staff who had to spend up to 80 per cent of their time in front of computers, doing administration.

David Osborne, one of Gore's Performance Review founders, estimated in the 1990s that 20 per cent of American government spending was devoted to controlling the other 80 per cent, via armies of auditors and inspectors.[68] The review itself found that one in three federal employees were there to oversee, control, audit or investigate the other two.

In the UK, the situation then was almost as hazy as it is now. The first person to investigate the bizarre growth of auditing in the UK was the accountancy professor Michael Power. He estimated that 10 per cent of UK public spending went on auditing – again that estimate is more than a decade old – which might come to around £50–60 billion. There is some confirmation of this because, if you work it out the other way round – as Osborne did in the USA – it comes to somewhere around the same figure.

It was not just the public sector that was wrestling with these issues. The corporate world was doing the same, if less wastefully, as they handed over responsibility for managing their staff to the distant contract culture of the human resources department. It made sense to automate it as much as they could. The stage was set for a merger between the controlled time-and-motion world of Frederick Winslow Taylor and McKinsey measurement. Meanwhile the whole thing was being bundled up in new software that was creating a new straitjacket for employees, not only in factories but in offices too. That big idea came along in 1993 with the publication of the bestseller *Re-engineering the Corporation*, by mathematician Michael Hammer and computer scientist James Champy. Hammer had begun what became the 're-engineering' revolution three years before with a typically aggressive article in the *Harvard Business Review* called 'Don't Automate, Obliterate'. It was a management philosophy that denied there were such things as economies of scale. It said that it made no sense to split up the functions of a company and carry them out separately. They needed to be brought together in one system, and that meant that middle managers no longer had any real function.

Champy and Hammer behaved like prophets of the new way, with all the intensity of the Inquisition. 'Leniency toward those who refuse to co-operate with the re-engineering effort gives the lie to the leader's pronouncements about re-engineering's critical importance,' warned Hammer.[69]

There certainly was resistance, because in practice re-engineering meant huge redundancies – a third of BT staff in the mid-1990s, for example, with a massive impact on morale. It also carried within it a major problem when re-engineering met IT. Re-engineering was supposed to make organisations more flexible. But as Champy and Hammer were putting the finishing touches to their book, the first enterprise resource planning (ERP) software – the earliest attempt to centralise decisions for the core functions of a company – was put on sale by the German software giant SAP. Their English version of ERP R/3 was available in 1993, and by 1994 it was earning over $1 billion.

ERP dovetailed with re-engineering. It offered to pull together all the functions of an organisation and the big corporates lapped it up. The trouble was that it failed to work very well for them. A 2000 report showed that 92 per cent of American companies were disappointed in their vast investments. They carried on with the idea, but increasingly bought software off the shelf from SAP or Oracle which was often even less suited to the particular needs of individual companies, let alone individual members of staff. The management consultancies had a brief moment of panic and then looked towards the public sector.

It was no coincidence that 2000 was also the first year of the most disastrous government investments in IT systems – many of them related to ERP, dividing heavily monitored front-line call centre staff from back-office experts. The huge tax credits IT system, bought from the US presidential hopeful Ross Perot's old company EDS, managed to pay out £2.2 billion too much in the first year. Even now, HMRC is reckoned to ignore about four million calls a year.[70] That is the pattern.

There is no doubt that, among the reasons why the Home Office was operating dysfunctional software to run the immigration service, you should find the big IT consultancies shifting their evangelising from the private to the public sector.

This is how it works. The software teams look in detail at all the processes, find the best employees and set down what they do into processes staff are led through on the screen, just like Taylor with his precious stopwatch. The tragedy of ERP and the apps which followed it is that they set best practice in concrete, so that it can never be changed without more huge investment.

They also build in onerous reporting, tickboxing and measurement systems to satisfy managers addicted to the McKinsey Fallacy. Such managers want to be able to stare at a complete picture of the machine in motion until they can find who to blame, and ERP gives them the illusion that they can do so. It is as much about control as it is about defining processes. It also imposes enormous new measurement burdens on front-line staff. That explains why, when I turned up at A&E at a London hospital some years ago, there was twenty pages of software to go through before staff could begin to deal with whatever emergency I had arrived for.

'These are the assembly lines of the digital age,' wrote Simon Head, one of the few academics from outside the IT industries to study the phenomenon, 'complete with their own digital proletariat.'[71]

There is a great deal of rhetoric from Silicon Valley about the potential for software to give power and responsibility to frontline staff, and you can see why. But if IT investment was really about empowering ordinary employees, then you would expect companies to value their middle- and lower-income staff as experts on the front line, said Head. In fact, they were de-skilling them and, wherever they could, making them redundant. People like John Seely Brown, a former director of IT think tank Xerox-PARC, saw what was happening as early as 2002 and described it as 'technologically inspired vandalism'.[72]

What was emerging instead was a series of 'monolithic blocks of concrete', where the accumulated experience of staff, and their ability to make human relationships – even brief ones over the phone – were being lost. And trapped inside these blocks of concrete are not only public employees, but call centre staff and anyone who deals with them – in fact, practically every large organisation, public and private, and nearly all of us in the modern world. What that means is a subject for other chapters, but it is worth noticing how far from the original purpose we have drifted.

Hammer first imagined re-engineering as the antidote to the fantasy of economies of scale, but the whole of tickbox is a testament to another continuing fantasy among those who rule us. It was supposed to end the divisions between different functions, but in practice it underpins even bigger ones – between front office and back office, between commissioners and suppliers, between those who count and those who *do* stuff.

IT was supposed to give responsibility to front-line staff; it actually removed it. Contract culture was supposed to help managers focus on what was really important; but it actually forced them to pay attention to what was less important. In the same way, privatisation was supposed to inject a kind of entrepreneurial flexibility into public services; it actually encased them in concrete.

This is important for the tickbox story, because it shows just how fast political language can be corroded. It shifts faster than you can tick the boxes. The best example applies especially to those of us who campaigned for 'patient-centred healthcare', because it used to mean being flexible enough to look after anybody, whatever their particular needs. Standing in for a colleague of mine, I had a peculiar experience after waxing lyrical about 'patient-centred care' in a lecture I gave to nurses. I began to fear some of them were looking at me as if I were from another planet. In fact, it became clear towards the end that they had a very different understanding of what the phrase meant in practice than I did. I thought it still meant what the Royal College of Nursing says ('compassionate and respectful'), or maybe what the NICE guidelines say ('take into account individual needs and preferences'). Apparently not.

In practice, it now means bending over backwards not to impose any agenda on patients, which includes not asking them any leading questions – and then, if they don't take the pills or do the exercises or arrive on time for their next appointment, striking them off your list as 'non-compliant'.

It hardly needs saying that this is not the official definition of 'patient-centred'. I had to take my audience's interpretation seriously because so many of them agreed that this was how they were told to act. There is also some evidence from medical studies which recognise that too many patients are labelled non-compliant just because they ask more questions than are entirely comfortable.[73] But the main reason I believed the nurses was that I recognised the idea of not 'imposing' your agenda on patients from the economists' playbook of public service choice. In my experience, economists are terrified that patients will ask doctors for advice, and will as a result not make a free choice. In fact, of course, the one thing patients want to ask is 'What would you do, doctor?' Because of this, I felt sure that – although the NHS guidance suggests otherwise – that is how NHS clinics often interpret the previously radical idea of patient-centred care.

It is an open question in medicine what non-compliance means. It is a tickbox concept in itself – it describes, on the face of it, patients who don't do what they are told. And it can be frustrating for doctors that they don't. New England doctor Toyin Ajayi described in 2017 talking to a particularly frustrating patient with a long history of chronic conditions, mental and physical, who had just been rushed to hospital in an eminently avoidable crisis. It was only when she took the patient, Mary-Beth, outside for a walk that she said, 'I'm not non-compliant – I'm defiant!' She was rejecting her allotted role in the healthcare system.

Mary-Beth was exactly the kind of person that 'patient-centred care' was designed for. Yet, in just a few years, the meaning has reversed itself. It is bizarre and rather terrifying what senior managers can achieve with one simple box, turning it inside out to suit their overall process as they understand it. Yet it is still the same box to tick.

It is fascinating to see that this kind of reversal can happen without any individual saying that it should. It happens because this is the process that takes place as the boxes that need ticking, and the targets and KPIs that lie behind them, descend down the layers of management and get translated into something a little easier to deliver. It is not perverted by some evil bureaucrat or middle manager, because they are scarce these days. A combination of New Public Management, re-engineering, contract culture and tickbox has abolished them. They have been replaced by machine minders, phone operators and all the rest of us, as part-time tickers of boxes on their behalf.

Oh yes, and a very small number of rather well-paid and select coders-in-chief who fix the boxes and set the concrete.

3

The Tickbox Men

You cannot run a highly complex technologically based society by centralised control at the top. You cannot have an emperor run it . . . Russia hasn't been able to. China can't. It is perfectly clear that we are really moving towards this same complex interdependent form. Now that frees up the capacity of society to move.

Rensis Likert on what he dubbed 'System 4
management style', 1973

The five-point scoring system that lets us grade our response to political opinions, job satisfaction or how well we were served, is now utterly ubiquitous. We are asked to respond to it practically every time we approach a counter or buy anything online or come within a whiff of a hospital. So it is a strange thought that it was invented by a particular individual and on a particular date.

And yet it was. The Likert Scale, as it is called, was the brainchild of the pioneering sociologist Rensis Likert, an engineer turned psychologist from Cheyenne, Wyoming. Likert was all set to follow his father into a career with the Union Pacific Railroad, where he was interning during the big 1922 railway strike. The experience gave him a fascination with organisations and the way they behaved. So he went to university to study psychology and it was his 1932 PhD thesis that started the ball rolling.

It was called 'A Technique for the Measurement of Attitudes' and it demonstrated how his five-point scale worked, categorising opinions simply as strong agreement, weak agreement, don't know, weak disagreement or strong disagreement. It showed how it operated much more flexibly, but just as accurately, as the Thurstone method, developed by the psychometric testing pioneer Louis Leon Thurstone for measuring attitudes to religion.

Likert was driven by memories of the First World War, and of the sheer 'irrationality' of the Union Pacific strike. So he stopped studying the stresses of metals and began studying the stresses of people instead. In fact, he stayed rather divided between the data approach and a more relaxed interviewing approach in which he tried to ask people open questions as a way of finding out what they really felt. And here, Likert also became a controversial pioneer of this style of market research – part data, part conversation.

He was a quietly spoken man, fascinated by a range of subjects and not given to public spats, but he knew what he believed. So when he managed to persuade forty New York University students to help him find out about people's attitudes to race – and other controversial issues like smoking and the Depression Bonus, a sum of money awarded to people who had fought in the war – the professor moved to stop them taking part, because he disapproved of so much controversy – and Likert left. In general, when it came to the bonus, the students found that people tended to be more in favour of the idea the closer they were related to someone receiving it – in all cases except for their in-laws. It was a fascinating discovery from what we might now call data mining.

Then, on 1 September 1939, the day the Second World War broke out, Likert went to Washington to meet Agriculture

Secretary Henry Wallace, and agreed to run his Division of Program Surveys at the Bureau of Agriculture Statistics, to help work out the attitude in rural communities to some of the New Deal programmes. Regular surveys were already being carried out, but in an unsystematic way. One rural researcher called Jay Whitson used to take his questions and put them in his hat; if he forgot one, to keep up the illusion that he and the participant were having an informal unrecorded conversation, he would take his hat off, look at the next question, and carry on. Then he would go back to his office and write up the interview for Wallace.

Likert was developing his own more scientific system, based partly on his five-point scale and partly on open-ended questions which would allow him to interpret what people meant. He also used a sophisticated probability system involving maps and aerial photos to work out which farms should be 'sampled', so that the results could be measured and built up into a representative picture. Both elements were controversial, and they became increasingly so as demands for food from war-torn Europe and the UK began to increase, and farmers – burned and bruised by the Depression – were reluctant to invest to boost production.

It was his experience with the internment of 'enemy aliens' after Pearl Harbor in 1941 that convinced Likert of the critical importance of interpreting the numerical data with open-ended questions, when the interviewers would write down exactly what the person said. The security authorities, unsure what to do, had been carrying out opinion research to find out people's views about internment on both sides of the nation. On the Pacific coast, surveys had found people very nervous about enemy aliens, and most people of Japanese origin were rounded up and put into camps. It remains one of the most painful blots on the US war record.

Likert had his doubts. When he was asked to run a parallel survey on the east coast about ethnic Germans, he made sure open-ended questions were asked. He found that people were indeed nervous of anyone dubbed an 'enemy alien' – like the little green men of science fiction – but what they really wanted was for the authorities to keep an eye on anyone suspicious. There was no appetite for camps. As a result, neither Germans nor Italians were ever interned in the USA. To the end of his life, Likert felt that – had he exerted himself more to interpret the Pacific coast results – the Japanese Americans too would have been left alone. In fact, all he probably needed to do was to avoid the frightening term 'aliens'.

But Likert's biggest controversy came at the end of the war. These were the heady days when people like George Gallup were pioneering opinion polls and Freud's nephew Edward Bernays was pioneering public relations. But Likert feared that their sampling was unrepresentative. It would, he wrote in an article for *Scientific American* in 1948, lead to a ridiculous muddle one day.

Scientific American sat on his article for five months, then – out of the blue – the predicted muddle suddenly happened. Gallup's polling organisation found that Harry Truman's Republican challenger, Governor Thomas Dewey, was well in the lead for the presidential election that November. The polls showed the same result consistently across the United States, and did so right up to the count, when it emerged that, in fact, he had lost. Far from a sweeping Republican victory, Truman's Democrats took control of both houses of Congress. This was particularly unfortunate for the Republican paper the *Chicago Daily Tribune*, which because of a printers' strike needed to go to press before the polls had closed. The headline for their early edition was 'DEWEY DEFEATS TRUMAN!'

The *Tribune* had famously called Truman a 'nincompoop' during the campaign, so when he reached St Louis by train the following day, he held up a copy of the front page for the photographers – sealing the incident in the memory of the public.

Scientific American immediately dusted down Likert's article, and published it as if it had been written in response to the pollsters' humiliation. Gallup never forgave him.

Interviewing the enemy

Likert's major contribution to his own nation's history came in November 1944. The campaigns of aerial bombardment over Germany and Japan were reaching their joint crescendos. The terrifying firebombing of Dresden by the RAF followed a month later; the firebombing of Tokyo by the US air force in March.

But were they effective? They were hugely expensive in terms of money, planes and aircrew, and utterly brutal to civilians who happened to live or work underneath. Everyone understood the theory, though there were humane voices beginning to speak out against it, including the bishop of Chichester, George Bell. It made sense to find out as soon as possible, which was why President Franklin Roosevelt set up his Strategic Bombing Survey to discover the truth – while it could still be useful to know.

It was a vast project, and part of a wider undertaking in the economic war, involving a tall young economist called John Kenneth Galbraith. With his opinion research experience, Likert was an obvious recruit for the main board, along with a team of over 1200 people drawn from across the armed forces and from civilian life. The project director, banker Paul Nitze, said he aimed to avoid involving anyone who knew too much about bombing already. He also preferred social scientists, who could use partial statistics, to the kind of scientists who demanded laboratory conditions before they could come to any conclusions.

When Galbraith hurried into Germany the following year just behind the front-line troops to seize documents, he struck

gold by managing to interrogate Albert Speer, Hitler's armaments minister, for ten days. Speer bent over backwards to help,
directing Galbraith to a safe in Munich that held key economic
documents and even giving him the combination for the lock.
Likert meanwhile was put in charge of interview techniques for
enemy civilians, first in Germany and then in Japan. Some of the
first interviews in which the general public used the five-point
Likert Scale were conducted here, though it seems a slightly
strange idea – categorising people's feelings about their own
morale and being bombed. And it was Likert's conclusions that
there was indeed an impact of bombing on civilian morale that
proved decisive. There was controversy about the two reports
in air force circles – air force chief Carl Spaatz is supposed to
have refused to read them – but they were unequivocal in their
findings that the bombing campaigns had been decisive. More
detailed readings revealed, more than a little uncomfortably, the
brutality of the firebombing of Japanese cities, and the terror of
the raids on German cities too.

They also, paradoxically, revealed some doubts, especially in
Germany, where peak tank and aircraft production happened to
coincide with the fiercest raids. Similarly in Japan, production in
war factories which had been bombed appeared for some reason
to be higher than in those which had not.

Given that the economic impact of bombing was so disputed,
Likert's work on civilian morale was doubly important. In fact,
Paul Nitze became convinced as attention shifted to the Pacific
war that Japan would inevitably surrender – and that the Allies
could therefore stop firebombing and let events take their course.
His views cut no ice with the chiefs of staff, who pressed ahead
with plans to drop atomic bombs on Hiroshima and Nagasaki.
They were helped unexpectedly by a captured American pilot,
who was tortured after the Hiroshima bomb; he knew nothing

about it, but 'confessed' that the USA had a hundred more bombs and were about to hit Tokyo with one.

Doubts such as Nitze's have persisted to this day in the form of arguments about whether it was right to vaporise two Japanese cities, and exactly what was going on within the different factions inside the Japanese government. The issue partly relates to the question of morale, and exactly what it means.

General Tojo, Japan's wartime leader, had no interest in civilian morale. According to the final bombing survey, it wasn't that he believed his nation's morale was strong enough to survive, it was that he never considered the matter. As far as he was concerned, morale was completely irrelevant. And, of course, as always with tickbox, the data looks objective and robust – but it rather depends on what is being counted. If you think morale means the will to resist, then that was blown to smithereens by the bombing and the huge exodus to the countryside during 1945. But if you think – as the strategists believed at the time – that it was about people's willingness to overthrow their own government, then the research makes it clear that this was never likely to happen, either in Germany or Japan.

This was because the main effect of bombing on civilians was to force them to concentrate on small details that would allow themselves and their families to survive. Far from overthrowing their governments – however much they might hate them – the bombs had a numbing effect that seemed to undermine their belief in their own efficacy.

And as it turned out, as many as a quarter of Likert's respondents in Japan refused to answer his question about what they thought of the Americans. Therein lay the problem for this kind of tickbox inquiry – too many people were unwilling to displease their questioners. Among Japanese or UK audiences, certainly, basic diffidence or politeness often kicks in.

Nor did Likert rely on his five-point scale, perhaps not surprisingly. The idea, as far as possible, was to avoid leading the interviewees and then to categorise their answers – there were ten possible points for the question about what they felt when they heard about the Japanese surrender. It was also difficult that the Japanese appeared to have no word that exactly corresponded to *morale*, so researchers had to ask about confidence in various different aspects of the conflict – victory, their leaders, each other. It was fascinating to find that morale collapsed among educated people much earlier than among others, for whom all propaganda simply increased their cynicism.

It is easy to be sceptical about the survey reports. They concluded that the bombing had been 'decisive' because it had destroyed the economies and productive capacity of both Germany and Japan – which was precisely what they were intended to conclude. The firebombing of Japanese cities in the final five months of the war killed more than half a million people, most of them civilians – it *required* some serious justification. Yet the weight of evidence on both sides still makes these pretty impressive documents. It is just that, from what we know about the later development of tickbox, we need to be a little careful before we completely take their word for it.

The first of these raids took place on the night of 9–10 March 1945, when more than two hundred B-29 Superfortresses, packed with magnesium, napalm and phosphorus bombs, began dropping them over the Tokyo suburbs from as little as 5000 feet – low enough that the aircrews could smell the burning human flesh below. The bombing chief in the Pacific war, General Curtis LeMay, said that if the war was lost he expected to be tried for war crimes. The justification for an operation like this was that the Japanese had moved their war production to small workshops in the suburbs.

It is true that resources had to be diverted to cope with the losses, just as they had been in Germany, which faced an onslaught from the USAAF by day and the RAF by night, designed to destroy enemy morale. What the strategists failed to understand was that, as we know now, if you destroy the homes and family lives of enemy civilians, they tend to feel they have nothing more to lose and cling on to their remaining lives with a ferocious intensity. The constant moving of production also meant that it became more efficient with every move. The loss of oil destroyed the Nazi war economy; it isn't clear that the bombing of civilians was worth the moral horror. Certainly, that was not how Britons regarded their own response to being bombed ('plucky Britain carries on'). Nor does it appear to have the same effect on Afghans who are bombed endlessly by drones.

There was the question about Likert's tickbox tests. It was not clear then, any more than it is now, whether or not opinion surveys of this kind simply reflect the bias and opinions of the organisations and the people who set the questions. Both the questions and the answers require interpretation, which tends to be biased as well. It is certainly not objective.

So was the firebombing of Germany and Japan worth the horror and the loss of life? Likert's surveys are probably no longer enough to justify the answers.

An IBM machine with legs

Attached to Curtis LeMay's staff at his headquarters at Wright's Field, Ohio, was a former Harvard statistician with slicked-back hair and a distinctively boyish face, who was destined to embed tickbox firmly into government policy at every level. His name was Robert McNamara.

It is not clear whether he and Likert met, but McNamara was certainly involved with the Strategic Bombing Survey. But while Likert was developing reservations about policy by measurement, McNamara would go on to exemplify the basics of tickbox. In two prestigious jobs through the 1960s and 1970s – as US Secretary of Defense during most of the Vietnam War and then as president of the World Bank during its years of massive expansion – McNamara dominated the policy world. And in both those herculean tasks, he played the role of what Senator Barry Goldwater called 'an IBM machine with legs'. Even more than Likert, he exemplified both the ambition and the failures of tickbox.

McNamara was born into relative poverty in San Francisco in 1916, the son of a sales manager for a wholesale shoe company. He was turned down for active service in 1942 because his eyesight was poor – but still, having attached himself to the Statistical Control Unit, managed to end the war as a lieutenant-colonel. His boss there, Colonel 'Tex' Thornton, reached the conclusion – in a triumph for statistical thinking – that the US should stop making aircraft around 1944, and start managing down ready for the end of the war.

It was Thornton who offered the services of his protégés to Henry Ford II, just back from the navy to take over his grandfather's ailing Detroit car manufacturing firm. McNamara was not keen but decided to join the company in order to help with his sick wife's medical bills. Christened the 'quiz kids' by the existing management thanks to their incessant Likert-style surveying, their team managed to rebrand themselves as the 'whiz kids'.

McNamara rose up the hierarchy quickly to become company president, all the while concerned – as he had been in the USAAF – with cost-cutting and safety (he introduced seat belts in Ford cars). He also had the big idea of producing smaller cars, where he was decades ahead of his time, though the proposal led to tension with Ford himself. But, according to one executive, McNamara 'ruled the place by fear'.[74] Reserved and aloof, the archetypal statistical mind, at Ford he set the pattern for the rest of his career. He had been president for just five weeks when the Kennedys' brother-in-law Sargent Shriver approached him to be Defense Secretary in the new Kennedy administration.

But the peculiar thing about the 'IBM machine with legs' was that, like other highly logical people in public life, McNamara was not simply determined to change the world – he was also a romantic. Not only in his belief that change was possible, but in his hero worship of the handful of people he looked up to. He would be a pall-bearer at Bobby Kennedy's funeral. And, five years after the assassination of JFK in 1963, standing next to Jackie Kennedy and the Kennedy children dressed in white, he broke down at the launch ceremony of an aircraft carrier bearing the dead president's name: 'Those who knew him will never be the same,' he said.[75]

McNamara's career was characterised by extreme loyalty, not just to Kennedy, but for a time also to Lyndon Johnson, his successor. It was a passion that nearly sent him insane, but it also led him to develop the egregious habit of quoting selective numbers in public to defend his president – even, as it turned out, when he turned against the Vietnam War. This was seen as part of the McNamara cult, which took possession of his ambitious assistants, the core of which he described as 'better a wrong decision than no decision at all'.[76] In itself a highly romantic view, this also contradicts one of the central tenets of tickbox (the one which we know under the shorthand of 'evidence-based policy').

Still, it was the calculating element of McNamara's personality, not the romantic side, that first brought him into conflict with the US defence establishment – and particularly with his old boss, Curtis LeMay.

Ironically, given what was about to happen, McNamara was

making his name as a cost-cutter, enraging the admirals in particular, whose favourite home bases were being closed, and closed
as fast as possible. Not a penny was to be spent on anything ob-
solete, and the old idea of massive retaliation by nuclear bombers
was being replaced with an emphasis on flexible response and a
second-strike capacity by submarines that could be anywhere on
the planet. The bomber types hated it. So when McNamara began to promote his and Kennedy's approach – that missiles were
better than bombers – he soon found himself with enemies. How
many Polaris nuclear missile submarines should he ask for from
Congress, he asked one Washington insider.

'Seven,' he was told. Why? Because that was what the chairman
of the House Appropriations Committee wanted.

'That's a hell of a way to build a programme,' said McNamara.
'It's not logical.'[77]

Nor is it. But then, defence is a highly political business, because it is so ferociously expensive. When you try to take the politics out of it, attempting to measure precisely the correct answer
to a question like the number of submarines you need, you very
quickly offend those who used to take the decisions on a less logical basis.

Nevertheless, McNamara stood next to Kennedy throughout
the Cuban missile crisis in 1962, urging a blockade rather than
the massive strike favoured by some of the top brass. The most
implacable of his opponents was his old chief Curtis LeMay, who
was also reputed to be the original for the Peter Sellers character
in the film *Dr Strangelove*.

'Kennedy was trying to keep us out of war,' McNamara said
much later.[78] 'I was trying to help him keep us out of war but
General Curtis LeMay, with whom I served ... in World War II,
was saying; "Let's go in. Let's totally destroy Cuba".' More help-
fully, the US ambassador to Moscow, Tommy Thompson, urged

Kennedy to reply directly to Soviet leader Nikita Khrushchev's earlier, less aggressive message, where he promised to remove the missiles in return for a face-saving undertaking that the US would not invade Cuba. There were tougher, more intransigent messages later. Thompson worked out that Khrushchev needed a device to allow him to step back. As it turned out, he was right.

Apart from the romanticism, McNamara and LeMay had nothing in common except their background in B-29 Superfortresses and the memory of the Strategic Bombing Survey. As McNamara tightened his grip over US defence policy, LeMay became increasingly implacable. He ended his career as running mate to the racist governor George Wallace in the 1968 presidential election.

Meanwhile, McNamara was enraging the old guard further by removing intelligence and procurement from the military and naval chiefs, and entrusting them to two new technocratic agencies, the Defense Intelligence Agency and the Defense Logistics Agency. Again, this was an early tickbox battle – tickbox regards it as anathema for professionals to handle any functions except their own. But it was McNamara's system analysis techniques, breaking decisions down systematically so that the context was fully understood, which most infuriated LeMay's allies. The old guard suspected that his system analysis was not actually objective, but was being manipulated to support decisions that McNamara had already made.

Yet there is, and was, a more fundamental issue, which is emerging only now, in the manipulation of big data. McNamara asked his comptroller Charles Hitch to produce a long-term defence budget, based on a combination of strategic needs and costs and a comparison between the two. The PPBS – the Planning, Programming and Budgeting System – was intended to be an 'open and explicit analysis' that should be completely transparent and available to anyone with a legitimate interest. In practice, it was so huge and complicated that no outsider could use it to challenge any conclusions.

It did not, in fact, make decisions any more transparent. But it added to the mystique of those who took them. Like the sophisticated data mining and analysis used by government and retailers, for example, these days, in practice few people had the time or the skills to make head or tail of it.

Then everything changed and the cost-cutter presided over one of the biggest, and most secretive, cost increases in history. It began in earnest in 1964, with two incidents in the Gulf of Tonkin, when a US destroyer, USS *Maddox*, came under attack from North Vietnamese forces. Three decades later, McNamara came to believe that the second incident had never actually happened. But, at the time, he was instrumental in using it to justify the retaliatory strikes and the military build-up that followed.

The fog of war

Ironically for the great rational policy-maker, the insanity of Vietnam cast its long shadow over McNamara's period of office – longer than anyone else has ever been US Defense Secretary. The defence budget rose from \$48 billion in 1962 to \$74 billion in 1968; it would not reach that level again until Ronald Reagan's presidency in 1984. By 1968, there were half a million American troops in Vietnam and the bodybags were coming home in increasing numbers.

McNamara was a true believer. It was an element of his mystery and his romanticism. Not only did he take on Curtis LeMay and other dyed-in-the-wool militarists, he took on the racists too: from 1963 onwards, commanding officers were under a legal obligation to use their powers to influence local businesses to serve black and white soldiers on equal terms, and to ban their troops from any that failed to do so.

But he was, above all, a numbers man. Vietnam was a war of attrition and, for McNamara, there was one number above all that could make a difference: the enemy's ability to replace dead troops with live ones, and the limited number of Viet Cong fighters ranged against them. The faster they killed the Viet Cong, the quicker their resistance would run out of steam – or so he calculated. Looked at like that, it should be possible to measure progress in the war purely by the enemy body count. 'Close attention to the battleground facts would help the anti-communists win,' he told the Washington press corps.[79] It was to be the classic example of tickbox in action.

It was no easy matter, however, to estimate body count. By 1963, McNamara's statisticians were guessing that their South Vietnamese allies had been overestimating the numbers of the enemy killed by about 40 per cent. For one thing, the Viet Cong tried to remove the bodies of their dead comrades by taking them away. The key estimate was even more difficult: the notorious KBA, or Killed by Air, fuelled by Lyndon Johnson's peculiar evenings choosing bombing targets from the safety of the Oval Office in what was becoming an increasingly violent campaign.

There were other problems. American soldiers were losing their lives just counting bodies. Worse, the focus on the ground became increasingly to provide the metrics the hierarchy craved, which meant more killing. Perhaps this fed into the horrors of the March 1968 massacre when US soldiers ran amok in the village of My Lai, killing up to 500 men, women, children and babies with horrifying savagery. Only one soldier was ever convicted and three who had tried to shield villagers were initially denounced in Congress as traitors. It seems likely that My Lai was somewhere near the top of a huge, unseen iceberg, testament to what happens when war is reduced to tickbox.

If you need metrics to show whether you are winning or not, there will always be a tension – and it is a familiar one to anyone who sees tickbox in action. The Australian-American officer David Kilcullen wrote in his book *Counterinsurgency* that good military metrics mean that you really have to know the area you are fighting over.[80] It could be that body counts are simply a distortion of the meaningful statistics about the wellbeing and safety of the locals. You might just gain yourself more enemies the more you kill.

The same goes for any old statistic, and here Kilcullen won praise from the veteran military correspondent of the *Wall Street Journal* and *Washington Post*, Thomas Ricks, who wrote: 'This was another thing that used to drive me nuts in Iraq, listening to Americans boast about money spent, projects initiated, patrols conducted, and such.'[81]

In fact, said Kilcullen, the best statistic in Afghanistan would have been the price of exotic vegetables, which showed more accurately than anything else how calm or otherwise the situation was. It might not have meant much in Vietnam, but it would have tracked something meaningful in Afghanistan. It would have indicated that life had become stable enough for the local population to truck in vegetables from outside the area by road. It would demonstrate road security, and imply that the number of bribes you had to pay to use the roads was low enough to be affordable. The same with indicators based on the repayment of debts.

The difficulty – as always with tickbox – is to find the kind of ubiquitous blueprint indicators that your superiors back home can understand. The chances of those having a real meaning are pretty slim, but the generals and politicians are not usually very keen on vegetable statistics. In fact, Kilcullen suggested that any measure that embarrassed whoever was reporting it probably made better sense.

And therein lies the very practical tickbox dilemma. Do you choose metrics that actually mean something, but which your bosses dismiss, or do you chose the meaningless stuff that board members can boast about? It is a problem, and a very modern one, about the dysfunctional nature of big hierarchies; about central versus local decision-making.

And what happens when the distant hierarchies latch on to the wrong number was horribly apparent in Vietnam. Because, despite the rising level of enemy dead – and their families, who were counted too – McNamara was losing his war. The mismatch was driving him inwards, so that he increasingly looked at the tickbox figures instead of anything else. He no longer heard the sceptical voices of reporters like Neil Sheehan (later the author of *A Bright Shining Lie*), and the military bureaucracy around him managed to massage the figures so that only positive news would reach him.

Johnson would call McNamara's home at all times of the day or night and launch straight away into scatological rants, even passing on some of the FBI files on his friend Bobby Kennedy for his edification. And all the time, despite his own doubts about the war, McNamara was carrying on in public with the fantasy that they would be able to pull out of Vietnam, job done, by the middle of 1966. So he helped Johnson push for a bigger budget. He was still telling Congress that the war would cost $10 billion in 1967 when it was actually – as he must have known – going to cost twice that.

Where was your miscalculation, one congressman asked him.

'I don't know if you would call it a miscalculation,' said McNamara.[82] And there was the problem: when you are using figures to tell a story, it is ever so tempting to tweak them a little to demonstrate what you 'know' is true. Even if you would never do anything of the kind yourself, there will always be an underling prepared to find the figures you crave.

The uncrowned king

By 1967, McNamara had lost his faith in bombing altogether and was openly looking for a way to launch peace talks. That was the year he quietly told Johnson he must negotiate. As a result, he was losing his influence in the Johnson administration. The same year, he commissioned the Vietnam Study Task Force to look at these issues. The report it produced was not just top secret, it was also three thousand pages long, and in due course it was leaked to the *New York Times* by an aide to his assistant secretary, John McNaughton.

The 'Pentagon Papers' were a hugely important revelation of what McNamara really thought about the war (it led to the Nixon's administration's later horror of leaks, which in turn led to their involvement in the Watergate scandal). But even then, he could not bring himself to be disloyal to Johnson. Until, in a confusing flurry, Johnson rid himself of the man by nominating him to be the head of the World Bank.

By now, McNamara had become a clearly defined personality in the political world. Commentators watched his ability to issue streams of figures on television, and the hardness with which he dismissed searching questions. There is a sense in which his move to the World Bank was a continuation of his Kennedy years, and with what JFK had called the 'battle for minds and souls as well as lives and territories' – and in the sheer ambition of Johnson's ill-fated War on Poverty, from which McNamara clearly learned in the massive expansion in foreign aid over which he presided at the World Bank. There was a huge rise in the ambition and the status of this global institution; and, once again, McNamara brought his own system analysis to the problem of poverty – focusing then, as the bank does now, on the income levels of small farmers.

The tragedy of McNamara, then the uncrowned King of

Tickbox, was not that he lacked ambition – quite the reverse. It was that he could not see clearly enough to make the difference he wanted. New high-yield crop varieties and mechanisation were introduced from the 1960s onwards in a move dubbed by the US government the 'Green Revolution'. Intended to showcase what a peaceful revolution, rather than a Red one, might be like, it worked at first in India and Mexico by enormously increasing the yield of those countries' crops. It succeeded on its own terms, but that involved turning a blind eye to some of the unwanted side-effects – like rising debt, the loss of local knowhow and, for example, the high levels of suicide among indebted small farmers in India which now suggest that all was not well even then.

Yet even if it seemed to work in some pioneering locations, it didn't work nearly as well everywhere, perhaps not surprisingly. Brazilian farmers rejected the new crops because in their own dry climate the new varieties seemed to be bred only for yield, not hardiness. In sub-Saharan Africa, where the problems were particularly intense, and where the new crops would not grow, World Bank staff began to lend only on projects they knew would work towards meeting their targets. Roads were popular because they were easy to lend on, but they tended only to help the richest, and often forced poorer people off the land. Dam projects were even more damaging.

But, just as at the Department of Defense, McNamara's style was too aloof to hear these negatives. He was never seen in the World Bank building, except on formal occasions. He was never in the dining room talking to staff. He sat in the front with his wife in the plane when they travelled anywhere. Management By Walking Around it wasn't.

One staff member claimed that this led to other inaccuracies. 'Without knowing it, he manufactured data. If there was a gap in the numbers, he would ask staff to fill it, and others made it up for him. The practice was not widespread but it was habitual.'[83]

It was not the endless measurement that was faulty in itself, it was measurement without Likert's open-ended questions – without checking with real people who knew. He had succumbed to the fantasy of data at the centre, and was hardly the first or the last to do so.

And so it was that McNamara could not understand why the poor in Latin America destroyed the homes they were given. He called it the 'pathology of poverty', and similar conundrums about the War on Poverty presented themselves back home in the USA. The urban poor in American ghettos also rejected their new housing because of the way they were described – as hopeless or feckless, or both. 'Charity wounds,' said the great anthropologist Marcel Mauss, and this is a real phenomenon. This rejection of welfare consistently confuses well-meaning officials, but is not necessarily surprising that poorer people might prefer to avoid the implication – and sometimes the description – that they are feckless. To take an example from the UK, slum-dwellers, according to Wilfred Burns, chief planning officer for Newcastle in the same period, had 'no initiative or civic pride'.[84] Anyone with either might tell them to go to hell.

Worse, this particular pathology of data hunger meant that the World Bank was taken for a ride disastrously by some of the less salubrious tyrants they were dealing with. Hastings Banda in Malawi, for example, accepted the loans but pocketed the money himself.

In other words, McNamara was flying blind. What he took to be objective numbers were not providing him with a helpful picture. And there was a sense – as there often is with tickbox – that the data was not there to be objective, but as a means of what he called 'managing reality'. In a 1967 speech, he talked about how, if you need to take on the big issues, you must 'manage reality' to give yourself the authority to carry on.[85] You can detect a pattern here about tickbox, which is in practice the opposite of General Electric CEO Jack Welch's famous injunction to 'face reality ... see the world the way it is, not the way you wish it were'.[86] The problem for McNamara was that the data was also managing his own reality, which was not nearly so effective. If he thought the data *allowed* him to be aloof, the combination led to a catastrophic loss of trust. He certainly trusted nobody himself, except his wife Margaret.

This had consequences. By the mid-1970s, developing countries had got into the borrowing habit. Private banks were awash with petro-dollars and were happy to lend to such countries without the kind of stipulations that came with a World Bank loan. Still, they could afford the interest burden as long as economic growth continued – which was also McNamara's plan: to pump the countries with economic growth so they could pay back the loans. Unfortunately, the global economy was slowing down, partly because of the US inflation that followed its spending on the Vietnam War. The first debt crisis was on the horizon.

That was how the unexpected side-effects of McNamara's first big project emerged to undermine his second. But then it is precisely such side-effects that tickbox data ignores.

Here was the problem. To measure effectively, you need an underlying theory, and you have to be flexible enough to change it as you find out whether it works or not. It is an art, not a science. The War on Poverty threw up a critique of the theory behind it – partly that, to change people's lives effectively, you need it to be somehow reciprocal. Simply spending money helps nobody and serves to cement existing power relations. Charity disempowers if it carries on for too long. The World Bank was hardly in the business of charity. Their loans were designed to be paid back – but by somebody else. Worse, if they got it wrong on the ground – and they often did – it was because they were not really listening to the poor recipients. In the same way, McNamara's massive expansion at the World Bank – $13 billion lent on five hundred projects over thirteen years, with an annual increase in developing countries' debt of up to 20 per cent – led to a radical rethink of the theory of development. McNamara's assumptions came under scrutiny, and they have done ever since.

For one thing, there was a new understanding about famine. The economist Amartya Sen showed that it wasn't to do with there being too little food. It was more to do with economics than agronomy – that the poor were no longer able to *command* food during famines, although almost as much of it might have been produced as usual. As it turned out, the real killer during famine periods was actually waterborne diseases, not malnutrition.

Which means that the huge investment in grain storage, before and during McNamara's reign – because it was thought conventional storage methods were inadequate – was largely irrelevant. Most communities were losing less than 5 per cent of their grain in storage. That was a vital mistake made by McNamara's data-driven staff. That more food meant less famine and that existing storage arrangements were actually fine. The next was that yield was not the only measure that was important: small farmers in India or Africa also felt that hardiness was at least as important as yield, but the World Bank found that hard to grasp.

But it was the third mistake which goes to the heart of the tickbox problem, just as McNamara's body count figures deluded him about progress in Vietnam. McNamara truly believed in the simple, single figure, and his regime believed you could sum up the productivity of a rural community by looking at the amount of grain it produced. That was therefore the only data they examined. All crops except for the main grain crop were ignored. The huge productivity in the most diverse and successful communities was ignored: breadfruit, mangoes, bananas, potatoes, sweet potatoes and all the rest. So was the basic productivity of their gardens. It made the most resilient communities seem like the most desperate, and it rendered genuinely threatened communities more vulnerable.

It has taken decades to shift this apparently tickbox-driven approach to development. Plant your one crop, make it high yield or famine threatens – it is not the way the world is. But billions have been squandered by big biotech companies developing genetically modified crops to meet problems that don't exist.

Why does data do this? The answer was summed up by the development economist Robert Chambers in his aphorism 'power hinders learning'.[87] McNamara was employing powerful technocrats, mainly white men, and they did not listen. The World Bank at the time employed only twenty sociologists, and they were outnumbered by economists fifty to one.[88] Data skills were valued considerably more highly than local knowledge, and those who wielded the former were paid much more than those who could interpret the latter.

This was, oddly enough, the very problem that was beginning to concern Rensis Likert.

System 4

'What the world cannot afford is procrastination and delay,' McNamara used to say, and nothing distinguishes his approach from that of today's tickbox more than that statement.[89] These days, thanks to so-called 'evidence-based policy', there is always a ready excuse for doing nothing whatever – because the narrow definition of 'evidence' means that the information required never arrives in the right form (see for example the way the Home Office tickbox system treated Anthony Bryan in Chapter 1). But

McNamara himself is a flawed hero. He wanted to make a difference and believed, passionately and romantically, that he could. Yet under his watch, the poor of the world were getting poorer, however many metrics he could produce to show otherwise.

Likert was never remotely so well known. As far as I know, his path and McNamara's never crossed again after the Bombing Survey. Yet Likert was beginning to seek out solutions to the organisational problem which had so stymied McNamara.

In 1946, with the findings on Japan wrapped up, Likert and his closest colleagues developed a new kind of institution, based at Michigan University but earning consultancy in the world outside. The model represented by the Institute for Social Research is a familiar one now, but back then its approach was original. Likert had become fascinated with how organisations worked, and this arrangement gave him the academic respectability to ask difficult questions. Just as both Taylor and McNamara had cut their teeth on institutions managing or supplying the US navy, it was the Department of Naval Research which first backed Likert in his study of management styles.

For the rest of his career, and past retirement until his death in 1981, Likert developed his management theories. Together with Jane Gibson Likert, his wife and collaborator, he wrote *New Patterns of Management* (1961), then *The Human Organisation* (1967), and finally *New Ways of Managing Conflict* (1976). By the end of this period, the Likerts and their team had studied nearly five hundred different companies in a range of sectors to confirm their theory – which was that, normally, organisations evolve in the same way that species do. At the outset their management is essentially tyrannical, a form which Likert called System 1. Then they go through a period of 'benevolent dictatorship' (System 2), before reaching 'consultative' (System 3) and 'participative' (System 4) stages.

Over and over again, Likert found that business units run under System 4 – which combined teamwork, interest and concern with staff as individuals and high expectations for their performance – performed more productively than the others. 'The most successful managers were more approachable, more interested in the problems of their men, more interested in their careers, were eager to be more constructive and helpful,' Likert wrote. Yet there was a 'but'. Once managers had been able to get this system working, it always took three or four years to produce results. Some companies were not prepared to wait.

Most of Likert's research work was carried out in the 1950s, with particular attention being paid to an unnamed clerical company; its four identical divisions carried out the same work, allowing him to demonstrate in research conditions that System 4-style managers tended to achieve better productivity.[90] But then, in 1962, Likert made a real breakthrough. Harwood, a successful pyjama manufacturer in Virginia, bought its loss-making rival, Weldon Company based in Williamsport, Pennsylvania. Harwood was an enlightened company where a team of researchers from Likert's institute were already working. The purchase gave him the opportunity to see if the Weldon plant, and its eight hundred employees, could be brought up to speed.

The answer was that it could. Within two years, productivity had increased by over a quarter, piece-rate workers' earnings had risen by 30 per cent and manufacturing costs were down by 20 per cent.[91] It was hard to think of any reason why that might be so if it was not that the new management had introduced Likert's System 4.

Likert's team found that the process was also multi-faceted. It could not be measured simply, using what he called a 'fever chart' – like a one-dimensional thermometer which went only up or down. But human beings could manage it. 'High productivity, high quality products, high earnings and successful use of resources and development are not accomplished by impersonal equipment or computers; these goals are achieved by human beings,' he wrote later.[92]

The broad results were pretty clear too. People managed under System 1 tended to have more accidents. It was never obvious why people should fall off telegraph poles more often when they were managed in an authoritarian way, and yet they did.

Research carried out more recently in hospitals has come up with similar results, thanks to former Indian banker turned management researcher Naresh Khatri.[93] Having returned to the American healthcare system after two decades away, Khatri was confused to be told by everyone how much it had changed, when – as far as he could see – it felt exactly the same. There were still hugely expensive law suits, and the same vast insurance bills, the same huge hospital corporations and the same mistakes. Nearly 100,000 patients die in the USA every year because of mistakes, more than deaths from car accidents and breast cancer (in England and Wales, the equivalent figures about hospital errors are contested). He came to the conclusion that the hierarchical management style, the blame culture, and the obsession with top-down IT systems had continued regardless. If the new systems, which caused so much argument, were really more efficient, you might expect that there would be fewer mistakes too. Actually there were still much the same number. Health reformers were even using the burgeoning cost of hospital mistakes as a reason for standardising, controlling and tickboxing even more, but there was little evidence that this was effective.

Khatri's research surveyed over a thousand health providers across the USA, showing clearly that fewer mistakes were made when the medical staff trusted and felt good about each other, while more drug-related errors occurred in hospital cultures where the most detailed control was exerted. The alternative – he called it 'commitment-based management' – meant self-regulation based on trust among staff. This resembled Likert's System 4, which is the opposite of a tickbox system: it deliberately regards staff as individuals and ignores the fundamental metrics.

Likert was a data guy. He believed companies needed 'asset accounting' – what we might now call the measurement of social or intellectual capital – so that finance departments would have to take staff into account. Otherwise, he believed, there was always the temptation to go back to a tyrannical System 1 to force more out of staff, but at the cost of their loyalty and the company's long-term reputation. Yet, paradoxically, it was only when managers set aside those metrics and took an interest in their staff that the benefits of System 4 began slowly to kick in. Likert came to believe also that System 4 might be the key to managing human conflict. If you do things by numbers, you tend towards a punitive way of tackling differences – no negotiation, arbitrary impositions of terms – but using this kind of natural human complexity forces you to get a glimpse of where the other side is coming from.[94]

The question for us, some generations later – when Likert could see all around him evidence that organisations were evolving into System 4 – is why so many of them have reverted to the data-driven tyranny of System 1. But then, Likert warned against that eventuality: the people with the power try to constrain an organisation's evolution, he said. There is a tendency for bad managers to destroy staff productivity in the name of short-term profits and to rise up the hierarchy as a result, leaving the good managers to cope with the mess.

Herein is a partial explanation of why, for example, staff are timed when they go to the loo, and employed on a basis of major distrust, and why this should now appear to be the direction of travel. We will come back to this question in Chapter 5.

The five-point failure

By the 1960s, the other side of Likert's career had taken on a life of its own. His five-point surveys became widely used, mainly as a way of testing how the company that used them was progressing towards his System 4. They became especially popular in the insurance industry as a means of testing staff satisfaction.

'I feel satisfied/fairly satisfied with my present job', or 'I don't know', or 'I am not happy with/I definitely dislike my work'. Such assessments are tremendously familiar and look hard-nosed and thoroughly objective. But they were not, as it turned out, much of a measure of whether employees were more productive. Nor, to be fair to Likert, did he ever suggest that they might be.

This was because the link between job satisfaction and productivity was assumed rather than proved. And, as Likert believed, productivity tends to follow satisfaction some years later: job satisfaction by itself is not System 4. Staff might, after all, be satisfied with their jobs because they are able to relax at work – who knows. Or to snooze under their desks.

By the 1980s, the human resources professionals had realised this little flaw at the heart of their surveys, and were beginning to wonder what really motivated their employees and what might engage them. Likert himself was no longer alive and there is only a ten-year horizon or similar for even the best management ideas, before managers begin to forget them. Even so, System 4 was part of the zeitgeist, even if the name had disappeared. By the mid-1990s, phone giant GTE was able to improve the accuracy of its billing by adjusting the leadership style of its unit managers. And leadership and management style does seem to be a deciding factor in what makes staff engaged, just as Likert claimed it was – though both tend to slip through the radar when tickbox is employed. They are instantly recognisable but impossible to measure.

By 1997, the parcel delivery company UPS was congratulating itself on an impressive score for the morale of its workforce, only to find itself ten months later in the middle of a bitter strike. Complaints about part-time jobs had not shown up in the survey data. Worse, employees were beginning to feel uncomfortable about the incessant measurement. The retailer Dayton-Hudson, meanwhile, had to reach an out-of-court settlement with a group of employees who felt that standardised personality tests were an invasion of privacy.

Then, according to one recent survey (slight paradox here), while managers felt that such surveys were helpful, it was found that the people actually being surveyed – the employees – usually felt they were unlikely to be of any use.[95] Who knew best? Chances are it was those at the sharp end.

There have also been sceptics who notice that figures for staff or customer satisfaction very rarely change, so really what is the point? Perhaps they are right to watch out for real change, but even if they did change, the surveys would not be able to tell you why. That would require some interpretation using non-tickbox skills like imagination, theory and intuition. And probably more than a dollop of common sense.

Yet Robert McNamara believed the data. Managers and board members are peculiarly prone to some of the delusions of tickbox. They really believe in the single metric. So when senior managers try to influence their senior staff using bonuses, because they only really believe in money, morale tends to unravel. Of course, if you pay staff more for achieving certain targets, they will tend to achieve those targets. They will adopt the same one-eyed framing that you have assumed they should have adopted. If you standardise jobs, as Taylor would have you do, then you will get Taylor's ideal – an employee whose sole attention is focused on your single measures, and who pays little or no attention to anything else.

This single-measure approach tends not only to undermine the ability of employees to deal with complexity, but also their willingness to do so. It all goes to confirm Likert's assertion that you only get what you want – more productivity – if you ignore the productivity metrics. In fact, according to recent research, if you pay someone for behaving ethically, they will stop behaving ethically when you stop paying them – even if they had been happy to do so without payment before. The most recent example of this was 2008 American research involving forty-eight 20-month-old toddlers nudged into helping the grown-ups and then either rewarded by being allowed to play with a particularly cute toy or not. After the rewards had been removed, the group of toddlers who got no reward carried on wanting to help, but the group which had been rewarded with the toy went off the whole idea of helping.[96]

In fact, as we know now, paying employees for particular behaviour – whether by using bonuses or by any other means – can mean *lower* productivity, less engagement and collaboration and more mistrust.[97] Senior managers believe – it is one of the illusions of tickbox – that employees need to compete with each other for rewards. Likert came to believe that it was far more effective to find ways in which employees could compete with their own past performance. There, in a nutshell, is the difference between tickboxes and checklists – tickbox keeps tabs on people from above and perhaps, these days, also makes it possible for them to earn more money. Checklists allow you to keep better tabs on yourself.

Then along came the banking crash of 2008, and it was clear

early on that the disaster of collateralised debt obligations – as it turned out, valueless mixtures of good and bad mortgage debt – was at least partly to do with performance-related pay, which led those who should have known better to ignore people's ability to repay when they signed them up for mortgages, and then mixed flawed mortgages together with safer ones on the grounds that the good would make the bad invisible. Tickbox seems also to have been the flaw that led the ratings agencies to judge these financial instruments as safe investments, because ratings agency staff bonuses depended on them ticking the box marked AA or AAA for safety.

Since these bonuses played their part in blowing up the global economy, human resources departments have been reluctantly letting go of some of their bonus systems. The big American investment management company Woodford was one of the first in its sector to do so. The trouble is that tickbox is now so ingrained in other managements that they keep on making the same mistakes.

The American bank Wells Fargo, for example, set ambitious targets for each relevant employee for cross-selling their products. Bonuses were offered to those who sold to existing customers, and the employment of those who failed to do so was reviewed. The managers were surprised to find that some employees were opening false accounts in the name of customers in order to boost their figures. When the news broke in 2016, the company was fined a total of $185 million and 5300 employees were sacked. It was, wrote history professor Jerry Muller in his book *The Tyranny of Metrics*, 'a predictable response to the performance quotas that the company managers had set for their employees'.[98]

Quite right. If you treat your employees as if they were Pavlovian dogs, then that is the kind of one-eyed behaviour you will get.

For all these reasons, at the turn of the century, HR departments began to use a different approach. They redirected Likert's five-point surveys at the customer. As a result, there is hardly any interaction with staff in any agency, public or private, that will not involve a request to 'feed back'. This is irritating and entirely voluntary – though I have noticed that one big agency in the UK usually fails to return my calls if I have asked not to give feedback. There is a sense of addiction, almost, in the zeal with which organisations crave our feedback.

What I find annoying about it is that they very rarely allow you to feed back what you really think. It is, after all, primarily a way of keeping their eye on front-line staff. The surveys are designed to find out only whether staff are sticking to the company's often inadequate processes. That is the best you can expect. If you don't like the way the processes work, or you have an issue that staff don't have a space for on their computer screen, this version of tickbox will take no notice.

It hardly needs saying, but I am not a big fan of customer surveys. They are far too long; I once clicked delete on a 75-question survey from an airline. They ask irritatingly pointless questions – I know it would help them gain some kind of imprimatur from an institute of sociological research, but I don't really want to tell them whether I am a man or a woman. Some of them infuriatingly make certain answers compulsory, so that you feel you have wasted your time when you delete the rest.

But one of the most infuriating aspects of tickbox is that so many surveys are designed to exclude certain answers completely. Such surveys are designed to look objective, but are actually there to provide the authors with marketing or PR ammunition. So they will not allow you to complain about a more obvious point, like their system.

Tickbox

Our proposals will make financial contributions to improving local infrastructure at ███████████████ – we welcome your views on the importance of the following projects. *Please tick as appropriate.*

	Very Important	Important	Quite Important	Not Important	Neutral / Don't Know
Improvements to the ███████████	☐	☐	☐	☐	☐
Improvements to the roundabouts on ███████████	☐	☐	☐	☐	☐
Improvements to parking in the town centre	☐	☐	☐	☐	☐
Provision of new leisure facilities	☐	☐	☐	☐	☐
Improvements to the existing Town Council offices	☐	☐	☐	☐	☐
Traffic calming measures at the southern entrance to ████████	☐	☐	☐	☐	☐

Do you have any comments about the projects mentioned above or are there any others you would like ████████ to consider?

Are you happy for ███████████████ to contact you in future? *Please circle as appropriate.*

Yes / No

Once completed, please post your form in the box provided. Thank you.

The survey was sent to me by a friend who received it from a developer at her home. It is clearly designed for the developers to be able to crow about most of the answers on the five-point scale – which is extremely unbalanced (Likert would turn in his grave). But there is nowhere to say you would actually like them to take their money and push off – except for the box at the bottom, which excludes negative answers from the survey.

Let's take a closer look at the survey I have just been sent by my bank (the Co-op) about our last phone call. There are batteries of questions about Ivan (let's call him that), who handled the call, all couched using the Likert Scale. He was fine at it, efficient and friendly, and I know my answers will make a difference to him. But how do I tell the bank that my previous call handler cut me off in mid-sentence when she discovered I had a non-standard request? And how do I complain about how long the system took to answer? The truth is that they are only really interested in how well their staff performed and not terribly interested in their bank's systems.

To be fair, there is a catch-all question at the end with a ten-point scale about how likely I am to 'recommend' their services. I mean, how often do I go around *recommending* banks to people? How often do people ask for recommendations for a bank? But if I tick the box marked *never*, I know I am misunderstanding the purpose of the question. I also have no idea if I will damage poor Ivan's prospects of clinging onto his job. So I bail out and abandon the questionnaire – and also refuse the request for another five-minute telephone interview. The conversation only took a couple of minutes and I could carry on raking over the entrails of this encounter for ages afterwards – as I am now, I suppose.

So much for customer surveys. Even with respect to the very narrow element they are measuring in staff surveys, the data will be inaccurate. Another friend of mine went into their bank recently and was asked by the counter staff if they wouldn't mind scoring them a straight five this time. Being of a challenging disposition, my friend then spent some time discussing with the staff what might constitute service so excellent that it should get the top score. Following the procedure certainly wouldn't be enough.

Again, here is the great tickbox gap between what managers think and what front-line staff know, because they can see it. Nobody benefits if you ask staff to go beyond their procedure for a moment, though that is the logical extension of the whole idea, but managers are usually solely interested in whether procedures have been followed. If they just follow the process – even magnificently – managers think they should get a 5, but as far as customers are concerned, there seems no obvious reason why they should get more than a 3 or 4. And if the system itself is demeaning or robotic, or makes you feel like an inconvenient cog, then you want to give them a 2. Yet, as you know very well, this will reflect badly on the blameless staff member in front of you.

The misunderstanding is worse than that. What would customer service that went beyond the system look like? It would have to involve a human touch beyond the procedures. And there the management would be less happy, because the human touch gets in the way of efficiency – or they think it can.

It is hardly Likert's fault that his five-point surveys have become so ambiguous that they are misused and misunderstood. But there is something familiar about the basic problem here – the gap between the numbers and the reality on the ground that gives you more than a whiff of tickbox.

4

Goodhart's Law

Decline of language is the decline of the life of the people who use it.

Ian Robinson, *The Survival of English*, 1973

Professor Charles Goodhart sat back ruminatively and looked out of the window. 'It all goes back,' he said, with a perceptible hint of disapproval, 'to a slightly throwaway line in a speech I gave in Sydney.'

The speech which gave rise to the law that now bears his name was actually called 'Problems of Monetary Management'.[99] It was a comparatively dry piece of econometrics at a conference called by the Reserve Bank of Australia in 1975, the participants mainly being eminent monetary economists. In his discussion of the new-fangled doctrine of monetary targeting, Goodhart suggested that 'Any observed statistical regularity will tend to collapse once pressure is placed upon it for control purposes.'[100]

It seems extraordinary that his self-styled 'throwaway remark' on monetary targets should now be in the social theory textbooks as 'Goodhart's Law', and yet it is. But more than that, it has developed into one of those priceless pieces of theory that might be the antidote to all things tickbox, and their most assertive and troublesome unwanted consequences.

To understand why it happened, and what Goodhart's Law means, we have first to go back to the heady days of 1968. Not just the student uprisings, the summer of riots in American cities, and the spreading civil rights movement. It was the moment in the 1960s when everything unravelled – race riots in Detroit, the Tet offensive in Vietnam, the immediate aftermath of the devaluation of the pound, the twin assassinations of Martin Luther King and Bobby Kennedy. It was the end of the Indian summer for technocracy and Keynesian economics, as it had developed.

Two other events that took place that year are relevant to our story here. First, the pioneering monetary economist Milton Friedman – soon to be adviser to Ronald Reagan and a major influence on global economic policy – set out his stall in his presidential address to the American Economics Association, at which his bundle of monetarist concepts went live. The other event was that Goodhart, a young economist fresh from a PhD in monetary economics at Harvard University, joined the staff of the Bank of England.

Goodhart had done well at Cambridge, and had the cleverness or excellent luck to do his PhD in the USA at the moment of this crucial switch in economic thinking. He had read the manuscript of Friedman's forthcoming book. He was familiar with the technical mathematics behind monetarism, probably more so than any of the senior economists in the UK. So when he arrived at the Bank of England as a junior economist, as the UK economy was reeling from the devaluation of the pound, he found himself a valued expert.

Very much in demand, Goodhart quickly rose to be a chief monetary economist, then a chief adviser. It was a thrilling moment to find yourself in senior policy circles. The UK economy was sinking into what was known at the time as 'stagflation', a combination – believed until then to be impossible – of stagnation and inflation, which combined high unemployment with rampaging price increases; inflation would reach a nerve-wracking 25 per cent in the mid-1970s. And equally rampaging, over the corpse of the British economy, ran the battles between the monetarists and Keynesian economists. Goodhart says now that his role was 'to explain monetarism to the Bank of England, and to explain the Bank of England to the monetarists'. His specialist knowledge began to propel him upwards in policy circles.

By the early 1970s, most countries had begun to adopt monetary targets to regulate how much money was going into the economy, which was not an easy task in a market where banks created money in the form of loans whenever they felt like it. Central bankers would track 'broad money' or 'narrow money' – each a different interpretation of how much money there was, and in different combinations of cash or bank deposits.

The whole idea of money targets was an odd one. It derived partly from the even odder idea that the UK banks could be controlled by good behaviour on their part, plus the occasional interest rate tweak. It used to be said that bank lending was controlled by the eyebrows of the governor of the Bank of England. In fact, there had been little need for raised eyebrows during the 1960s, because the value of the pound was pegged to the dollar, which was at least nominally linked to the value of gold.

All that began to unravel as the vast sums that Robert McNamara was spending in Vietnam began to undermine these cosy fictions about the dollar and the gold standard. When Richard Nixon's administration cut the link in the summer of 1971, the UK banking authorities reverted to the eyebrows solution, backed by interest rate rises and monetary targets. Perhaps it was hardly surprising that the banks let rip and their lending shot up by a quarter between 1971 and 1972, flinging the UK economy into its famous inflationary spiral. Something had to shift. But the question was: which lending target should they focus on?

The issue seemed a simple one to solve. Everyone seemed to agree that it was. They would focus on measures of monetary growth, and when the money supply began to grow too much, interest rates would rise and gently ease it back down again. The trouble was that it didn't work. As he was going through the figures that came across his desk from most countries every month, Goodhart began to notice something peculiar. It didn't matter which country it was, or which target they chose – the act of establishing a target seemed to change it. Whatever monetary target was chosen, because of its relationship to incomes or inflation, would lose that relationship pretty quickly. It was certainly not what was supposed to happen.

Having realised this, the governments that followed, battling the inflation that was a direct result of this failure, kept on having another go and found that it never really worked. In the 1970s, they fell back on the control on mortgage lending known as the 'Corset', which was abolished again under Margaret Thatcher in 1980.[101]

These were the bones of Goodhart's Law. It was clear that the very act of making one figure a target and paying attention to it changed the behaviour of bankers. They would put in extra effort, or interpret their work in slightly different ways, to please their superiors and to meet the target. It was this quirk of monetary theory that Goodhart pointed out in Sydney in 1975.

By doing so, he guaranteed a place for himself in the encyclopaedias. He also upstaged – though he did not know it at the time – the American economist Robert Lucas, who was in the process of setting out in the traditional academic format what became the Lucas Critique. On its appearance in 1976, Lucas said something similar: if there is a relationship between two variables, and this relationship depends on policy, then changing the policy is likely to change the relationship. Or, as one academic simplified

Goodhart's Law: 'When a measure becomes a target, it ceases to be a good measure.'[102]

So Lucas took the credit in the economics community, but by then Goodhart's Law was being studied by theorists of social policy instead. Perhaps that is appropriate, because it is really a statement about how people behave – so that, if you use a piece of data as a target or as a box that must be ticked, then the data will become inaccurate.

Take for example the idea set out in cartoon form by the American cartoonist Zack Weinersmith, which imagines that – through some hideous policy brainwave – all children have to stop studying poetry or the arts and start practising clock-mending, and the number of hours spent mending clocks becomes the target for success among schools.[103] It all seems logical, given that so many top engineers are known to have been keen on taking clocks apart when they were children. But the policy has the reverse effect, as one might expect. 'Science is dead, engineering is static, humanities are unknown,' says the penultimate picture. 'All is clock.'

The final comic picture shows the policy-makers congratulating each other, because 'according to our clock-based metric, everything is great!'

This little story has not actually come to pass – yet – but it does demonstrate the issue that Goodhart's Law poses to organisations, especially large or centralised ones. Not only does the target skew everything, so that the original relationship – in this case, the link between great engineers and clock-mending – is no more, but the target then blinds the distant policy-makers to the truth because they have over-simplified the world and perhaps even lost a way to describe what is now missing.

Just as exam results tend to improve over time, because teachers teach to the test, so target figures tend to get better too, because front-line staff learn – not necessarily how to fake it, but how to make the numbers look better, how to burnish their reputations.

For example, when the Metropolitan Police announced in 2000 that it had recruited 218 people from ethnic minorities, it transpired that it had included Irish people, Australians and New Zealanders in its definition. The meaningful figure was actually just four. Or when the Soviet authorities used to measure the output of their glass factories in tons, they made the glass too thick. When they measured it in square metres, they made it too thin. There is also an explanation here for Robert McNamara's disastrous use of body count to measure success in Vietnam.

It happens in perfectly respectable ways, as Goodhart explains. Imagine you have an NHS target to ensure that patients arriving at accident and emergency departments are seen within four hours. It will be achieved simply because the hospital authorities are paying attention to the target and prioritising its achievement at the expense of other patients, who will have to wait longer as a result. Of course, in those circumstances, the target figures are achieved and the boxes can be ticked.

Then there is the method by which the definitions are tweaked. In the early days of the A&E target, when treatment was often defined as getting patients off a trolley in the corridor and into bed, some hospitals dealt with it by buying more expensive trolleys and designating them as 'mobile beds'.[104]

Even so, it is strange that so eminent a macro-economist should be known more for his social policy theory – but such is the world. 'You never know which bit of your work will be influential or widely read,' says Goodhart now, like Sir Arthur Sullivan agonising that he was better known for his comic sketches than his grand opera. Or Hilaire Belloc, better known for his *Cautionary Tales* than his history. 'The fact is that I'm better known for a throwaway line in a speech than I am for maybe hundreds of more serious academic articles.'

That may be so, but Goodhart's Law is a profound thought and it has huge implications for tickbox. Because it is not just that the act of setting out the tickbox that needs to be ticked skews the data, it also skews everything else.

Goodhart was there at the beginning of the data revolution and he responded to one of its peculiarities. Let's look at what data tends to be correlated with success, said senior managers. Let's make that the target! Sensible idea, but then they found people's behaviour changing because managers found they could sum up in numbers what seemed to be the essence of their job. This narrowed the job so miserably that staff found they could make the numbers change just by tweaking a few definitions.

'It was other people who saw its wider implications, not me,' says Goodhart modestly. 'If you are an academic, you want to have a wider influence. I'd rather be known for this than not be known for anything.'

What Goodhart's Law is unable to do is to work out how *much* the data has been skewed, or how much time and public money has been wasted skewing it. It has been assumed over the years that it points out a small peculiarity, but actually the implications may be huge. Just imagine for a moment that every front-line public servant, and their bosses, have had their judgement skewed and have changed the way they work to meet the targets they are set, rather than what their professional judgement is telling them they should do. Say they have they wasted 5 or 10 per cent of their time, or 5 or 10 per cent of their professionalism has been suborned to turn the service into more of a machine. Taken across the whole public sector, that is a great deal of money.

Goodhart himself suggests that digitalisation offers some answer because you have now a much wider range of data at your disposal. But his law still applies when regulators choose one piece of data on which to make a judgement. 'You could decide internally which one to assess, but then – if they are going to be transparent – the government has to publish the weightings and then, once again, you have a series of targets.'

Therein lies the power of Goodhart's Law. There appears to be no escape from its effects. And if you try to escape from it, it simply turns more of your system into the kind of judgement-free machine that tickbox seems to prefer – and all in the name of transparency.

Nil-qualify and failure demand

What sort of waste has this kind of tickbox thinking caused to our services? The person who has come closest to working this out is the British industrial psychologist John Seddon, now one of the leading systems thinkers in the UK.

His interest began as he was asked to review the first British quality standard in businesses, known as BS 5750, and couldn't see how it related to quality – at least as understood by the Japanese quality pioneers he had been studying. This revelation led him to take on the bureaucrats behind the international quality standard ISO 9000 (the successor to BS 5750), convinced that it was making organisations less effective and less efficient by creating exhausting tickbox systems rather than assessing people face to face. The standard actually 'encourages managers to act on their organisations in ways which undermine performance', he said.[105]

Time after time, he found himself helping organisations which had signed up to ISO 9000, with its reams of paperwork and fearsome inspectors, and found their service deteriorating as a result. Far from increasing trust in organisations, or engaging staff in constantly making the service they offered better, ISO 9000 meant blind obedience to procedures. Companies like the haulage contractor Eddie Stobart, which steadfastly refused to sign up – despite government instructions to do so – found themselves racing ahead.

In one company, Seddon found people made the sign of the cross when the quality managers arrived. 'The ISO campaign taught me that it was okay to question orthodoxy,' he told me. Nearly three decades on, he is one of the most trenchant critics of the process whereby companies or services are turned into modern versions of Taylor's shop floor or Ford's assembly line, where employees are instructed to master one tiny stage of a job in precisely the specified way.

This is an entrenched battle because, for well over a decade, the management consultants who advise the UK government believed that public services should process jobs by dividing front-office call centres from back-office functions. From claiming benefits to buying computers, this is the system we usually find ourselves inside, from the moment we hear the first recorded message about which button we should press.

Seddon proposed an alternative, which puts these two sides back together again, so that the experts can speak directly to the customers, and each task is completed right first time by someone who can see it through from start to finish. He put this into effect in a series of private companies, but then encountered the same problem in the public sector. More than a decade after his ISO campaign, his work drew him into a series of furious arguments with government auditors, first in New Zealand and then in the UK. His angry monthly emails tracked his various engagements with them. But what really drew him into the public-sector battles was his experience of what happens when you subdivide the task of processing housing benefit claims. The revelation was a result of being asked to advise Swale District Council in Kent in 2004.

Swale council, based in the town of Sittingbourne, had difficulties. There were 8000 people waiting for their housing benefit claims to be processed, the government fraud inspectors were due in for an unprecedented third visit, and the local MP was furious. Swale had done everything it was supposed to, dividing its front-office call centre from the experts in the back office – but was still bouncing along the bottom of the league tables. Something was going wrong.

Swale was operating a system for processing housing benefit claims that was the result of a £200 million investment by the Department for Work and Pensions (DWP). People would apply by phoning the call centre. The call centre staff would send the applications for processing to the experts in the back office, and their every move was then measured – how quickly the phones were answered, how quickly letters were answered, how long the claim took to calculate, and so on.

In the case of Swale, Seddon found it took an average of fifty-two days for people claiming housing benefits to get the money, but sometimes as much as 152 days, nearly six months, which is a great deal if you are a tenant – or a landlord, come to that.[106] Seddon has worked on a range of public services since, and he clearly relishes the moment he shows the real figures to managers. They often seem shocked, because they watch the delusory tickbox figures, which usually show something very different. Some councils which were given four stars for excellence by government inspectors turned out to be no better than those which were doing badly. But of course this was so, he says – they were getting their four stars for doing it the wrong way.

As regards housing benefit, this was because targets measured the time between the arrival of a claim at the front office and the moment a decision was made. This was one of the government's 'best value performance indicators', but in practice it didn't measure the time it actually took for the average person to have their claim settled. This is where Goodhart's Law came in, because staff subjected to targets will always find ruses to make the figures look better. In this case, they kept the forms out of the statistics until they had nearly finished them. Then the inspectors would find out, add in more rules, and they would have to use their ingenuity to massage the figures some other way.

Seddon uncovered the use of a rule called 'nil-qualify', which disqualified claimants who had failed to produce all the information needed within a month. The case was then closed and the applicant had to start again from scratch, which stopped cases which might fail the target going through into the figures. In one council, he found that 40 per cent of claims were being nil-qualified. It meant that managers could say that the average length of time spent dealing with a claim was twenty-eight days, when it was actually ninety-eight days.

Often this was nothing to do with the claimants, who were asked to bring in documents they had already supplied. The system was being used to protect front-line staff from the inspectors and to make their managers look effective, rather than to help housing benefit claimants. It fed the delusions of those higher up the hierarchy that things were working when they weren't. In Swale, only 3 per cent of claimants were getting their claim settled in one call or one visit.

'We've forgotten our purpose,' one member of staff said. 'We're pushing paper to satisfy official specifications, not the claimants.'[107]

Of course, there were targets to make sure people were seen within fifteen minutes. In practice, managers often met this target by giving people a form, then sending them home to get more information. When the queues began to gather outside from early in the morning, some managers in other local authorities hit on the idea of giving people numbers and letting the first fifty ask a question (only one, mind) while everyone else could only hand in documents.

When he spoke to claimants in the housing benefits queues, Seddon found people who were coming back for the fifth or sixth time, even sometimes the tenth, bringing in yet more documents. The system was clogged up with its own processes and duplications, bouncing parts of applications backwards and forwards between front and back offices.

The system sounds insane, but it is used in one form or another in many businesses and public services. The front office tends to fragment jobs, which then have to be put together again by the back office – in the absence of any human contact with the person who is claiming, and without taking any responsibility for them. If the case is 'incomplete', there are no qualms about taking it out of the target statistics and sending it back to the front office for more information. And so the volume of work grows – a huge machine for creating work, at vast expense. The targets are met but the service is awful.

To stop fraud in housing benefit, on the part of either the claimants or the front office, the DWP began asking back-office staff to use what they called a Verification Framework. This was a checklist of information they would need before any claim could be processed. Yet in practice it meant more room for misunderstanding, because the back-office experts took a different view about how much of the framework applied to the human being on the end of the phone. One side was using their human skills, despite all efforts to root these out, and the other was applying a set of rules. The framework was designed to be inflexible, so of course it failed to deal easily with lots of different kinds of people. Or, as Seddon said, it stopped the system from 'absorbing variety'.

It is precisely this phenomenon that has so undermined the

introduction of universal credit in recent years – it is deliberately inflexible, so it deals very badly and exhaustingly with human beings. After eight years, the Verification Framework was abolished, by which time the DWP had spent nearly £320 million on it, largely on IT. It had become clear that it was actually raising costs.

It was the inflexible system that was making things so inefficient in Swale too, and this was Seddon's great discovery: the key problem about inflexible systems is that many of the cases they deal with don't fit neatly into the approved categories or boxes – of course they don't, because people are different. And those cases hang around unsolved, clogging things up. Staff who are trained not to use their initiative just pass them on elsewhere, and the poor clients keep phoning and the work mounts up.

Perhaps the best example is the planning departments of local councils, most of which claim to be responsive – because it smoothes the path to solutions, after all – but most of which now, as a matter of policy, no longer answer their phone at all.

Seddon called this *failure demand*. He meant all those people contacting the call centre because something has gone wrong, or because they haven't had a reply – all that extra work which an effective system shouldn't have to do at all. In Swale, he discovered that up to 78 per cent of calls were not from people calling with new claims but from people trying to find out what was causing the delay in current claims. This added to the workload and provided him with his big idea: that there are two kinds of demands on call centres or public services – real demand and failure demand. Real demand has to be catered for; failure demand needs to be diverted. But most organisations don't distinguish between the two, partly because the experts are divided from the people who are calling. Or, worse, because they are paid according to the number of calls they get.

Seddon's answer, which he developed working in the private

sector, was to bring the front office and back office together again so that people could speak directly to the experts with the power to do something about their cases. That meant the system needed to be flexible enough to solve people's problems there and then. It would give staff the responsibility to do the job in the way they knew best, and to judge that according to their own criteria.

Seddon managed to reduce the time Swale took to process housing benefit claims right down to five or six days. Within five months, they had gone from one of the worst in the country to one of the best. Soon they were able to boast that they were 'dealing with the claim as it comes in', which is the way to do it. Yet other local authorities which similarly ended the split between front and back offices then risked being rapped over the knuckles by government inspectors (in those days the Audit Commission). The inspectors demanded that councils show them plans for 'shared services' with other local authorities, so that they could tick that box, and expected to check out aspects of a system which were no longer in existence.

The problem was that the government relied on experts in the management and IT consultancies who were completely committed to the same split. They were not exactly open to Seddon's message.

Now here is the point. Failure demand isn't a small matter. Seddon believes that the proportion of demand on call centres in financial services which is the result of failure elsewhere can be anything from 20 to 40 per cent. In utilities and local authorities, it is sometimes as much as 80 per cent, or occasionally even more.[108] That in itself has frightening implications for the cost of public services.

This may not be the same as the money wasted by using targets, through the application of Goodhart's Law. In fact, failure demand is, strictly speaking, wasted money that is hidden as a result of the tickbox regime. It is one of the effects of Goodhart's Law, but not the only one. There is also the literally incalculable cost of shifting the focus of services from supporting customers and users to what managers want. It would be silly to pretend there is no overlap, but equally silly to pretend that the two amount to the same thing – and the closer you work to the front line, the better you tend to grasp that.

It is also worth relating this to tickbox itself. Where exactly does the box-ticking come in? The answer is that it may be a shorthand way of demonstrating the public sector's compliance. There may not actually be boxes to tick – though often there are, either on forms or online – which show that an organisation or branch meets certain standards, and which are usually based on numerical approximations.

The issue here, as throughout the tickbox phenomenon, is the gulf between the boxes ticked and the reality outside. I would not want to suggest that a mildly corrupt sleight of hand is evident throughout the public sector. What I am suggesting is that there exists a kind of tickbox disease, ferocious in the way it has spread, which blinds managers to the difference between a ticked box and reality – not because they have been corrupted, but because they have developed a habit of seeing the box ticked, breathing a small sigh of relief and moving on.

I first came across this phenomenon in the voluntary sector, at a public meeting where the charity involved had to feed back the numbers attending to their funder, to show 'impact'. The manager said to their employee on the door: 'If any couples come in, can you mark them down as women – we don't have many of those!'

It was only a small bending of the definitions. But I realised also how tickbox encourages a tolerance of small lies. It certainly does on those unusual occasions when I want to take my children out of school for some non-medical issue, maybe a phenomenal educational opportunity or rare family party. I am usually too disorganised, or too busy, to fill in the school's online form two weeks ahead and to wait patiently for 'permission'. It used to seem disrespectful of the office staff to lie to them, so we used to tell the truth. Then I realised the awkward position I was putting them in when they had attendance boxes to tick. So now I just lie, as I am clearly supposed to.

Such small untruths are what smooths an awkward system along, but people get into the habit. Again, it is only a small untruth to forget about the gap between a ticked box and reality. It makes things smoother and easier, but it can sometimes lead to disaster. 'We were always ticking boxes and the focus was on meeting targets rather than doing what matters, and we lost the customer in the whole thing,' explained estate manager Sekandar Ravi, from Hounslow Homes, where Seddon took on the task of improving the antisocial behaviour unit.[109] It was ostensibly meeting its target of responding to 100 per cent of calls within twenty-four hours. In practice, Seddon's team found that three-quarters of callers were actually chasing officers to find out why nothing was happening.

Seddon's team discovered that officers were meeting the target by calling people back, even if they couldn't get through, and leaving a message – so people had to call again. It could take two or three weeks to speak to someone who wasn't just ticking the boxes using customer management software. Cases took up to two years to actually solve.

The 'nil-qualify' rule has been adopted by many local authorities as they desperately try to stretch their budgets. For some years now, planning departments have been using the rule, telling clients that they must withdraw their planning application to fix unspecified issues before the deadline for ticking the box is reached. That means they can keep to their target of the number of applications decided – partly by sending the rest away. I've often found the same is true when trying to open a business bank account.

It is peculiar that a target imposed on planning departments to help the public ends up being used against them.

A new Boyle's Law

Nearly two decades ago, I had a brief but revealing conversation with a prominent member of the New Labour cabinet, who asked me what book I was going to write next. I told him I was questioning the idea of targets. These were the days before opposition to targets had become relatively fashionable, and he was enjoyably astonished. 'But what else can we do?' he asked.

It was a rhetorical question back then. Ten years later, targets had fallen out of fashion, along with much of the detritus of what used to be called the New Public Management. Instead, the new coalition government which took office in 2010 planned to measure by 'outcomes' – measuring the effects of an activity rather than the activity itself. It was a core element of the coalition's conviction that these outcomes should be paid for only when they appeared.

In theory, it certainly makes sense to pay only for what is achieved, despite the practical difficulty of withholding payment and the narrowed field of contractors and bidders that would result from such a move. But, to release the money, boxes still had to be ticked. It seemed to me then – and seems to me now, a decade later – that it was always going to fall foul of precisely the same difficulties that had beset the previous Labour government's targets infrastructure. It would still fail to avoid the sheer power of Goodhart's Law.

For some reason – I never was clear why – I had been invited to a seminar to unveil the new approach at the Department for Communities in 2010. As the acting permanent secretary set out her understanding of the payment-by-results idea, I got more and more confused. Surely it would change nothing; yet, by introducing money, it threatened to turbocharge the same infuriating failure to deliver. If Goodhart's Law had applied before, it would do so in spades once you introduced money, because money would simply increase the power of the target. It would also bizarrely begin to elide control issues with economic ones.

That is the essence of what I said, once I had screwed up the courage to put up my hand. She denied it – and, for an hour or so, I thought I was crazy. Yet I was right. The problem was that the same kind of 'fantasy efficiency' that had so gripped New Labour, and the management consultants behind it, was still influential in Whitehall. It remains so even now.[110]

There was agreement by then that targets should be dumped, but ignorance about quite why. Worse, if Whitehall was really to dispense with targets, what kind of pressure would it be able to bring to bear on public services? There was even a small doubt in the back of the minds of civil servants: what was the purpose of Whitehall without some means of exerting control?

There is also a problem about the whole concept of outcomes. Most consultants talk about outputs and outcomes as if they were absolute categories, as if an outcome was a concrete thing beyond argument. This is not the case. What is the *outcome* of the NHS for example? Is it the number of patients successfully treated? Or is it the health of the population? Because those are diametrically different ideas, and require different measurements and probably different institutions.

Outcome measurements assume that our institutions should be permanent. They are about organisational control. They don't let us imagine whether we might be better off with different institutions instead.

There is actually a continuum of potential outcomes, none of which are definitive. At one end of the continuum, they are little more than a restatement of the simple purpose of existing institutions. At the other end, they are usually outside the control of institutions altogether. The Environment Agency, for example, announced in 2005 that it would measure its success partly by limiting the rise in sea levels, which it had almost no power to affect one way or the other. King Canute tried a similar indicator himself.

Of course, if you can pay people directly for what you can see they have achieved – oil delivered through a pipeline, potatoes by lorry, for example – that might work. But the moment it becomes more complicated, so that the measures stand for something else, then Goodhart's Law kicks in. Payment-by-results has been described as 'performance management with teeth'.[111] This is precisely the problem: giving teeth to a flawed system that measures and rewards the wrong thing, and distorts services, can in practice only lead to more distortion.

So here is the difficulty: you can pay contractors for what they do, even for an immediate treatment (which is what the NHS, quite inaccurately, calls 'payment by results'). You can even make an attempt to measure the long-term effects of actions (outcomes). What you can't do, without running foul of Goodhart's Law, is to stick the two together. Who achieved these outcomes precisely? Where is the causality? When is the cut-off point at which the outcome is defined as permanent? Those are problems even before we start to look at how the definitions of success were manipulated, as they inevitably were.

So here let me humbly submit a new Boyle's Law: *When you use numbers as the basis for payment, they become irrelevant to the broader objectives of the service.*

I used to argue that payment-by-results contracts would hollow out and subvert the services being paid for. They would shift the energy and focus – not to the encouragement of services which can genuinely prevent future demand, but to selecting the clients who could fulfil the definitions of the outcome with the minimum effort. Worse, they meant excluding difficult clients, or even those who were simply difficult to define, because the effort involved for the money on offer would make them too expensive.

Defenders of the system say that you can pay more for the difficult cases, and indeed you can – but that still leaves those on the border between categories to get lost. The alternative is that agencies are allowed to cherry-pick their cases so that they are paid for the easiest, when most anecdotes about successful policy initiatives – like Louise Casey's Rough Sleepers Initiative – suggest that they succeed because they target the toughest cases first.[112]

You can usually recognise effective, tickbox-free systems by their ambition not to go first for the low-hanging fruit (as they tend to put it), but to start by tackling the most difficult cases. But then Casey, a civil servant who didn't really behave like one, didn't have a payment-by-results contract. She did, however, have a prime ministerial target to meet – which she managed by 2002 (achieving a 70 per cent reduction in rough sleeping). There were mutterings from homelessness charities that her methods of counting rather underestimated the situation, but she was certainly helped to achieve what she did by rejecting most of the detailed targets imposed from outside.

She was afraid that they would encourage those at the sharp end to tackle the easiest cases first, to make the figures look good, as they had in so many other areas. For her, the key objective was to go for those who had lived out of doors longest, were the sickest, most drug-addicted and most difficult. If permanent housing could be provided for the most vulnerable people, then those who were less vulnerable would be swept up at the same time.

It may have been that Casey was so high profile that she was constantly in conflict with those, inside and outside government, who were suspicious about being too effective for various reasons of their own; they felt either that being a civil servant meant defending the status quo, or that it was somehow dishonest to actually *solve* a problem. Some in the voluntary sector earned their money out of homelessness, after all, and had a financial stake in the continuance of the problem. There were also people who felt that admitting that progress was being made was somehow compromising the cause. Either way, a quick wander through London's West End today would put these fleeting successes into perspective.

One of Louise Casey's most important contributions was to be recorded at a private dinner in 2005 using the phrase: 'If No. 10 says bloody "evidence-based policy" to me once more I'll deck them.' The speech was leaked to the *Daily Mail*. It was a wonderfully unlikely thing for a senior civil servant to say, and shed some light on an official dilemma. On one hand policy-makers could be heard complaining that policy was being pushed through without a scrap of evidence to support it. One study found – for all the talk of evidence-based policy – that what really influenced ministers was a human anecdote told to them at a critical moment. On the other hand was the tyranny of evidence, where sceptical men – it often was men – waited endlessly for proof that never arrived. As one contemporary said of the philosopher Bertrand Russell, they had an open mind for so long that they couldn't get the damn thing shut. Demanding evidence that could never be forthcoming in the way they expected simply meant delaying action.

The transformation of services from enabling institutions that can bring professional expertise to bear into a kind of game where you push buttons and tick boxes and try to get the money, is partly thanks to targets and payment-by-results. It is the same endeavour, but leached of humanity and morality. Which is why, unsurprisingly, shocked regulators find themselves prosecuting teachers and doctors for fiddling their target results. With payment-by-results, this is now financial fraud.

Rewarding work with high-risk groups more highly, or rewarding for distance travelled, or distinguishing between a range of client groups according to price, certainly reduced the opportunities for cherry-picking, but it also emphasised the main problem: making payment-by-results work requires a whole range of additional rules and complexities, which may seem to reduce gaming but will actually increase it – because rules and incentives inevitably do. Really, the very last thing we should do is to muddle those measurements up with money. Remember Boyle's Law.

I believe that, nearly a decade on, these laws (Goodhart's and Boyle's) have done their damage, but in peculiarly unpredictable ways. The big outsourcing giants, like G4S or Capita, became adept at producing the target numbers. But it was, unfortunately, what they became best at.[113] They did so by narrowing what the service was doing, making it efficient in a purely financial sense, by removing all the most effective human elements – relationships between service users and professionals are not effective for the bottom line. The result was to spray the costs of failure demand across the rest of the system.

The collapse early in 2019 of the probation provider Working Links (Employment) Ltd came the same day that a report by the probation watchdog called for 'urgent remedial action' on one of their contracts, covering Dorset, Devon and Cornwall. Inspectors warned of 'professional ethics ... compromised and immutable lines crossed' because of cost pressures. Staff had avoided giving offenders the highest 'red' risk rating because they did not have enough resources to undertake the level of contact and supervision such a rating required. There appears to have been a deliberate policy to downgrade risk so that they could deal with their workload. Worse, at least for the twenty-one subcontractors, only a handful managed to reduce reoffending enough to earn their payouts.[114]

It was actually the second time the Ministry of Justice had been forced to bail out its privatised probation services. This time, the report made particularly difficult reading. It painted a picture of staff staying in touch with clients by phone, rather than face-to-face, in order to save money. And of clients doing community service being set pointless tasks like moving mud from one pile to another around the same graveyard.

But the real mistake had been around risk, as if risk remains constant. As the Howard League for Penal Reform said at the start, risk can increase or decrease – you can't just assign some kind of numerical assessment and stick to it.

As usual with tickbox, the real world just does not work like that.

The whistleblower's nightmare

Throughout a childhood in Birmingham reading about Nurse Nancy in *Twinkle* comics or watching episodes of *Angels*, Bernie Rochford always wanted to be a nurse. She duly became one, and she also studied to postgraduate level and became proficient in account management, auditing, writing contracts and all the palaver of the modern NHS.

When I met her for the first time, she was working for a London primary care trust (PCT). The trust was about to undergo a period of what they call, in the somewhat brutal world of health administration, 'staff consultations'. As so often with management speak, this meant the absolute opposite – it meant the kind of internal restructuring that set colleagues at each other's throats as they battled over the remaining jobs, like a horrible grown-up version of musical chairs. The purpose was to climb through the hoops required to be among the early PCTs to transform itself into one of the new clinical commissioning groups, forever known by the acronym CCGs.

This is in itself slightly depressing. It reveals the process that so often happens with organisational reform in the public services: the existing staff, leadership and structures simply transform themselves into the new shape and carry on as before. It is a more complex version of Goodhart's Law in action. In this case, as usual, huge egos were at stake in the process. Targets had to be met so that boxes could be ticked. It was a challenging time, and not just for senior managers.

In 2011, Rochford won her particular struggle and was appointed a clinical commissioner for continuing healthcare (CHC) – which again has to be translated for outsiders. It means the person responsible for assessing CHC applications and organising services for the most vulnerable patients – very sick children, those needing end-of-life care and people with serious mental, learning or physical disabilities, all of which must reach a defined threshold of care needs. Some of these care packages cost the PCT up to £6000 a week.

Just two days into her new role, things began to unravel. There were some anomalies. 'Nobody could tell me how many patients we were the responsible commissioner for,' she said. The database didn't add up, and neither did the records or the paperwork. Files, contracts and patients would disappear and others would reappear in duplicate or triplicate. It would be hard for her to do her work unless this could be resolved, but there was an even bigger worry. These vulnerable patients had been sent outside the area to care homes or other facilities and had effectively been lost. Who was responsible for checking up on them and making sure they were OK? Well, the PCT was – or *should* be …

But instead of helping her find some of the answers that she needed, her managers got cross. The situation deteriorated and the anger spread once other staff members realised the records didn't match the patients and they were afraid they would be blamed. Months later, in preparation for becoming a CCG, the team undertook another tickbox exercise to match individual patients to GPs as remarkably it wasn't documented in the database. After a lot of cross-referencing, including phoning up nursing homes to see if their patients were still at that address, the team did a best guess of patient numbers. It discovered that approximately two-thirds of the PCT's named continuing healthcare patients were actually dead or lost somewhere in the UK. Their care hadn't been reviewed for years, there had been multiple breaches of confidential patient-sensitive data, and hundreds of the invoices hadn't been processed for years. You might have expected the PCT to be grateful to Rochford for instigating these discoveries, but instead things got worse for her. As a result, she had begun to fear being alone in the office with some of her colleagues.

'It didn't stop there,' she says. 'In fact, it became a lot worse ... This, in turn, caused sleep deprivation, which impacted on all aspects of my life. All control was taken from me, as I was left waiting for pseudo-investigations or meetings. If it felt scary and unsafe to be at work, it wasn't safe to be off work either, as management wrote to me stating I needed to inform them of my whereabouts and contact details of whomever I was with, when I wasn't at home. It was like being under curfew. And all I had done was ask: "Who are and where are our patients?"'[115]

She found that what she said in meetings was later contradicted in the minutes. When she secretly recorded a meeting to provide objective back-up about what was said, she was told she was guilty of 'gross misconduct'.

What Bernie Rochford later concluded was that all the meetings and quasi-investigations acted like a smokescreen, a waiting game, a means to keep her out of the office and delay the evidence being revealed before the PCT could became a clinical commissioning group. 'Once the PCT ticked the box to become a clinical commissioning group, it would not be regulated by anybody and no one would have the authority to stop the cover-up.'[116]

She found herself at the heart of an increasingly insane world. She also later discovered her senior managers were in the same union as her but the union hadn't declared the conflict of interest when they advised her to drop the case. The nightmare world she found herself in – forced to say where she was day and night, hanging onto her job by the skin of her teeth, subjected to barrages of phone calls and emails, refusing to back down – was taking a serious toll on her health. Sometimes the pain in her legs as a result of the fear and threats was so intense that she could barely walk.

After nearly two years, it was clear that she would have to take the newly approved CCG to an employment tribunal for constructive dismissal – if only to clear her name. In the end, she went to court three times, each experience more painful than the last – representing herself while the CCG was able to employ a highly educated barrister at public expense. She heard her words twisted in other people's mouths. Nor is this an uncommon experience for whistleblowers. And after all that, by the end of the process, she found she had been blacklisted across the NHS: job offers were mysteriously withdrawn. She was stuck.

'I realised we had played the same game, but with different rules,' says Bernie Rochford now. 'I went to court to reveal the truth, while they went in to win. They won – but they didn't, really. Nobody wins in these cases, most especially not the patients or the public, who pay the price.' What happened to all those patients? The duty of candour to the families? They were simply tickboxed out of existence.

She was shunned by some friends and colleagues who were afraid to be seen talking to her. Her MP gave her the brush-off. During the period, she contacted fifty different layers of management or official NHS regulators or watchdogs, and every one of them passed the buck, despite having ticked boxes claiming to provide 'patient safety', 'governance' and 'support for whistleblowers'. She never did find out who regulates the CCGs. But then again neither did the Department of Health, the Care Quality Commission, NHS England, the CCG clinical chair, the HR director helicoptered in to advise the CCG or the Whistleblow Helplines when she approached and asked them – each in turn didn't know and passed the buck to the next organisation. Her experiences appeared in *Private Eye* and in Sir Robert Francis' *Speak Up* report on whistleblowing after the Mid Staffs affair, as a prime example of the tortuous journey many whistleblowers in the NHS face.[117]

Worse, she found that her choice to go to a tribunal meant that the NHS agencies and MPs said they could not intervene while legal processes were going on. But when her case was over, they could not intervene either – because the case was then closed. She and the patients fell down the gap between the NHS and legal tickbox cultures. She was also threatened by her PCT with costs of more than £200,000 if she pursued the case. That threat did not eventually materialise but it hung over her as long as she dared to pursue justice.

All those boxes ticked to support whistleblowers and patients, for the good of the NHS, and nobody helped. There were processes in place, but in practice those processes meant next to nothing. Tickboxes and hoops to gain CCG status were masking the failings in continuing healthcare and commissioning.

'I recognise the need for and benefits of risk assessments, policies, processes, targets, and so on, but trying to pin everything down into certainties and assurances when life isn't like that is a conundrum,' Rochford says now. 'Organisational resilience won't come from doing another restructure, merger, redundancies or pay freezes – but by living and breathing core values. Organisations can either ignore or explore whistleblowers, but the issues won't disappear – the evidence might, but that's another story. It's the taxpayer that pays for the patient care provided – or not – then pays for the staff to not notice it, then for the bullying, threats and intimidation if someone speaks up about something unpopular, the quasi-investigations and kangaroo courts and then the white-wash of issues.'

One of the recommendations of the Francis report is that every NHS trust needs to have a 'Freedom to Speak Up' guardian to support and protect staff and whistleblowers when they speak out. And the good news for Bernie Rochford is that she is now employed as one such guardian, hundreds of miles away from her former PCT in London.

It is now a contractual requirement for any provider offering NHS services to have a Speak Up guardian, but they don't have to believe in it. Her experiences pursuing similar jobs before securing this one convinced her that the same tickbox mentality still applies. One hospital trust CEO who interviewed her responded to her question about the trusts' aims for the Speak Up guardian role, while flopping back in their chair, with: 'I hope in a year's time, I'll understand what this role is about and why there's a need.' That trust was rated as outstanding by the Care Quality Commission.

'They were just ticking the box,' says Rochford. 'If I'd been offered the job by them, I wouldn't have wanted it.'

Still, the use of public funds has to be justified, and so there are more and different tickboxes to complete. Opinion varies on which boxes to tick and what KPIs and data it is useful to collect.

Some favour collecting data on the number of staff who raise concerns to the Speak Up guardians, and thereby measuring what they hope will be increasing confidence among staff in speaking up; others instead suggest measuring the number of concerns that are raised, rather than the number of staff raising them, because this would give an indicator of the number of problem areas in the organisation. But does any of this demonstrate whether the guardian is effective, whether they are just another person in the grip of organisational groupthink, or whether the whistleblowing concerns are ever really resolved?

Maybe identifying the time lag from when a concern is raised until it is resolved is a more useful measure of how responsive an organisation really is, at least when things don't go as well as expected. How much of John Seddon's failure demand is there within the processing of these cases? And at what cost to patients, staff, taxpayers or the NHS as a whole? Perhaps it would be more useful to explore, for example, why it took years to look into concerns raised by a member of staff because, in Bernie Rochford's case, it was just one member of staff raising just one concern.

Rochford recognises that steps are being taken to make it safer for staff to raise concerns in the NHS, but there is still a long way to go. Promoting a 'Speak Up' culture of courageous conversations in the NHS seems to be at odds with fostering a dutiful compliance tickbox culture. Mere tickboxing enables a *lack* of accountability. All these systemic failures have to be measured against the extreme pressure on services brought about by the austerity policies of successive governments, which is why NHS managers are trying to tickbox compassion into the mix, fearful perhaps that the real thing is unaffordable. But that may mean that there is now an urgent job for whistleblowers to flag up what is unseen, dangerous or unravelling. Because they are often the only people who can make visible the reality behind the ticked boxes.

'Otherwise, what's it all for?' asks Bernie Rochford. 'This isn't a mission to save the NHS – it is to save the spirit of the NHS. Once you start ticking boxes and turning a blind eye, the spirit of the NHS has gone. Tickboxing has no real energy behind it. If you just tick the boxes, there is no energy or passion to drive it, it loses momentum. It is short-term thinking and unlikely to be able to go the distance in the long term. Everyone knows it has no value, nor the passion or determination or group cohesion to achieve anything. It's like driving down the motorway in second gear all the way.'

A tickbox education

'Like driving down the motorway in second gear': almost anyone you talk to involved in public services could tell you similar stories to Bernie Rochford's – though few of them can be quoted so that they can be identified, for fear that they will suffer as Rochford suffered. I have covered tickbox local government and tickbox healthcare, but the real worry is tickbox education, because of its deadening potential effects on the next generation, which in practice means a combination of testing, testing again and technocratic inspection regimes. Here is another of my friends, this time working in a pupil referral unit in the south of England. Let's call her Frances.

Pupil referral units are the places you get sent to when you are behaving too badly to stay in the classroom. Staff at the units are able to give more individual attention to the children who really need it, giving their long-suffering classmates and teachers a break. But the process tends too often to be complicated by the way the tickbox targets for absentees are organised. If a difficult pupil goes absent from school, for whatever reason, then they count as an absentee and the school's tickbox position suffers. Handing difficult pupils over to a pupil referral unit means that, if they then go absent, it will be a black mark against the unit, not the school.

Frances tells me about the way that schools dispose of some of their pupils, once their boxes are ticked – in ways that show how little attention they have been giving those who fit no obvious category. She describes a twelve-year-old boy sent to a unit recently who could neither read nor write. He was clearly in need of attention, but the school was so intent on keeping its boxes ticked that it was living a little lie about what this boy could do. He was nice enough, she says. Then she looked at the work the school had sent him with, as schools must do when they send anyone to a pupil referral unit. Instead of an appropriate piece of maths that he might have had some chance of doing, it was a German translation.

Frances told me she went to an empty classroom and wept. It was not that the school was deliberately trying to humiliate this boy; but equally they had shown him so little attention that all they could do was look at what his age group was learning that day, and send him with that.

As we were having this conversation, along came another example. Her unit was sent a ten-year-old boy because he kept refusing to do homework, or to go to the detentions they gave him for not doing homework. He told them later that he had not done any homework for three years, though only now was the school making an issue of it. He was always polite about it. He just calmly informed teachers that he wouldn't be doing his homework.

'Almost as an afterthought on the boy's referral notes to us, it says he is of low academic ability,' Frances tells me. 'Yet once we have him and chat to him, it is clear that he gets no help at school when he is struggling and doesn't do homework because he doesn't know where to start with it. He's a lovely polite, warm boy, who asked for help today when he needed it – because someone is right there for him – and responded well to help given.'

Yet sadly, she says, the situation is getting worse. Rather than send him permanently to the unit, the school is putting him in isolation for missing his detentions. Which means, of course, that he is missing an increasing number of lessons while in isolation for not going to detentions. 'It's a mess,' says Frances. 'If it was an exception, it wouldn't be interesting, but it is typical – and it makes me furious.' How, we should ask ourselves, have our schools become so rigid? How have they ended up such mugs that they are happy to tick a box that says 'zero tolerance', yet have ceased to be interested in flexible solutions?

I am only too aware from talking to my children's teachers how much they feel constrained by the regime imposed on the school from outside, and thence by the school authorities. Despite the undoubted ambition of the best teachers, and of the hierarchy in the school, I have been wondering why my son's best teacher felt compelled to leave so that she could teach as she saw fit. I'm also aware of the pressures on primary schools to ban children from talking in corridors, or parents from classrooms, or to continually squeeze creativity – the arts, poetry and music. Because those things suffer from the ultimate tickbox sin: they are difficult to measure. Meanwhile, the school reports I used to receive have been replaced by numerical estimations of my children's 'grit'.

Perhaps most worrying is what has happened to the English curriculum, which has been reduced to a rump of its former self, partly through the introduction of tests on obscure parts of speech, which no sane person unaffected by tickbox would possibly waste their time with, and partly by the transformation of our greatest works of literature into the subject of multiple choice questionnaires, so that pupils never enjoy literature as a whole – just miserably chopped and diced for comprehension tests. I have a feeling that this may have been what *Northern Lights* author Philip Pullman meant when he described the desolation that faces children when they have their daemons surgically removed.

The number of drama, arts and music teachers in the school system has dropped by about two thousand in each category.[118] But listen to the former Children's Laureate Michael Rosen, who said that 'Our school system is skewed as never before to testing and exams.'[119] Or the educationalist Ken Robinson, whose TED talk called 'Do Schools Kill Creativity?' garnered a staggering 53 million hits.[120] Rosen describes four-year-olds as 'GCSE apprentices', being taught exceedingly narrow slices of knowledge – or 'attainment targets' – which all relate to exam tickboxes. The sad fact is that maths remains the official obsession because it is easy to score and therefore to tickbox. Creativity slips irritatingly through the tickbox cracks.

One reason that so many children with special educational needs (about 15 per cent of them) are being excluded by schools is to maintain those schools' positions in the league tables.[121] Targets again, and their disturbing influence, via Goodhart's Law. 'I have external moderation coming up,' wrote one teacher.[122] 'But am very worried as we're being forced to report children as "working towards" [a certain level] who cannot string a sentence together, use full stops. I don't know what to do.' What is the truth? All we know is that the data won't tell us.

In fact, the whole educational world seems to be pulling in opposite directions. On the one hand, Ofsted inspectors will now look for 'broad curriculum' in schools rather than narrow exam results. 'A focus on performance data is coming at the expense of what is taught in schools,' said Ofsted chief executive Amanda Spielman, who had to come from outside the education sector to see this clearly. We need to go back to treating teachers like 'experts in their field, not just data managers'.[123]

On the other hand, the regime in too many schools has become far too inflexible, thanks to the tickbox approach and the slow war of attrition against any kind of experimental education. Since the closure of the flagship Dartington School in 1987, schools with different approaches to education have increasingly been side-lined. Now it is the turn of the Steiner schools, given that at the end of 2018, three of their secondary schools were put in special measures – and are now being managed by a conventional academy chain – and another one closed down.[124] I am an outsider, and I have no idea how far Ofsted's concerns are due to genuine worries about safeguarding and how far they are simply nervous of variation (education goes at the speed of the pupil in Steiner schools, which is not the way Ofsted sees things). But, even if I doubt whether my own children will benefit from alternative education, I know perfectly well that others will. In fact, we will all be poorer without experimentation, in schools as elsewhere.

Processing by numbers

Let me end this chapter with another story, this time from the most outrageous extremes of the public sector. Once again it is about the Home Office, and it concerns someone I will call Petra. Like many European Union nationals, she lives in her birth country but works in London. One provision of the treaties which allowed EU nationals to access health insurance at home, when they work elsewhere, is that they first need to obtain the relevant paperwork from the country where they work. That is because that is where we pay or have paid our national insurance dues.

Since Petra moved home to her birth country eight years ago, she has been trying to get the paperwork out of the Home Office department responsible. It has been slow progress: at first, the department denied knowledge of any such arrangement. Then, for eighteen months, she received no reply.

'Deliberately, they make sure they publish no postal address to reach them, nor phone numbers. If you phone up, they just repeat that they can't help you until you submit a claim. They did this to me on one occasion for four hours,' says Petra. 'Every hurdle was put in place, so you couldn't reach anyone or communicate with anyone.'

When she did finally receive a reply by post, it took six weeks to arrive and had been posted from abroad, confirming her suspicion that the decision had been processed offshore and had therefore been seriously tickboxed. But when she opened the envelope, to her horror, she found scrawled across the form the words 'employment ended, no grant of insurance, claim denied'.

'It wasn't true. None of it. I had been in the same job with the same company for ten years,' she says.

Finally, in 2015, she made her annual application in January and received the correct paperwork on 9 December. This allowed her a couple of weeks' health insurance coverage at home before she had to apply again. To be fair, by 2018, they were getting the hang of things and she now receives the paperwork within a few weeks. So something is improving, but she remains suspicious.

'Things improved once the UK was going to leave the EU,' she says. 'I couldn't believe they can't reply for a year to a form of their own design. It had to be deliberate.'

I am not sure if Petra is right about this, though of course we don't know what the rules for dealing with these applications were when they were sent offshore for processing. Because, once you start processing forms by numbers, then pride in your work and the ability to empathise with those on the other end of the forms, so to speak, both disappear. As long as the process is complete and staff meet their complex targets, their managers assume that everything is going fine.

So there we are: Goodhart's Law has a terrifying logic to it that starts by bending the definitions of words or processes to make the data look better – so that the box can be ticked – and ends by permanently limiting the meaning of words. If we let it.

5

The Empty Corporation

Corporations have to show more developed emotions than just fear and greed ...

Anita Roddick, founder of the Body Shop
retailing chain, 2001

There I was in the rabbit warren of tunnels in King's Cross Underground station last year when a woman collapsed just ahead of me. The tunnels were soon clogged up with bad-tempered people, stepping around the few passengers who were looking after her and the American woman who had taken it upon herself to direct the human traffic.

I found myself next to one of London Underground's round, white information points. On the rare occasions that I've pressed the information button, nobody has answered. This time, a genuine emergency, it beeped at me for what seemed like an unnecessarily long time, before saying: 'Your call has been redirected to the British Transport Police.'

There were some longer beeps. Then: 'No British Transport Police lines are available.' Finally, there was a crunching noise which indicated that my call had ended.

Now the usual reaction to this kind of dysfunctionality – which, let's face it, happens all the time with most of the public and private organisations we deal with over the phone – is to wonder why they bother installing emergency buttons all over the transport system if they are not going to staff them. But there is another question, which has not really been asked in this way before: *Is there actually anyone there?*

Maybe the emergency department was elsewhere when I tried to call them, having a cup of tea or in a forward planning meeting – or maybe there actually wasn't one. Maybe, like so many other customer-facing functions, it has been excised and handed over to some other harassed tickbox official to do if they have time – or turned into software. Maybe at the heart of these organisations, there is actually now a great emptiness, a silence interrupted only by the buzzing of computer programs and the occasional meeting of the finance department.

Welcome to the world of the absent or empty corporation. It is a rather familiar phenomenon.[125] Try contacting YouTube because your children are being harassed by online bullies, or Virgin Media because you want to cancel your phone contract, and you often find that nobody replies. Some will have experienced the double bind used by Microsoft – perhaps we should call it Catch-23 – when you try to reload your ancient version of Word, that the facility for verifying your software online no longer exists and it has to be done by phone. But hey, guess what, 'no phone facilities' exist for that either.

We have all been there in one way or another, but we tend to think of it as an aberration, an irritating dysfunctionality. We don't assume that this is the way it has been planned. But tickbox and its development in business among the biggest companies has led to the peculiar phenomenon that – as my colleague Lindsay Mackie and I wrote in our pamphlet introducing it – the companies we buy from don't really want to hear from us.[126] They certainly don't want to see us, but they would like us to reply to their five-point surveys to check on their remaining front-line staff.

This is a disease which, as we will see, tends to afflict bigger companies, which are more susceptible to the fantasies that the boxes ticked relate to anything real – and where, partly because of Goodhart's Law, the data from the front line bears only a vague relationship with the real world.

It gives their managers a sort of one-eyed relationship with reality, a belief in single bottom lines and single measures. Years of being managed by KPIs has blunted their ability to deal with complexity. The result, especially if their company has some kind of monopolistic hold on the market – BT springs to mind – is that they begin to limit what they do to the finance function. All the rest gets outsourced, starting with customer service. They really don't want to hear from us – and if they can possibly interact with us via an algorithm, all the better.

What we find in practice is that staff in contact with customers are transformed into security personnel, whose task is to prevent those customers from messing with the machinery. (I recently rescued an old lady from some closing train doors, only to be bawled at by the platform staff for obstructing them.)

'Please continue to hold,' says the call centre recording. 'Your call is important to us and will be answered by the next available operator ...' Here is the evidence that your call is not important to them at all. Nor does the invariable message that 'we are receiving an unprecedented number of calls at the moment' feel at all convincing. Call rates vary only rarely from week to week in their frequency patterns, and these variations are nearly always predictable. The company or government department is unable to bring themselves to meet the demand because, actually, the calls are not very important to them after all.

It would be good to be able to choose a different company with better customer service, but that is increasingly difficult because our governments have become a little pusillanimous when it comes to tackling monopolies. So, for the time being, we are often stuck in the land of tickbox, where the one-eyed man is king.

The one-eyed man

I moved house to Sussex a few years ago. None of the public services I used found it easy to grasp this idea. Some proved incompetent; some proved downright malevolent. But by the end, all of them, in their different ways, managed to sort out the glitches – except one. Southern Water.

The problem stems from the fact that my new house boasts both a number and a name. I enrolled with Southern Water (not that I had much choice) using the number; though I didn't realise it at the time, it used the name. I started receiving letters addressed to the named house, asking me who I was, and I phoned Southern Water back a couple of times to explain the situation. But the letters kept coming. A year after I moved in, it sent round a real person to find out why there seemed to be only one water meter for two properties. I explained the situation to him. He grasped it immediately. But the company itself was too focused on the data to grasp this simple truth. I began to worry about it when I started getting letters warning me that the named house would have its water cut off.

This letter led to a long conversation with the company's call centre. I insisted I should have a second letter accepting that it now understood that it was only one house, and withdrawing the threat. It promised. Unfortunately, the next letter I received said that it had closed my account at the numbered address (which was now an 'uncharged property', apparently) and opened a new account for me at the named address.

I rang the company back and told it that this was wrong. Not a bit of it, I was told. Everything was fine, everything I had paid had been transferred and there would be no further problems. After a flash of inspiration, I asked that my new named address should be changed so that it also had a number. But I was told this could only be done 'offshore'. A week later, I started getting bills for 34p at the numbered address to close my account, and letters asking me if I had moved elsewhere in the Southern area.

Everyone will know the journey from mild irritation, to frustration, to rage that processes like that give us. But I am now out the other side and no longer raging about the waste of my time. Actually, I started feeling rather sorry for Southern Water or, more particularly, for the people who work there. They have a tickbox system, managed offshore, which has rendered them unable to deal with variety – the fatal cause of the extra costs identified by John Seddon.

All that investment in tickbox had rendered their system stupid, because it wasn't flexible enough to deal with very mild human variations. It may be that data provided them with just a pale reflection of what they really wanted to know – so often, tickbox lets the truth slip through its fingers. But by itself, the data also can't predict, can't imagine, can't adapt, and so can't move the problem forward.

Obviously, my address is in itself irrelevant to national wellbeing. But, if the story sounds alarmingly familiar, imagine the effect repeated time after time – across not just Southern Water but every utility using the same kind of inflexible tickbox system – and then multiply it by social services, healthcare, banking and so on. Just imagine. The costs are incalculable, the inefficiency is staggering, and the blind rush towards automation at all costs is really alarming. Especially when, as we all know, a more human, less controlled, less tickboxed system would be able to deal with these sort of problems instantly.

I am not suggesting that we should avoid *facts*. Facts are elements of the truth. But data is just raw figures built around definitions. It looks objective because of the precision, but the numbers are chained to hopelessly malleable definitions. Of course there is some overlap between tickbox data and reality, but that is all.

One of the problems is that our understanding of the companies that run our lives is stuck in a former age. Billy Wilder's 1960 film *The Apartment* was a vision of the great corporation as it used to be, complete with keys to the executive washroom and Mr Sheldrake on the twenty-seventh floor.

It was unusual for Hollywood to tackle the world of work, and so the picture of great tides of people pouring down the lifts and out into the Manhattan streets was an unfamiliar one to us – though it was as much a part of life as our own working schedules today, five decades later, so much more intense. It was the same picture that Walt Whitman painted a century before of the great tides of people emerging from the black ferries across the Delaware and into work in Philadelphia.

Whatever else you might have said about the immense corporate names of two generations ago – General Electric, Grand Metropolitan, National Provincial Bank – they were not, in any sense, empty or absent. Except perhaps in their vulnerability: despite those marble porticos with their denotation of permanence, only GE still exists from the first Dow Jones Index in 1896.

So in what sense are such corporations empty or absent now? Big organisations, in both the public and the private sector, have a special kind of absence or emptiness, one which is hidden but horribly obvious when you point it out. I don't mean that the people are gone, though that is a symptom. Whitman's tides of men are with us still, but they aren't pouring through the portals of the great organisations. The aim of the new corporations today is to cut back on the use of human beings, which requires them in turn to limit their contact with us: we who used to be customers or passengers or buyers or a whole range of things, and are now – in a subtle shift – consumers. In the private sector, tickbox tends to be used to replace anyone who can take a decision, in middle management and on the front line. A similar process has been going on in the public sector, where tickbox has replaced bureaucrats.

The great global corporations, which dominate our lives to a degree unimaginable thirty years ago, have begun to remove themselves from the traditional relationship of the market – a relationship that once gave citizens some power. Once upon a time, if customers, users or purchasers did not like the product or service offered, they could change to another one. Not so much these days, when five banks control around 85 per cent of the UK banking market, when one company dominates more than 85 per cent of the ebook market, when two companies dominate 90 per cent of the US beer market, and when three companies control 70 per cent of the world pesticide market. I could go on; suffice to say that these markets aren't exactly free and open.

One of the great unacknowledged truths about the current era is not that nationalised state services now resemble the multiplicity of private market services, but the other way around. Big corporates feel like the nationalised industries of the past, if they are fully present at all.

When the 'revolution' in public services began in earnest under New Labour, baby steps having been made under the Major government, we were promised more choice. This was the gold-plated carrot for us as we prepared to countenance some privatisation of hitherto stolidly public services.

There were improvements. Train services did get better – cleaner, more comfortable, and temporarily more punctual (though ending the practice of holding connections helped targets rather than passengers). Schools certainly improved, largely as a result of the public money that was poured into buildings, staffing and teacher training. Local authorities became more innovative.

But what we did not see was that this new agenda was emerging at a time of growth in the strength of the financial industry, which – in its insatiable search for organisations to buy up (the unkind might say, assets to strip) – in turn imposed its own corporate mantras and tickboxes on both private and public goods and services. And the principal mantra was that people were expensive, and so was contact with them.

The result was that, for the leviathans which dominate our high streets, our communications, our finances, our public services, our transport, people – both staff and consumers – became primarily a cost and no longer an asset or an investment. A waste, even.

Reductions in staff numbers are now an accepted form of asset-building. They provide, often, the only remaining, easily accomplished, increase in profits. From automatic shopping tills, to automated payment systems, to complex online banking systems, the removal of skilled people, used to helping customers, continues.

In more grandiose language, it is thanks to a fatal tolerance for monopoly and a commitment to economies of scale, and therefore to economic specialisation – the ideology, as much as anything, of the Chicago School of Economics – that our corporations have been hollowed out. In the process, it was necessary to demote customers from a position of some market power, to one where their choices had to fit a new definition of competition.

This absence has allowed both businesses and public services to break their link with their customers and users, backed up, in a sort of perfect storm, by their commitment to a tickbox version of Taylorisation. The remaining finance function believes it can control what happens in every corner of its empire. That is a more or less hidden agenda of tickbox.

Politicians and corporates have been following parallel paths in this respect. As politics has suffered by attempting to simplify itself, and more in a machine-like way than a human way, by focusing on one box or one number, so business has gone the same way. This version of obsession with the bottom line has, paradoxically, left the actual bottom line behind. You could imagine some focus on company profits might be useful. Instead, it is often about some other key figure like EBITDA (earnings before interest, tax, depreciation and amortisation), or the share price, or the GPM (gross profit margin).

Focusing simply on one element of company performance is a kind of short-termism, a kind of paint-by-numbers management. It isn't so much a checklist, because it is too simplistic for that. Short-termism has emerged in economic policy because you can to some extent fake the results – either as a minister or as a chief executive – to create the *belief* that things are getting better. That's your main objective, after all. Growth figures are themselves no longer enough: there needs to be some other measure of what is critical in running the economy. And yet growth figures were a legacy of tickbox, in the sense that they allowed governments to sum up their success in one single number.

The zombie organisation

Not all organisations are empty, absent corporations like this, but most of the big ones are. They have emptied themselves for different reasons: the private ones so they can control their share price better – and speculators prefer companies which have small payrolls and can give the impression of what they call 'efficiency'; the public-sector ones are often private too, because they have been privatised or contracted out, or are otherwise aping private-sector patterns because – quite mistakenly – they seem efficient.

There are still big employers: the big supermarkets or the big online sales companies, or the big public services, where not everything can be automated. All these will take automation as far as it will go, whether appropriately or, sometimes, less so, but there remains – for the time being, at least – the need for some mass employment. This has led to the phenomenon of the outsourcing specialist.

These are a threatened species, for reasons which may be inevitable – they are not in fact terribly competent. Yet at the high tide of outsourcing, their names became ubiquitous. Serco, Capita, Carillion, Interserve, A4E, G4S – all emerged as specialists which could take the business of employment away from other organisations and deliver services on their behalf. As we shall see, this was a little delusory. Their main expertise was not, as it turned out, the delivery of services; it was the delivery of service target data for the ministers who craved it. They are brilliant at ticking boxes; not necessarily at anything else.

But these organisations are also empty in a more fundamental sense, having removed their human functions and replaced them with simplistic and largely dysfunctional algorithms – a process which has also removed something of their moral sense. They are controlled from a great distance by means of a pathetically unambitious series of numbers, to the extent that their human attributes have also corroded. They are, as Body Shop founder Anita Roddick used to say, dinosaurs which can only feel two emotions: greed and fear. That is what lies at the heart of our empty corporations.

Perhaps now, ten years since Anita Roddick died, a dinosaur is itself somehow too much a creature of flesh and blood to be an adequate metaphor. There is something of the zombie about empty corporations. Something of the undead. We shrink from their touch, just as we do from their voice when one of their robots phones us.

The complicated data rules enforced by the software that staff are using have ushered in an era when customers are very much less important than processes. These rules create an intractable combination of such processes with Kafkaesque customer service and a peculiar belief that whatever comes up on the screen is real. Plus of course, the withdrawal from anything that is not focused on the single bottom line.

Take the domestic banks in the UK, for example. The great banks of a generation past had local branches, with local managers, who took local decisions which were based on helping sustain local economies. Over twenty-five years, the mammoth withdrawal of attention and resources from domestic banking, especially in poorer areas – the closing of bank branches and the retreat from small business lending – has taken place because the potential rewards from investment banking (as well, it turned out, as the potential losses) were so much more exciting. Bank managers who knew their localities have largely been replaced with risk software, running a system of credit scoring and operated from a regional office.[127]

This process has taken place across the Western world, but it matters more in the UK because the UK domestic banking market has been so reliant on the big banks. By 1919, the UK banks had been consolidated to a rump of what was known as the Big Five (Barclays, Lloyds, Midland, National Provincial and Westminster), so the UK banking market included little competition from small, local banks, the kind of network which has done so much to redress the balance in many of the countries we work, trade and compete with in the UK.

Lending to small- and medium-sized enterprises (SMEs) fell by nearly one-fifth after the financial crisis, and many more loan requests were turned down. One in four SMEs that applied for bank finance in 2010 were refused outright, compared to just one in twenty-five in 2007, and the smallest firms were hit the hardest.[128] The terms of loans were also changed, in ways that have yet to be properly researched. The level of SME lending only returned to pre-crash levels in 2016. The resulting under-provision to SMEs may seem rational for individual commercial banks, but it damages the economy because it means that wealth-creating enterprises so often fail to get the finance they need to expand.

Most SME credit applications are filtered out before they even reach the credit scoring stage. Evidence suggests that small banks are better at using the 'soft' information needed to assess the prospects of small firms, because they have the banking equivalent of boots on the ground.[129] What this amounts to is that not only do big banks lack the infrastructure to price local risk effectively, there are virtually no small banks to take their place – only 3 per cent of UK banks are local, compared to 34 per cent in the USA, 33 per cent in Germany and 44 per cent in Japan.[130]

Then there are the physical banking structures on which so many ordinary businesses rely. The small Sussex town where I live has just lost two banks and ATMs, and seems likely shortly to lose the last. The customers, whose decades of loyalty have been so badly let down, are told that they can use the post office to bank takings, and they can – though the post office in the next village has closed (there are two ATMs there too, which charge £1.99 to disgorge your cash).

The point is that, without any response from policy-makers, and for the reason that neither the post office nor the bank branches are selling enough insurance or other financial products, banks have withdrawn from their marginal service role, to the great detriment of local businesses. Nor are there enough 'scale up' companies – companies that have a chance of being household names one day – opening accounts. That isn't supposed to be the purpose of banks, but that is how their success is measured, so that is what it becomes. We are not rich; and if you are not rich, you are expected to pay.

Otherwise, the banks have withdrawn their attention to their core functions, focusing their service energy on places that can maximise profits. Their version of tickbox is one that tries to keep the risks at bay, but at a cost – which is that they have withdrawn from activities that might allow them to support, understand, glean information from and ultimately profit from local business.

Perhaps the most egregious example came from the Royal Bank of Scotland's global restructuring group, which after 2008 was supposed to be helping small business customers in financial difficulties. It turned out to have a very different purpose, harrying 12,000 small businesses, some of them into bankruptcy, which meant that the bank could seize their assets. The role of tickbox was made clear in an internal memo written in 2009. 'Sometimes you have to let customers hang themselves' when in financial difficulty, it stated, explaining that 'missed opportunities will mean missed bonuses'.[131] RBS said later that the memo did not reflect bank policy.

That is logical, in a sense, as are many of the trends suggested here. But it means that resources are increasingly concentrated on the handful of businesses with growth potential as conventionally measured. A few of those might help my town, but what it actually needs are ordinary businesses, shops and services, which will not demonstrate stratospheric growth rates. Unfortunately, resources are now so closely targeted that such businesses will have nowhere to bank cash apart from queuing up at the equally scarce post offices.

So who is going to provide for the rest? Should the market involve more than the maximising of profit for asset-holders in far-off lands, on Wiltshire estates and in ludicrously expensive houses in Notting Hill? It certainly used to. But then, senior managers and economists have persuaded themselves that there is no such thing as 'soft information'.

Oddly enough, there is a parallel debate in the medical profession about whether soft information, the kind of understanding you can get about patients from their context, or the story they tell, is important or not. The process was dubbed 'narrative-based medicine' by Professor Trisha Greenhalgh, herself an experienced GP – not so much in opposition to the prevailing rule of evidence-based medicine, but as an addition to it.[132]

She told the story of Dr Jenkins' Hunch, based on the tale of a Cardiff GP who was called by a mother he knew who said that there wasn't much wrong with her daughter, but that she was 'behaving strangely'.[133] Dr Greenhalgh asks trainees to work out why it was that Dr Jenkins broke off his Monday morning surgery and went straight round to her home, where he diagnosed meningococcal meningitis in time to save the girl's life. Was it that he knew how level-headed the mother was? Was it something in the voice?

Whatever it was, it would have eluded a computer or a doctor – real or virtual – relying on checklists, who thought that medicine was just about formal evidence and coming up with a scientific hypothesis, just as it would have been impossible to input the critical data onto a record card. It wasn't that Dr Jenkins was *ignoring* the data or the information. He was expanding it in ways which a computer could not do – and certainly will be unable to do for some decades to come, if ever. He was doing so by using the soft information, the medical equivalent of gossip.

There is also a fringe of doctoring which regards narratives as more than the sum of their constituent facts. Lewis Mehl-Madrona is a doctor, but that isn't quite the end of the matter. He is part Scottish, part French, part Cherokee and part Lakota. He is also, as a result, a thorn in the side of the American medical establishment, because of his insistence that there are elements of traditional healing methods that work.[134]

His arrival at Stanford Medical School in California happened to coincide with that of a number of other rebels – his class included people who became barefoot doctors in Tibet, or studied by wandering around Mexico and Central America. This so irritated the authorities in the medical school that, the following year, they changed their entrance requirements. What had been bothering Mehl-Madrona was that, much as he enjoyed his work in the accident and emergency department where he was training – with all the technology and machinery – he could not forget the traditional healings he had witnessed as a child in the Lakota and Cherokee communities of his relatives, healings that his colleagues and teachers dismissed as 'miraculous'.

He began to study the traditional practices of his Native American relatives, and what he found flew in the face of mainstream medicine. When these healings took place, they tended to be experienced by patients in a relationship with the healer and who were not focused on a cure – and who were open-minded about the transformation of their lives that was required. Above all, they tended to involve telling a story.

The healings fitted well with other practices, like the twelve-step programme for curing alcoholism, but it didn't fit at all well with modern medicine. If all we need is simple data – symptoms and mechanical readouts – then a computer can and does provide at least as good a diagnosis as a human doctor. Trisha Greenhalgh and her narrative-based medicine movement may not subscribe to this kind of traditional healing – I have perhaps done her no favours putting her in the same chapter – but at the heart of both stories is a similar idea: that facts alone are not enough, that they can provide too little information for healing to take place.

Mehl-Madrona remains a doctor, and a professor of psychiatry, concentrating especially on geriatrics, but he has studied traditional healing for a quarter of a century and has tried to integrate the two – and he does that through stories. Stories are key, he says, not just to diagnosis but also to healing.

These examples say something about why reducing professional functions to numbers and then rearranging those numbers, or automating the functions – missing out on the tools and evidence that professionals need to function effectively – seems to render the professionals themselves less effective. Evidence without the narrative is just not enough, either in medicine or in banking. Yet that is what we tend to get when we empty our organisations of people, replacing them with automated algorithms based on incomplete data – watched by the technocrats at the heart of the great organisational machinery.

Ghost trains

It so happened that I was there, on the platform so to speak, just as one of the most notorious data-driven – indeed one of the emptiest – UK corporations began to unravel. This is because I make my way from Shoreham-by-Sea in West Sussex via Southern Rail to London Victoria once or twice every week.

I had been aware by June 2016 that all was not well with the franchise. There was nobody on the trains to sell me hot drinks or refreshments any more, and the regularity with which services were being cancelled was becoming ridiculous, laughable even, had it not been so infuriating.

By the first weeks of that month, the cancellations were mounting up until they seemed to include most of the timetable. Then one day, there I was, and none of the impersonal 'we apologise ...' messages could be heard. No explanation that it was all the fault of 'staff shortages'. Nothing. The trains had simply been removed from the indicators as if they had never existed at all.

Why? I asked a rare member of Southern staff.

'Staff shortages,' he said.

On an impulse, I said, 'But that's not true, is it?'

He stared at me for a moment, then said, rather unexpectedly, 'You're right, but I can't tell you the real reason or I would be sacked.'

The first blog I wrote on the subject was about that initial conversation, and I was pleased when as many as ten thousand people read it. But when, by the end of the first weekend, one hundred thousand people had read it, I began to feel scared. What had I unleashed? Members of Southern staff were writing to me or calling me anonymously. One of them even resigned his job on the comments section of my blog. I wrote a short book on what I learned – it was called *Cancelled!*[135] And I borrowed a brilliant photo for the cover from Summer Dean, one of the duo who had launched the Association of British Commuters that same month, that showed almost the whole departure board at Brighton covered with cancelled trains.

It was frightening but it was also fascinating, because here – or so it seemed to me at the time – was a public service company that was so empty at the top, so data driven, that it was incapable of providing a proper service. I was determined to find out how this organisation had emptied itself – realising that I had been taking for granted that it had barely changed since 1948, when the old Southern Railways had been a byword for efficiency, from the red ties the staff wore in those days (for waving in an emergency) to the kippers they served to Laurence Olivier coming home on the Brighton Belle in the morning from first nights in the West End.

Why had it unravelled? Well, Govia Thameslink Railway

(Southern plus Thameslink plus the Gatwick Express) is an example of an outsourcing vehicle, owned in this case at arm's length by the French transport company Keolis and the train company Go Via – which is in turn a subsidiary of the bus giant, the Go Ahead Group, once from Newcastle, now rather disconnected from the world in its City of London offices in Museum Street.

Since it took over the franchise in 2014, GTR's performance had been lamentable. This was not entirely GTR's fault: it suffered from the mismanagement of a major redevelopment of London Bridge and the failure of Network Rail, the managers of the track and stations, to invest south of central London. The number of passenger journeys was increasing very rapidly and the entire infrastructure was under strain. By the spring of 2016, after two day-long strikes by guards angry at company plans – mandated by the Department of Transport – to make the whole franchise driver-only, the timekeeping collapsed, and more than a third of services were cancelled.

First, haphazardly and then, with Whitehall's agreement, the timetable changed, with about a quarter of services removed. But even the new temporary timetable proved too much for GTR. Day after day, services were cancelled at the last minute, driving passengers like cattle between non-existent trains. Often traffic controllers gave up and cancelled trains each day, aware that it was impossible to run them. And it was the front-line staff, on trains and platforms, who bore the brunt, day after day, of furious, exhausted and even fainting passengers, and contradictory, rapidly changing or non-existent information.

People depend on railways to get to work or to do business. Many lost jobs or were forced to resign. Many more were unable to see their own children because they arrived home so late every night. The traffic on the London–Brighton M23 increased to disastrous levels. Air pollution increased. In a desperate move to survive until they were allowed to impose new driver-only contracts, GTR reassigned eight managers from their Brighton depot to act as guards on the Seaford line. A campaign among commuters, which emerged to take the government to court over GTR, raised its initial target of £10,000 within a week. A sense of powerlessness and deep frustration made passengers horribly aware of their own weakness, despite the original idea that privatised services would be more responsive.

GTR is the quintessential empty company. It is run by the finance function of Go Ahead, and is primarily a vehicle for maximising Go Ahead's income. It runs its services by numbers, because it is so distant from the action; its managers are accountants who also happen to run a railway, and it is hardly surprising that they don't do it very well. Rather like schools with their difficult pupils, this tends to make the company inflexibly authoritarian with its otherwise loyal and hard-working staff.

It was a surprise to GTR managers that staff numbers when the company took over were lower than they expected. But the numbers have remained at least 20 per cent down on what is needed ever since, though there are always supposed to have been drivers and guards in training. GTR seems not to have the flexibility to fix this. The company also dispensed with station staff along the south coast, closing ticket offices with plans to rent them out as convenience stores. Ticket inspectors were replaced with contract staff and revenue protection teams were dispensed with.

All these actions were completely predictable given the structure of GTR's unusual franchise agreement with the Department of Transport. This set out that all the ticket money, less 3 per cent, would go direct to the government, and GTR would be paid a set fee – £8.9 billion over seven years. The Department even had to fork out for late payments to passengers who had been delayed. It seems obvious, in retrospect, that there were no economic motivations for GTR to keep its trains running to time, and that the only way for them to maximise income was to radically reduce costs – there were no benefits for the operator in increasing passenger numbers.

Not only is GTR an empty corporation in the sense that it is not primarily a train operator, but a virtual accountancy programme operating by numbers. It also has within it no human or economic motivations which might lead it to provide a good service for passengers.

As an empty corporation, GTR has taken on the obsessive fear of the rail unions that infects their real customer at the Department of Transport. This has led to the 'iron fist' policy of threats, and the docking of two days' pay for every day the guards stopped work during the two short strikes of April 2016, which led directly to the disaster two months later.

It was the problem of overtime that caused the bulk of the delays: there were too few staff to operate the timetable without it. GTR managers convinced themselves that the local flexibility that allowed depot managers to negotiate with guards and drivers to stay later or arrive earlier, or do half a shift, was somehow retrograde. The dip in overtime which caused the difficulties that began the following spring and summer was a direct result of this attitude – but because it was obsessed with the union threat, the company blamed delays on a 'sicknote strike'.

There was no evidence for this claim at all, but it appeared to let the Department of Transport off the hook, so it was widely repeated. It was true that sickness rates had gone up, but the growing stresses suffered by front-line staff were enough to explain it. The highly centralised company also compounded the error by insisting on doctors' notes for any absence, unaware perhaps that these are only available for *weeks* off work, not for days off. That regulation undoubtedly compounded the problem.

This kind of treatment had precisely the opposite effect to that intended, raising sickness rates, insulting loyal and exhausted staff and driving them into the arms of the very rail unions the company feared. Some of the unions were themselves no help, harking back to a boneheaded and nostalgic view of the great days of industrial disputes, which was almost as damaging to passengers as the original problem.

But there was GTR, its refurbished offices in Matthew Parker Street echoingly empty, its long-suffering staff organised by spreadsheet, its management involving a tight group of colleagues and former colleagues – one of the side-effects of this style of franchising. Ask them for help with a wheelchair, phone them to ask their advice, and – as with other absent corporations – you find you can't. There is nobody there.

Mind the doors!

As I have already observed, one of the peculiar implications of empty corporations is that they transform customer-facing staff into the minders, security guards and defenders of machinery. Sometimes that machinery is the software that gives them a script and undermines their ability to help customers solve non-standard problems. Sometimes, the task of the machine-minders is to make sure that customers stay passive and easy to process, and don't obstruct the doors.

At manned railway stations, there are often more staff guarding the barriers than there are selling tickets. But the best example may be supermarkets, where numbers of checkout staff are shrinking as they are replaced by security staff and robot-minders, there to make sure you treat their automated checkouts properly. As always with empty corporations, customer service staff tend to get transformed into security staff whose job it is to guard the technology.

By the way, there is a sense in which the station gates are a fascinating metaphor for tickbox. Their purpose is to be implacable and inflexible, to allow no human judgement. But in practice, so many tickets fail to work that the gates have to be either manned or left open. So it is with tickbox.

It began to annoy me that, after each wasted evening waiting for Southern trains, I still had to show my ticket. As the months went by, and the emergency timetable showed little improvement, and then we were caught in a real strike, this time by the train drivers, I began to get very cross.

I never did talk to Go Ahead chief executive David Brown, but I understood that he and government ministers had convinced themselves that they had been the victims of a vicious trade union conspiracy, that militants had cooked up the 'sicknote strike' that so torpedoed their services in 2016. This seemed to me to be another example of how insulated those at the top of empty corporations can be (and when the sickness rates went back down again, the service was still appalling). In fact, most of the militant trade unionists I met turned out to be, when asked, very cross Conservative voters.

But no, ministers and executives alike were able to avoid personal responsibility in their own eyes – because, first, they were the victims and, second, the whole operation had been a game of chess between management and staff, where passengers irritatingly got in the way.

It was hard for them to grasp, just by looking at their data, that if you reduce crew numbers at the same time as platform staff to the extent they have, it will inevitably constrain the ability of people in wheelchairs to travel. This was almost as irritating as the shiny Thameslink trains, the insides of which looked as if they had been designed to be hosed down every night.

I began to wonder what Gandhi would have done in the same situation, if he had been a passenger. It was a bit like going to a restaurant and finding it couldn't provide you with what was on the menu, or maybe with any food at all – but you still had to pay for the steak tartare you'd ordered, even though you only got a cheese sandwich for which you had to wait an hour. Then, as an extra humiliation, you also had to prove you had paid when you left, by handing over your receipt to a security guard.

In such a situation, I reasoned, it wouldn't be an excuse that the restaurant's waiting staff were off sick or that the chef was on strike. Yet, when we complained to the government about this particular eating joint, they would blame striking waiters – though we might also notice that the disastrous service had gone on far longer than the strike.

It struck me that if Gandhi had unexpectedly been commuting alongside me, he might have refused to hand over his ticket at the resolutely guarded gates of Brighton station. This would force the rail managers into either climbing down and opening the gates, or confronting the passengers they constantly apologised to. It would hardly make a difference to the service, but it would constitute one of those symbolic victories that Gandhi set such store by. I also realised that, to kickstart #passengerstrike, I would probably have to do this myself.

I am not naturally brave. I am certainly no organiser or conventional protester. But I took a deep breath, put on my suit, printed out a letter to passengers explaining what I was doing and handed it out on the 16:22 from Blackfriars to Brighton.

Summer, the photographer, very kindly joined me, or I would have done it entirely alone. I went through the train asking people if they would join me by the gates, refusing to show our tickets – and have some cake. One passenger said she wouldn't because she was backing the strikers; two others said they wouldn't because I was clearly a troublemaker (I don't think they were backing the strikers). Apart from them, I was surprised at how many people said they would join us, including the Brighton MP Caroline Lucas. Many more promised to give us a thumbs-up as they went by.

Either opening the gates or keeping them closed would embarrass Southern's managers, but it took me by surprise quite how quickly we managed to stir them into action. The passengers in the final carriage I went into included a Southern executive. He was later overheard phoning ahead to staff at the station: 'We've got a problem,' he said. 'Get everyone out by the gates!'

So when we arrived, ten minutes or so later, although we were met by a line of security guards – Southern's main recent investment – the gates had been opened. We cheered, claimed victory, and categorised GTR's action as a humiliating climbdown. It was exciting, and I am very glad we did it. But half an hour later, when we had finished our victory party, the gates were closed again.

I have no idea whether #passengerstrike would have had the desired effect if we had carried on with it. But we never had to find out. Hours after the *Guardian* published my account of our day as Gandhiesque protesters, the government instructed the company to settle with the drivers' union, Aslef. I would like to think that the prospect of a peaceful uprising by middle England – the combination of angry people in suits with cake – scared them so much that they caved in. But actually I have no idea.

I published some advice for anyone who wanted to try it themselves, and I reproduce it here, in case train services go wrong next time you travel:

Take three friends on the train with you for moral support; understand that many people will be desperate to get home and won't be able to stay at the gates; be polite: don't browbeat the security staff – focus on the manager in charge; sing songs, eat cake, but – most of all – have fun.[136]

That is in fact rather a good recipe for life, and it is entirely unrelated to tickboxes of any kind.

Is big beautiful?

As I write, in 2018, two American thinkers, the IT think tanker Robert Atkinson and the public affairs academic Michael Lind, have teamed up to publish a defence of big business against what they regard as the privileging of small business. Statistics pour out of their book to defend the main proposition – that big business is more efficient, more innovative, better in every possible way. They call it *Big is Beautiful*.

I describe the book now because it is in every respect the op-posite of what I am advocating. It offers, though, if read carefully, some justification for my thesis that small organisations manage a more personal approach while big organisations fail to do this by relying on tickbox, algorithms and a slightly deluded imposition of central control. But that is not what the authors intended.

There is, of course, an argument that companies have to merge in order to pool resources or to avoid legislation on cartels so they could manage the variations in the price of raw materials or com-ponents – it doesn't really matter *why* they got big. *Big is Beautiful* is a hymn to scale and economies of scale in an age in which, despite everything, people are beginning to be a little sceptical of those things.

It is also a paean of praise for statistics. Some of them don't re-ally travel, like the decline in self-employment in the USA, which is certainly not the case in the UK. Others have been roundly rubbished by Stacy Mitchell of the Boston-based Centre for Local Self-reliance, whose work – because she has been such an effective anti-trust advocate battling against monopoly power – must have been one of the reasons the book was written. But it would be perverse of me to write an anti-tickbox book and then wrestle too much with statistics.

No, the real problem I have with Atkinson and Lind's thesis is what they say about the decline of start-ups: 'We see the decline in small businesses like Justin and Ashley's independent pizza parlour as a good thing, reflecting the growth of more efficient, more innovative larger firms.'[137]

That is so wrong-headed it could only have been written by someone in thrall to tickbox. Some parts of it are more obviously wrong than others, but let's just look at innovation. Atkinson and Lind say that big companies are more innovative than small ones – and, if you only look at official headline, tickbox figures, perhaps you might be forgiven for thinking so. The raw figures are the number of patents issued in the USA: large firms hold 37.4 per cent of patents and small businesses only 18.8 per cent. Case closed? Don't believe it.

Because one reason for those figures to appear as they do is that the multinational companies have been straining every sinew to buy up the innovative small companies that hold the patents, and have the creative power to get more.

This is true especially in big pharmaceuticals, but it is also true of food companies, where the big players have recognised that the small players have the edge in authenticity.[138] In fact, the demand for healthy, fresh, 'real' food is now so powerful in the USA that it is turning the food industry upside down, and beginning to re-localise the production of food. Hershey's have been taking BST milk, GM ingredients and artificial flavours out of their chocolate bars. Campbell's Soup has bought baby food maker Plum

Organics, and – to keep its authentic spirit – has made it a public benefit corporation. They are attempting to *feel* small-scale and personal, and spending a great deal of money doing so.

By 2015, there were also nearly 8300 farmers' markets in the USA, the figure having grown at an average of 19 per cent a year for nineteen years – the absolute mecca for small food producers.[139] People want it. A great deal of money is shifting out of big food corporations and into small-scale local production. (You can see similar trends emerging in the UK, if not nearly so fast.) The twenty-five biggest food and drink corporations in the USA have lost a total of $18 billion in market share since 2009. That seems to me to be good for the economy: it is $18 billion not going in mega-salaries and tickbox and dedicated to the wrong kind of efficiency, but shifting instead into local employment and innovation. I'm sure Atkinson and Lind would find such an idea completely incoherent.

This is what Campbell's CEO Denise Morrison said: 'We understand that increasing numbers of consumers are seeking authentic, genuine food experiences, and we know that they are sceptical of the ability of large, long-established food companies to deliver them.'[140] The problem for big companies is that this is very hard for them to deal with. To demonstrate the authenticity they seek, they are buying up small producers of healthy food, only to find that, in the stultifying big company culture, their new purchases shrivel up rather like an elderly organic lettuce. You can see something similar happening in the beer market. It is even happening slowly in the energy market. But the mere fact that it is possible at all – that we are not locked into buying from semi-monopolies as much as we feared we were – is a heartening thought.

If economies of scale were the only argument, none of this would be possible. The problem is not that there is no such thing as economies of scale – there is – but that they are very rapidly overtaken by diseconomies of scale. You can see how this is happening much faster when you look at the 'soft' data that economists don't trust. In fact, the diseconomies tend to remain invisible in someone else's budget, so tickbox tends to ignore them.

Every time I visit my child in primary school (my eldest left earlier last year), I am reminded of how this works in the education system. Despite the occasional blip, our primary schools are the jewel in the crown of UK public services. They are human in scale, widely involving parents in the process of schooling and extremely effective.

Secondary schools are not always so successful, and I've been puzzling out why, despite the rhetoric, they tend to be aloof, technocratic, somewhat intolerant and excessively concerned about appearances. They stress children out in the interests of their education and the children, in turn, stress each other. I'm particularly concerned about the failure of my son's new school to provide enough tables at lunchtime. It may seem a little thing, but it matters.

Why this gap? Because secondary schools are too big. They need technocratic systems to control them. They need to be managed by rules and computers, rather than by the human-scale, humane flexibility that most primary schools seem to manage. Educationalists obsess about 'maximising the teaching time' because actually the whole set-up is not very conducive to learning in the first place. Learning requires relationships, and the institutions are sometimes too big to manage relationships on the necessary scale.

Of course, this sounds a bit glib. You can imagine companies, factories, schools, hospitals and doctor's surgeries that are just *too* small, and rely too much on one individual. But the power of smaller educational institutions has certainly been confirmed by most research into small schools over the past generation, which has challenged the idea that schools are better when they are bigger. The mistake seems to have first been made in the USA after the successful Soviet launch of the *Sputnik* spacecraft. Educationalists persuaded themselves that somehow only huge schools could produce enough scientists to compete with the USSR. It is one of the peculiar ways that Soviet thinking filtered into the West.

The first challenge to this idea came from Roger Barker, describing himself as an environmental psychologist, who set up a statistical research centre in a small town in Kansas after the Second World War and researched the local schools to within an inch of their lives. His 1964 book *Big School, Small School*, written with his colleague Paul Gump, revealed that – despite what you might expect – more activities took place outside the classroom in the smaller schools than in the bigger schools.[141] More pupils were involved in those activities in the smaller schools, between three and twenty times more in fact. Barker also found that children were more tolerant of each other in small schools.

This was precisely the opposite of what the big-school advocates had suggested: big schools were supposed to mean more choice and opportunity. It wasn't so. Nor was this a research anomaly. Most similar research has been carried out in the United States rather than the UK, but it consistently shows that small schools (300–800 pupils at secondary level) have better results, better behaviour, less truancy and vandalism and better relationships than bigger schools. They show better achievement by pupils from ethnic minorities and from very poor families. If you take away the funding anomalies which privilege bigger institutions, they don't cost any more to run.[142]

But why should it be that smaller schools work better? There is some consensus among researchers about this. The answer is that small schools make transformational human relationships possible. Teachers can get to know pupils, and vice versa. 'Those of us who were researchers saw the damage caused by facelessness and namelessness,' said the Brown University educationalist Ted Sizer, who ran a five-year investigation into factory schooling in the 1970s. 'You cannot teach a child well unless you know that child well.'[143]

Frightening evidence of this came in 2008, when the *Times Educational Supplement* reported that 21 per cent of Year 8 pupils surveyed said they had never spoken to a teacher, even in class. 'Talk to the children, if you can,' one school volunteer I know was told by the headteacher on their first visit. 'Nobody talks to them these days.' That is evidence for a lot of peculiar things about our society, but it is also about the scale of organisations, and schools in particular.

It also seems pretty clear also that the smallest police forces are the most effective, catching more criminals for their population than the big ones.[144] That is another reason why American hospitals cost more to run per patient the bigger they get.[145] These are the costs of scale in the public sector, but – helped no doubt by the way the bigger institutions tend to pay higher salaries – tickbox seems to obscure them. It may be that higher salaries at the top are a benefit of scale: I would say that only if they were widely shared.

There is evidence of the costs of size in the private sector too. When the business writer Robert Waterman says that the key to business success is 'building relationships with customers, suppliers and employees that are exceptionally hard for competitors to duplicate', you know things may well have to shift.[146] Because, unless business as a whole shifts away from relationships, size will anyway get in the way of them.

There is evidence that the bigger companies get – and the more impersonal – the less innovative they are able to be. Which brings us back to innovation. More than half a century ago, the chairman of General Electric's finance board, T. K. Quinn, put it like this:

Not a single distinctively new electric home appliance has ever been created by one of the giant concerns – not the first washing machine, electric range, dryer, iron or ironer, electric lamp, refrigerator, radio, toaster, fan, heating pad, razor, lawn mower, freezer, air conditioner, vacuum cleaner, dishwasher or grill. The record of the giants is one of moving in, buying out, and absorbing after the fact.[147]

We have known this for years, but the system still struggles with the idea. It is time the issue of scale was placed centre stage, as it deserves to be.

Let's go back to Atkinson and Lind's hated pizza parlour (I don't know what they have against locally made pizza). If we really had fewer small businesses carrying out this kind of role, we know perfectly well what life would be like. Food would only be provided where extra profits could be made, town centres would be more empty, more bland, duller and less imaginative. There would be less local identity, probably more crime.[148] We would not be able to contact, still less talk to, those who took decisions in Tesco-Virgin Pizzas Ltd. We would be that much more enslaved to tickbox.

The real question is why anyone might think otherwise. Atkinson and Lind clearly believe what they write, but they are arguing on the side of the technocrats – the very people who have most faith in the tickbox figures, and who least understand Goodhart's Law.

Take Southern Rail owner Go Ahead, for example. Its annual report for 2017 – covering the year when the GTR service unravelled – gives you statistics on carbon emissions per passenger, EBITDA, dividend cover, bus accidents. It points out that the company now accounts for 35 per cent of journeys on the UK rail network. Every possible tickbox is rolled out, but we also know that, during the same period, the company failed miserably to operate the GTR network. And although there was an industrial relations issue at the time, and high absenteeism which the report says 'we believe' is linked, the boxes for rail figures are ticked and you can see little or no self-reflection – either in their rising customer satisfaction level (82 per cent) or in their rising rail revenues (+51 per cent).

Tickbox is absolutely in control. I am sure every figure is absolutely correct, but there is no recognition that they nearly lost their franchise through incompetent and disastrous organisation, nor that the rail minister resigned in despair. It is all both completely true and at the same time highly inaccurate. Perhaps this is why tickbox has become the favoured tool of marketers, diplomats, salesmen and annual report writers.

But what is most worrying is that, from their offices in Matthew Parker Street, the senior managers and board of Go Ahead clearly believe the whole thing. Just as Atkinson and Lind would. And here is the great technocratic divide – those who rule the world believe the figures; the rest of us know the truth because we can see it for ourselves.

It leads to a kind of craving among those at the top of big, centralised, imperial systems. They desperately want to know what is happening. Their staff bring them graphs and statistics, of which they are suspicious – but what else do they have?

I use the term *craving* advisedly, because there is something of an addiction here. 'Monitoring has become almost religious in status, as has centralised control,' said Richard Elliott, formerly of the Bristol Drugs Action Centre, after his resignation back in 2009 in frustration at the demands of tickbox – the nine different grids and eighty-two objectives imposed on him by managers, funders and the government (he reckoned that he and his colleagues spent less than 40 per cent of their time actually tackling drugs issues). 'The demand for quick hits and early wins is driven by a central desire analogous to the instant gratification demands made by drug users themselves.'[149]

That is telling, and it may be that there is something similarly unsatisfying – similarly unreal – about tickbox statistics which fuels the addiction. Michael Power – the LSE accountancy professor who first pointed out the modern obsession with auditing – said that any failures in accountancy are countered with demands for more accountancy.[150] In the same way, failures in tickbox are met with demands for more tickbox.

I am hoping to persuade Atkinson and Lind, should I ever meet them, that they have been taken in – perhaps not deliberately, but in the same way that so many technocrats, plutocrats and their hired hands are taken in. Not exactly by the numbers either, but by the way they are used – and in ways that are starkly obvious to those who can see for themselves. There is a clue in another of their conclusions: 'It doesn't matter for job creation whether a large firm or a small firm satisfies its demand; some firm will because consumers have money to be captured ...'[151]

This is of course nonsense, as anyone except a very orthodox economist will know. It is unpleasantly obvious, once you leave London and travel around some of our forgotten small towns, that big companies are not interested in any old demand or any old money. If they were, there would be food shops on every high street, not the sad mixture of charity shops and estate agents that you actually find in too many of them – because big companies have a different idea of efficiency from small ones. What can be a thin but reasonable profit for a small company is regarded by a big one as beneath its notice.

That is why they are also wrong about the employment implications. If demand is served by big companies, some of the profit will go to back to servicing the big salaries at head office. If it is served by small companies, some of it will go on local employment. The precise data in the UK about the contribution made by smaller businesses is not as well researched as it is in the USA, but we have to assume there are parallels. In 2010, *Harvard Business Review* published a graph along with the headline 'More small firms means more jobs'.[152] The article said: 'Our research shows that regional economic growth is highly correlated with the presence of many small, entrepreneurial employers – not a few big ones.' The authors argued that the arrival of a big company in a local or regional economy might have little comparative effect on employment, 'even when they are doing well'. There was more support for this position from *Economic Development Quarterly*, which found that:

> Economic growth models that control for other relevant factors reveal a positive relationship between density of locally owned firms and per capita income growth, but only for small (10–99 employees) firms, whereas the density of large (more than 500 workers) firms not owned locally has a negative effect.[153]

The implication is not just that SMEs are vital for local economies, especially when they are owned and managed nearby, but also for the national economy.

The real problem again is one of tickbox. Atkinson and Lind have become so fixated on one number – the money – that they think it is the only factor. They think money is money is money. They look at the bottom line and see nothing else. It is the slightly obsessive tickbox problem in economics. It means they really believe that the economic effect is the same with a corner store as with online retailers which suck out local spending power and redirect it somewhere else entirely.

On this particular topic, the bottom line, I think we should give the final word to the great American guru of total quality, W. Edwards Deming:

One cannot be successful on visible figures alone. Now of course, visible figures are important. There is payroll to meet, vendors to pay, taxes to pay; amortisation, pension funds, and contingency funds to meet. But he that would run his company on visible figures alone will in time have neither company nor figures. Actually, the most important figures that one needs for management are unknown or unknowable, but successful management must nevertheless take account of them.[154]

6

Tickbox Politics

The more one studies attempted solutions to problems in politics and economics, in art, philosophy and religion, the more one has the impression of extremely gifted people wearing out their ingenuity at the impossible and futile task of trying to get the water of life into neat and permanent packages.

Alan Watts, *The Wisdom of Insecurity*, 1951

The former senior civil servant Caroline Slocock spent the late 1990s at the Treasury, designing, among other things, new systems that would hold every public service, from fire stations to surgeries, accountable via numerical targets. She feels responsible for the tickbox disaster that followed – the chaos of ineffectiveness and disempowered staff and managers – but that is not quite the end of the story. The real question is how and why the political system became so fixated on the tickbox phenomenon – and her story provides us with a clue.

'I feel like I have a certain amount of blood on my hands,' she says now. Which is one reason why she has become such a vital advocate of rolling back tickbox.

What is most peculiar about this whole issue is how little public debate there has been about it, despite its importance in people's lives. It is as if the whole of the New Public Management – a term invented by the Oxford academic Christopher Hood in 1989 – was somehow outside legitimate political discussion.[155] Instead, the ideas are debated at abstruse academic conferences, far from the public gaze.

The ideas behind the New Public Management, introduced under Margaret Thatcher, came to a head on Labour's accession to power in 1997. Slocock found herself taking forward New Labour's ideas on this front – measure everything, hold managers to account, keep more than an eye on front-line staff by setting out how they must do their work. It was, as we have seen, nothing very new – a combination of Frederick Winslow Taylor and Jeremy Bentham, with McKinsey as the enforcer, and based on the idea that public services were businesses really, and ought to be run like that.

Yet even as all this was happening, the academic critique was becoming clear. The New Zealand academic Robert Gregory argued in 1995 that it fostered a 'production' approach to public services with unintended effects, including a downgrading of responsibility and the spread of what he called 'careful incompetence'.[156]

Slocock had a fascinating and varied career in government. She was private secretary to Margaret Thatcher in her final years as prime minister, a period of which she tells movingly and revealingly in her book *People Like Us*,[157] and was later employed in the wider public sector as chief executive of the Equal Opportunities Commission. At each stage, she learned important lessons about tickbox or numerical, technocratic solutions and why they fall short. When she was at the Department of Employment, she had discovered how the targeting of staff numbers in the Unemployment Benefit Service (what JobCentres were called then) had reduced the service's overall effectiveness.

When she started working on public expenditure at the Treasury early in 1997, preparations for 'resource accounting budgeting' were fully under way. Resource accounting was intended to bring public accounting practices in line with the private sector in the handling of capital expenditure. What was less well known was that departments were supposed to be specific about the outcomes they were seeking, and to allocate costs for each outcome in their accounts. As it turned out, this never quite happened.

Throughout the fraught final years of the Major government, officials had been preparing for this big shift. The arrival of Gordon Brown at the start of his decade as Chancellor of the Exchequer did not mean it all had to be flung away, but some important tweaks had to be carried out when it came to the setting of targets. These landed eventually on Slocock's desk at the Treasury, in the General Expenditure Policy team.

New Labour had come to power after eighteen years with a slogan – 'things can only get better' – and a great deal to prove. They had a diverse bundle of specific promises, ranging from waiting times in hospital (limit: four hours in A&E) to the size of classes in schools (limit: thirty children).

Gordon Brown himself also had something important to prove, as every new Labour chancellor has to. He needed to find ways of increasing spending without frightening the horses – the financial markets in particular. He needed to demonstrate what was called in those days 'prudence'. That was why he agreed to stay within the previous government's spending limits for two years, why he made the Bank of England independent, and why he came up with his 'golden rule' – that borrowing should be done only in order to invest. He also introduced three-year spending plans (instead of the normal one year) to give public services more time to deliver on their targets and to show the markets a clear future course for spending.

Brown needed an excuse – or, to use political language, a narrative – for funnelling money into services. He was, in short, determined he was going to 'get something for something'. In return for the new money, that something would be better, more efficient performance. Caroline Slocock was left with the problem of how this was to be measured. There had been targets before – via John Major's Citizen's Charter, for example – but now she had to negotiate targets for all the Whitehall departments.

She was already aware that there was a gap. One element of resource accounting was that departments were supposed to report on their performance by 'outcomes' – they had to show how their money matched their objectives. New Labour's promises were a much more careful version, consisting of so-called 'output targets', or in some cases 'input targets' – the numbers of people treated, hours in A&E or children in a class. The new targets that were developed under New Labour's 'Public Service Agreements' ended up being a mix of all of these forms. Although each department had to specify its objectives, it was the targets that became paramount and were passed down to front-line staff.

To carry out Gordon Brown's plans, Slocock developed three all-important acronyms, two of which still form the basis of UK public spending even now, two decades later:

- DEL was 'departmental expenditure limits', designed to help give the departments three years of stable budgets, but only including spending on the public services delivering key targets.
- AME was 'annually managed expenditure', such as spending on benefits, which tends to go up and down with the economic cycle and which in the past had led to cuts in public services when AME costs increased. Add AME to DEL and you get total spending.
- PSA, 'public service agreements', meant the contracts between the Treasury and the other departments drawn

up as spending was agreed. Both were overseen by a new cabinet committee under Brown codenamed PSX, which included the Northern Ireland Secretary Mo Mowlam.

It was clear from the start that Caroline Slocock's design was veering off in other directions. 'It was supposed to be a parallel process, but it turned out to be more chaotic than that,' she says now. 'The idea was that the PSAs should be negotiated along-side the talks on money, but actually Brown just tended to impose spending totals and the PSAs had to be delivered at great speed afterwards.'

Then there was the question of who was negotiating about the PSAs. 'We were only really talking to the principal finance officers in each department,' she says. 'They were a million miles away from people at the coalface, which meant that lots of targets were just made up by people who didn't know the consequences on the ground.'

It dawned on departmental managers that targets were a way of getting more money. They also found that, if you had no targets, your service was more likely to be cut. From a small trickle, a vast cascade of targets were being published, and there were extra sub-targets for all the other departments and services, with 'service level agreements' to cover those. 'Everyone had them,' she says now. 'If they didn't have targets, they seemed less important.

'By the time we reached the second round of PSAs, we tried to correct these problems. We set out guidelines which said that they had to talk to the people on the ground. The model in ministers' minds was that they were technocrats sat in the centre of the machine, and they only had to pull a lever and something happened. I felt at the time that it was extraordinarily damaging to their relations with public service staff. They had no idea they were dealing with people. But then they didn't realise that it matters whether you are engaging with staff on the ground. And when the staff don't feel appreciated or listened to, they start to game the system.'

Goodhart's Law strikes again. Which is why you still find hospitals repeatedly 'losing' letters from GPs, as a desperate attempt to manage their waiting lists. Or schools in London ridding themselves of responsibility for disruptive pupils by sending them for 'home schooling', knowing perfectly well there is nobody at home to educate them, and realising they may well join in with the gangs. These things matter, as we have seen. In fact, perhaps we should use the formula: Disruptive pupils + tickbox = knife crime.

'If hospital staff were in a position to see the health of their patients as paramount, they wouldn't play that game,' says Slocock. 'It is what happens when you impose targets from above. It has all led to a more punitive management regime. In the NHS, it stops people learning.'

Another problem in the early years of the Blair government was that the targets had begun to overshadow the most important element of the PSA design – setting out clearly the objectives of each government department. She had come to believe that, if you could describe the purpose of your job clearly, you would probably stick to it. Clarity of purpose matters. But she had learned in her human resources job at the Treasury that, if you asked civil servants to describe their job in one sentence, most of them would not be able to. It was therefore even more important to discuss what the job of each government department was. Was the purpose of the NHS, for example, to cure people, to promote health or to reduce health inequalities? If not, *should* it be? These issues really matter, but they require a great deal of discussion – and you won't get there by ministers arming themselves with figures to boast about the number of drugs they have distributed or how they have achieved their A&E waiting times target (or not, as it turns out). If many in the police, for example, believed that their job was to lock people up and that they would be judged on this – which they did – then that made it harder to put more emphasis on their preventative role.

Soon there were shared, cross-cutting targets too, which were on the face of it a good way of preventing thinking too narrowly within departmental boundaries. The danger was, at local level, that such targets led to disputes about who got to boast about achieving them. If there was any hint that the same achievement was being counted twice, the Audit Commission – part of Gordon Brown's new assessment infrastructure – would be down on you like a ton of bricks. As perhaps they should. If targets become a substitute for purpose, then services increasingly focus narrowly on delivering the target, with many unintended consequences.

We are approaching a reason for the phenomenon we found in Chapter 4: that when all your services are contracted out, their operators all start concentrating on their tickbox targets to the exclusion of everything else – and the one area that the big outsourcers like Carillion and Capita were experts in was delivering target numbers. Then the difficult cases are shunted out and bounce around the system until they finally appear in A&E or in a police cell, the last outposts of public services that will still take anyone.

'They think they are being efficient, but the costs are actually ballooning,' says Caroline Slocock. 'They believe the intuitive case for economies of scale is very strong, but they are doing it very badly because it is atomising services, and not dealing with the real problems. People have become units of production.'

Which is the logical direction of tickbox. If you believe our public services are giant machines, whirring away, then of course we do become widgets on the conveyor belt. But human beings are not widgets. If you treat them as if they were, then their sheer variety will eventually defeat your machine. They will gum it up with all the effort. Which is at least another explanation why our services have become so expensive – it is because Goodhart's Law has subverted their purpose more effectively than anyone realised.

So what went wrong with Slocock's 'public service agreements'? Was it something to do with the technocratic spirit in government that they fell victim so deeply to tickbox thinking? Was it perhaps the prevailing belief that IT systems, installed at vast expense, would solve any problem? Or was it just that there was not enough discussion? Caroline Slocock says she hardly ever talked to Gordon Brown, which is strange for such a senior Treasury official. He had very few meetings with officials, she says. He worked through his council of economic advisors, and his 'special advisers' – the so-called SPADs – like Ed Balls and Ed Miliband.

As she describes it, the central problem is the idea that public services are businesses in disguise and ought to be run like businesses. 'I fundamentally challenge that,' she says now. It's unquestionable that some public services were badly run, but that does not mean they would improve if they behaved like assembly lines.

I would probably go further, as I shall say in the next chapter. But that would be enough to explain why, although Brown and his control freakery have long gone, so little has changed. PSAs disappeared as part of the coalition's austerity programme, but Caroline Slocock's system of DEL and AME is still there. 'They take it completely as a given,' she says. 'Eighteen years on, nobody has questioned the system I put in place, even though it hasn't really delivered on making sure that public services have used their money wisely to really improve services.' Target culture and tickbox remain.

The great Ethereum robbery

Caroline Slocock explained that the direction of travel inside government has been towards arm's-length organisations, governed by contracts and automated as far as possible – with the money sloshing around the arteries of public services in accordance with KPIs and targets. That system became more entrenched with the new era ushered in by payment-by-results contracts.

It is also a fantasy along the lines of Jeremy Bentham's Panopticon, a system that would not just 'grind rogues honest', as he suggested, but was designed also to grind ill people well and to grind children into school. It does not work, partly because of Goodhart's Law and partly because all the grinding involved tends to be counter-productive.

The latest twist to this story – which is, in some ways, the prevailing story of our time, if it was written by those who run the world – has been in the field of new kinds of money. It was revealed in 2016, when the Ethereum system, the brainchild of 22-year-old data enthusiast and coder Vitalik Buterin, burst onto the world.

Ethereum had Wall Street and Silicon Valley shaking in anticipation, and it had a big idea behind it. Buterin wanted Ethereum to be more than just a currency. He wanted to use it to show how a new style of data management, based on a Bitcoin-style blockchain technology, could run contracts or corporations without human intervention, by making the tickboxes implied in contracts automatic.

On 17 June that year, Ethereum was given one of its biggest public outings, powering a new crowdfunded start-up called DAO – Decentralised Autonomous Organisation. DAO had raised more than $160 million from investors, all in 'ether', Ethereum's new virtual, decentralised currency. The money was 'more secure than every bank put together', according to the organisers. It was launch day – but it soon became clear, as the Silicon Valley investors' chat rooms went live, that something was going horribly wrong.[158] In fact, the worst thing possible. As they watched, hackers had penetrated DAO and were stealing the money. 'This is not a drill!' said the German tech company Slock.it, which was managing the launch.

The huge fraud became clear at 8.15 a.m. Berlin time, when Griff Green of Slock.it first sent the message 'Emergency Alert! Please DM a Slock.it member ASAP'. One of the immediate replies said simply 'Oh shit'. It should not have been happening to a project that had been hailed as the most successful crowdfunded scheme ever. And yet it was. Half an hour later, Green – a former Los Angeles massage therapist with one of the world's first master's degrees in digital currencies – posted the message: 'We aren't sure what is happening but the DAO is in an emergency situation.'[159]

By the time they stopped a few days later, the hackers had made off with $55 million of the investors' money, DAO was in ruins and Buterin had been called in to find a solution. (It has never been explained either who stole the money or why they stopped.)

In the manner of a semi-divine presence, Buterin simply wound back Ethereum's date to before the heist and started again by rewriting the code. It meant that the thieves would not be able to cash in their tokens and all the investors kept their money. Simple, when you have that kind of power.

After that, his currency ether seemed unstoppable, at least during the explosion of value in Bitcoin in 2017, when ether was not far behind. In a world which increasingly regards data, normally in the form of numerical information, as the solution to everything, anyone who shows a way to remove all humans (except perhaps themselves) from running the world thrills the investors and the business magazines. In this respect, Ethereum and DAO

were founded along similar lines: the idea was to turn corporations into automated vehicles run by digital contracts rather than
human beings.

Ether and Bitcoin have returned from the heights to more real-
istic values. What might concern anyone about tickbox is that this
kind of thinking is now so widespread. It isn't that you can never
automate decisions based on data, if the data is sound and if it is
about something that is reliably measurable – like the through-
put of a pipeline or the price of bread. Automated decisions suit
the powerful because they can insulate themselves from them – it
wasn't me, it was the software or the market, they might say. But
any decision that might be better taken in the light of wider information, like those about loans or pricing, or most medical matters,
ought at least to be overseen by a human being. Someone using the
algorithm as an aide or aide-memoire or checklist, maybe – but
not handing over all responsibility to a one-dimensional machine.

The automation of decisions seems to be the logical extension
of the attempt to codify everything. You set out the rules that
govern the relationship between the data and the decisions. Then
you find a way of getting feedback in a loop so that you constantly
analyse the decisions made and tweak the system so that it improves. Robots can do all that, faster and better; what they can't
always do is set the problem in a wider context to see how the data
falls short, how the boxes ticked fail to adequately describe the
world. You can of course find another algorithm that will identify
the exceptional cases that really need human oversight. But that in
itself will be based on data that is also subject to Goodhart's Law.

On the other hand, that is precisely what Google and Amazon
do, and it has given them virtual mastery of the world. So automation works – as long as you don't mind the side-effects of tickbox.

One of those side-effects is the phenomenon known as 'automation bias'. Three days after the start of the invasion of Iraq

in 2003, an American Patriot missile team shot down an RAF Tornado jet, killing both aircrew. It turned out later that the team were relying on a single radio link and were on heightened alert after a grenade attack the previous day. Their system gave them ten seconds to override it if they were in any doubt, and it was in fact falsely identifying targets many times a day. The situation was confusing, but they did not override. The problem was that they believed their IT too much.

The term 'automation bias' derives partly from research in 1998 by the Illinois University psychologist Linda Skitka and her colleagues, with some funding from NASA, who set out to ascertain whether automation did what it promised in reducing human error.[160] To do so, they looked at automated decision-making in a series of intensive care units and nuclear plants.

The first surprise was that those who worked without automated decision-making outperformed their machine-minding colleagues. Those who minded machines turned out to miss events to which they had not explicitly been alerted. They also 'did what an automated aid recommended, even when it contradicted their training and other 100 per cent valid and available indicators'.

It is not clear why this should be. I would suggest that the machine-minders had been de-skilled. They had become too dependent on the support. But the authors of the research paper fell back on a previous explanation, which is that they had become 'cognitive misers'. 'That is,' wrote Skitka and colleagues, 'most people will take the road of least cognitive effort and, rather than systematically analyse each decision, will use decision rules of thumb or heuristics.'

In other words, we may be heading towards a tickbox system that is complex, reliable and simple enough to manage whole corporations using data alone. That is certainly what the inventors of ether and DAO believe, and they do so in the name of digital libertarianism – though I am not sure if it is any less tyrannical to be managed by a machine than it is to be managed by a human being. But if we are managed by robots, we may transform our professionals into unskilled machine-minders, who still make mistakes – but different ones. Neither, from what we know about how tickbox works, will it be very effective. Automation bias is the other end of the problem from Goodhart's Law: it affects those at the controls of the machine, whether a Patriot missile system or a corporation or a government department. Unless those people are actively trained to doubt – as pilots now are – they will believe the faulty data. Why would they not?

These are the front lines of the political tickbox argument. Sometimes, the anti-tickbox forces lose and sometimes they prevail – as they did in the American Civil Liberties Union (ACLU) case against the Idaho Department of Health and Welfare. The state of Idaho had decided to reduce Medicaid support for health-care claimants and used a software package which arbitrarily cut people's money, without warning, by nearly a third. The Medicaid team refused to explain their calculations or to hand over the software, on the grounds that it was a trade secret. The judge disagreed: the software turned out to be an Excel spreadsheet using data so full of inaccuracies that the court ruled it unconstitutional.[161]

Richard Eppink, who took the case for ACLU, said afterwards: 'It's just this bias we all have for computerised results – we don't question them.'[162] He was, of course, right. But, just as the numbers are based on words and descriptions, so computerised results are based on data. Both may be faulty and are certainly prone to major massaging.

I can't think of many better arguments why we should not devolve power to robots to run our corporations, at least until they become more human (which, I realise, would defeat the purpose). But there is one better one: Stanislav Petrov.

It was September 1983. Three weeks before, the Soviet air force had shot down a Korean airliner and Cold War tensions were running high. Petrov was duty officer in the Soviet missile early warning centre at Oko, when the computers reported that a ballistic missile had been fired from the USA, closely followed by five more. Within seconds, the system had gone through thirty stages of confirmation. The attack was real.

What was he to do? His training and military protocol demanded that he should report it. His colleagues who had trained entirely in the military (Petrov was trained as an engineer) certainly would have done so. There then would have followed the most tremendous nuclear holocaust, resulting in death and destruction on both sides. But he had a nagging doubt. He had been led to expect that any attack from the Americans would be overwhelming. Why would they fire only six missiles? What was the point?

So Petrov reported a false alarm, and thereby saved the world. It transpired that the system had been triggered by an unusual combination of clouds and sunlight as the Soviet satellite flew over North Dakota. He was praised to start with, but was eventually reprimanded for failing to organise the paperwork properly (tickbox, Soviet-style). Then he was moved to a less sensitive position. Almost certainly, the NATO military would have acted the same way – missing the point, as tickbox does. The real point is that sometimes you have to break the rules or depart from the process to do a good job.

And in today's tickbox world, that may often happen.

At the same time, tickbox is expanding everywhere. Judges in some US states are using predictive software to work out how likely it is that a guilty prisoner will reoffend so that they can impose the right sentence. Bear in mind that the prisoners will not yet have reoffended and that the algorithm puts a great deal of weight on their answers to questions like: 'Is it ever right to steal to feed your children?' The software tends to predict that black people are twice as likely to reoffend as white people.

The problem is that human beings need to provide some oversight, as Stanislav Petrov managed to do so heroically. The *political* problem is that tickbox can't always tell the difference between what a group of people might need, sometimes for the good of the group as a whole, and what an individual might need. In medicine, it may only be a matter of time before some individuals can be treated entirely by algorithm, but it is not clear that any tickbox system – however sophisticated – can ever provide a fair assessment of how likely it is that a criminal will abscond or reoffend, or whether a small business owner will thrive or fail. In order to be fair, those kinds of decisions require an element of trust, intuition and understanding of context.

This is the opposite direction of travel from that currently occurring in politics. Politicians have automated decisions in order to excise human bias and prejudice. But you can't opt out of those things by using data, because the data already carries the bias.[163]

There are a few high-profile cases of obvious injustice, often caused by faulty data. Like that of Rabinah Ibrahim, an architect living with four children in California. She had to spend a decade fighting to clear her name, and get home again from an academic conference in Malaysia, after a policeman accidentally added her name to a security 'no-fly' list. There may have been some confusion between the name of the academic group which had invited her and the similarly named terrorist group that was behind the Bali bombing of 2002.[164] These are the tip of a vast iceberg of irritation, injustice and concern that are not yet political issues, but soon will be.

At the same time, human ingenuity is such that algorithms are emerging which hit back. Like Social Book Manager or TweetDelete, which let you clean up your own Facebook or Twitter pages to iron out youthful frolics which future employers might frown on. Or the HireVue app, or the £9000 Intro courses to help you learn how to beat the new tickbox methods of choosing job interviewees – mainly in the banking sector – by feeding back to their nervous tics and facial peculiarities during their interviews, so that interviewees can eradicate the so-called telltale signs that the tickbox systems use.[165]

When you have so many applications to be a junior master of the universe, it may not matter that talented people slip through the net of robots which are supposed to be able to 'understand'. But it will matter if most candidates have trained themselves to get through that kind of interview – as they will. Some other kind of giveaway sign will then be required, and it will be as vacuous and as susceptible to fakery as all the others. The fightback is inevitable.

A culture of inaction

Tickbox systems bear heavily, but in different ways, on the middle and working classes. They affect the middle classes because of the battery of KPIs to which the performance of so many profession-als is now reduced. But they bear most heavily on the poor, as the tentacles of tickboxes are wielded to check up on and generally humiliate them, in their child-rearing methods, their food skills, their mental state, the intensity of their searches for work, their contraceptive habits, and almost everything else. You would think then that politicians might have more to say about it. They do increasingly gargle with the word tickbox, but the real questions have yet to be articulated in the political world as they are in the policy world. There is unease, but it has yet to express itself as an-ger at the loss of control that tickbox represents.

In the meantime, politicians are by default caught in this ultimate data fantasy, a future of robot organisations, an ersatz world without human decision-making

Ironically, it may have been politicians who invented tickbox in the first place. Or, to be precise, it was developed on behalf of politicians by officials like Robert McNamara. They wanted to insulate themselves to some degree from responsibility for the failure of their policies, and officials took the battery of targets that politicians found themselves bound to – 500,000 new homes a year in Harold Wilson's day – and organised them around contracted organisations which could take responsibility for their delivery.

It was from this, from the loyalty of people like McNamara and Caroline Slocock to their political bosses, that tickbox has emerged. A combination of factors has led to a peculiar perversion of tickbox where politicians prefer the well-understood gesture to misunderstood effectiveness – and when those who run the world believe that the Great Tickbox Machine will somehow sort everything. How else can we possibly understand a contemporary political culture where the whole idea of action of any kind is discouraged?

This tendency goes very deep. Since its inception, the welfare state's service institutions have generally preferred their patients, pupils and service users to be as passive as possible to make them easier to process. This is despite ample evidence that active and involved service users recover faster, learn faster and spread their skills and knowhow better – but the prevailing, tickbox culture finds this extremely difficult to understand or act upon.

More recently, the same attitude seems to have spread to frontline staff. Their managers expect them to press the right buttons in the right order, to tick the right boxes and do what they are told, despite rhetoric about staff 'empowerment'. They are expected to be part of the machine. Worse, the same attitude has been spreading upwards through the hierarchies. I have met senior personnel on secondment in the civil service who find it next to impossible to persuade their staff to take any kind of decision. It seems just too risky. As if the ministers alone must take them all – while, at the same time, ministers have managed to insulate themselves from all day-to-day decisions by using arm's-length organisations to run the services. The result is a do-nothing culture that goes from top to bottom throughout government, and – as indicated by the chief executive of a regional authority I met recently who told me that the policies 'automatically follow' the data – tickbox is at the root of it.

Add to this the way our political parties prefer the right gesture, that one should give the right signals, rather than formulate a policy that might have some chance of actually tackling the problem it was supposed to. I was a member of the Liberal Democrat federal policy committee for twelve years and – although they were by no means the worst offenders – this was a besetting sin. The problem is that politicians are no longer judged by what they do – the news cycle is too short for that. They are judged by their seriousness, their ability to convince the public that they *want* to do something. Having their heart in the right place about an idea has become more important than a genuine ability to act effectively.

Then there is the way that evidence-based policy is understood. Nobody would want to advocate evidence-*free* policy, after all. But unfortunately, this excellent concept has become in the civil service an injunction to do nothing without evidence about the likely effects. Since such evidence is rarely available, at least about new systems that have yet to be tested on the scale envisaged, evidence-based policy becomes a reason for nothing to be done.

In short, our political culture has turned away from the importance of doing things to talking about things, or consulting on things or measuring things or communicating things. As always, those who measure are paid considerably more than those who just *do*.

This has serious consequences. It may have led to our widespread disaffection with formal politics – so incapable of acting, so miserably failing to *do* – that has in turn led to the election of populists peddling a simplistic, tickbox-style agenda. The prospect of a hollowing out of the political world is what we fear, and – looking closely – we find it has been hollowed out already. Politics has been overtaken by a kind of fearful lassitude which believes that doing is somehow too dangerous, too basic, too committed, too worrying, too complex – possibly even too vulgar.

The political world has bought into the traditional divide between professionals and their various shades in the class system. It is the same divide that used to lie between secondary moderns and grammar schools, between blue-collar and white-collar workers, between CSEs and GCEs, between apprenticeships and degrees – and all those other besetting sins of the UK educational elite. It is a more intensely snobbish divide in the UK than almost anywhere else in Europe, where engineers and practical people are valued. It is part and parcel of the long-standing Platonist division between those who *did*, the hewers of wood and the drawers of water, and those who simply thought, and who fancied themselves junior versions of philosopher kings.

Except that, in the Western world, that divide has crystallised into a distinction between those who do things and those who *measure* people doing things. Between those who make things happen and those who study them doing so and try to direct their experimentation more precisely. There is a hierarchy in economics which demonstrates this, between the highest caste, the econometrical mathematicians and theorists, who earn most, and the economic historians and policy experts.[166] Or below even them, those who criticise the prevailing model, who tend to drive second-hand cars. Those who try to make things happen are at the bottom of the heap.

My sense is that most non-political people prefer to do something, rather than to sit on a committee deciding things. I know all too well through the experience of time banks in health centres, where people provide each other with mutual support, the huge psychological difference it can make to someone who has never been asked to give back after a lifetime under professional care, when they find they suddenly have a useful role. It is an absolutely basic human need. Although there are individual politicians who understand this, they exist in a culture which can't – which believes that most people aspire to be at the table, discussing and taking decisions. Most people in my experience prefer to be almost anywhere else. But they do welcome the chance of doing something useful to help.

This snobbery about action has dovetailed with the tickbox approach to economics, as if it was a giant humming machine which does everything for us, called the *market*. Over the past forty years, a version of market liberalism has emerged, based on the work of Friedrich Hayek yet much more limited than he proposed, which believes that nothing is possible for us limited human beings unless the market wills it. And if the market wills it, of course then action will hardly be required anyway.

It was not really Hayek's fault. His 1944 book *The Road to Serfdom* set out a free-market approach that was a sceptical critique of state monopoly. This critique has been transformed more recently into a kind of lassitude, where human endeavour is pointless. All senior politicians have to do to prove their seriousness is to accept their own powerlessness and endorse the orthodoxy. As a result, absolutely the last thing they should do is to *act*. The tickbox approach to economics has led to a strange sense, not that nobody wants to act, but that nobody really should. Certainly that nobody really *can*.

The most obvious manifestation of this is the way that senior managers, ministers or those responsible for large organisations so often seem like deer caught in the headlights when anything goes wrong. Southern Rail was the worst example, when senior managers and the Department of Transport felt that the best option seemed to be to close their eyes and hope for the best, while maybe also blaming someone else (the DoT) or introducing some new marketing scheme (GTR). I notice that my dental practice, a member of a large group that serves southern England, is trying to operate with a total of one part-time dentist working a couple of days a week. This has been the case for some time, which is why they keep cancelling my appointments (though, to be fair to them, there is a serious national shortage of dentists that prefigures the coming shortage of professionals in many areas of life – who wants to live in thrall to tickbox, after all?). They appear to have addressed the problem, not by seeking out some new way of training or employing dentists, but by redecorating the public areas of the surgery.

When I briefly lived in Princeton in the US two decades ago, I remember the nervousness of the locals that a bear had come to live in the suburbs, living on scraps from people's dustbins. What are you going to do, the angry residents asked the local mayor. What is your policy? 'Our policy is,' he said, 'waiting for it to go away.' Sadly that appears to be a policy that derives from tickbox too. Because, as we have seen, the numbers keep you stuck in the current policy. Well, it is the 'one best way', isn't it? The numbers give no warning, because they see no context. The great machines that run the world are blind to wholly unpredictable black swan or even 'black elephant' events, like the 2008 banking crash. Or black bears, come to that.

In these circumstances it is hardly surprising that we are seeing a populist revolt in the Western world against an elite that can see that the poor of their countries have been suffering, can see how the middle classes have been overlooked, or have watched the evidence of rising global temperatures, but appear to be unable or unwilling to do anything about them. It is not that they believe any longer that the market will provide – that element of market fundamentalism has not survived the banking crisis of 2008 – but somehow the snobbery against action has outlived the original reasons for it.

Instead, we have developed a one-dimensional political discourse, filled with meaningless and disputed statistics, where simplistic solutions – full of tickbox assumptions – dominate debate. But, for me, the most worrying aspect of tickbox politics is about issues of identity.

Questions of identity

The Northern Ireland playwright David Ireland wrote a highly controversial play called *Cyprus Avenue*, which premiered at the Royal Court in London in 2016, about the disintegration of an Ulster loyalist called Eric Miller. Miller tells the story of a business trip he made to London, when he accidentally spent the evening in an Irish bar. It was filled, he said, with 'English voices, cockney voices, calling themselves Irish'. To his astonishment, he enjoyed it and found himself drinking Guinness and singing 'The Wearing of the Green' and other rebel nationalist songs. 'You've no idea what that does to a unionist mind like mine,' he says.

Borders have that effect on people, because they are like tickboxes: you are either one side or the other. And, if the world were really as simple as that – or so the argument for strong borders goes – there would be less confusion. As it is, especially in Ireland, borders simply create more confusion. They shape a muddle of identity that we all recognise to some extent in ourselves, but more intensely.

We are all of us a mixture of interlocking identities. Personally, I feel an emotional link to my home town of Steyning and my old home of Crystal Palace. I feel like a native of Sussex and the South Downs, a Crystal Palace supporter, an English, British European. I also sometimes feel like a human being and – if the conflict is not too intense – a Liberal Democrat. Most of the time, none of those identities struggling inside me overwhelms the others, so I don't regard myself as a nationalist.

But you only have to look at Twitter to see that is not how some people see themselves. I don't want to bring down their rage on my head, so I will just mention a short book I wrote about the Dublin gay scandal of 1884 and my great-great-grandfather's role in it.[167] Within hours of its publication, and for the only time in my career, I had acquired an online stalker who condemned the book roundly and in general terms. I struggled to understand this until I saw the comments below my article on the *Guardian* website, one of which cast doubt on whether it was possible to have a gay ancestor at all. Presumably because bisexuality is supposed to be impossible in the tickbox world.

The same identity politics would, I have to assume, not just refuse to accept bisexuality but also dual nationality, as if the existence of multiple identities was offensive to their particular chosen identity.

These are arguments about authenticity. And borders complicate them, as they do in places like Ireland or Korea. Which box do they tick, after all? Which box would they tick about more elusive categorisations like class? In my experience, most people you ask about such personal issues – and I don't recommend that you do – will reply in the form of a story: they were born to working-class parents, then sent on a scholarship to Eton, married a Spaniard, lived on a council estate, and so on. Stories are the antidote to tickbox and they communicate whole levels of truth about identity which slip through the net or the box. Is a person Irish or British? Often only a story will tell you, and you won't be certain even after hearing it.

The modern idea of identity draws on postmodern literary theory, to such an extent that you can find behind this kind of political 'correctness' a conviction that no one group can ever fully understand another, that men and women are not just from different planets but belong to different cultural species with very few points of connection. Oddly enough, this kind of mistake – human beings have enough in common to speak translatable languages that have similar structures – has also infected the political right. They are convinced that we have no human connection to the derided foreigners, who seem hell bent on bursting into our country to sponge off us (or worse). And if that doesn't work, they change the language: when you call a group of desperate people a 'caravan', they cease both to be individuals and to be completely human.

In case you think I am biased, the political left is barely any better. They have adopted their own tickbox-style politics that seems to derive from a conviction that nothing is possible – no action, and no change. Instead they try to change the language of politics, so that those outside the cognoscenti feel excluded for fear of offending them, and promote a series of symbolic gestures which have no effect, but which raise the political temperature. We should take down the statue of Cecil Rhodes in Oxford on the grounds that he is racist, or of Robert E. Lee in Charlottesville on the grounds that he supported slavery, or Nelson's Column on the grounds that he fought for the pro-slave trade status quo.[168]

Not one of these gestures would improve a single individual's life, but they would send the 'right signals'. That is tickbox politics. It seems to derive from a profound loss of belief in the possibility of genuine change. It therefore accepts the basic premise of tickbox political economy – that nothing is possible unless the market wills it.

The front line of the emerging identity battle is around the rights of transgender women, engaged in an epic struggle with feminists in the Labour Party about whether they should be allowed to qualify under all-women shortlists. Behind all that is, again, an argument about authenticity.[169] The feminist side sees the battle for all-women quotas unravelling. Both sides are radicals, but the transgender side is more protestant than catholic, preferring an inner reality, a more individualistic understanding. What I find hard to stomach is the way identity politics appears to encourage a kind of furious victimhood, which adds to the barriers. I am suspicious of those who patrol the boundaries of categories, like the shameful order to the Olympic champion athlete Caster Semenya by the IAAF to take hormones, in order to equal out her advantage against other women runners.

Identity politics seems a peculiar departure to someone like me, who has been brought up with the idea that we can be what we want to be – though we can't always expect people to call us what we ask. It is strange for those of us determined to break out of the definitions, to refuse to accept categorisation, no matter what identity we have accepted. Most women, men, children – people – are not quite as they are defined, after all. Within some basic constraints (mainly around brute facts), that is still my attitude. Even now, I will attempt to break out of whatever box I have been wrestled into by society. That seems to me to maximise individual freedom in a way that identity politics never can.

Machines of loving grace

Shoshana Zuboff is a social psychologist at Harvard University. She is now, thanks to the publication of a hugely important book, *The Age of Surveillance Capitalism*, in the eye of the storm over the way that Microsoft, Google and Facebook (and, to a lesser degree, Amazon) have woven around themselves a system that aspires to total knowledge and control about every individual, using data about their preferences, habits, loves and hates.[170]

It is a different argument to mine because it assumes an accuracy about data which I am sceptical about, thanks to the twin challenges of Goodhart's Law and automation bias, one of which twists the way employees behave and the other which blinds their bosses to it. But Zuboff's fears about the direction of travel are hugely relevant to the tickbox phenomenon because it leads to a kind of 'psychic numbing'. As she tells her children:

> It is not OK to have to hide in your own life; it is not normal. It is not OK to spend your lunchtime conversations comparing software that will camouflage you and protect you from continuous unwanted invasion ... It is not OK to have our best instincts for connection, empathy, and information, exploited by a draconian quid pro quo that holds these goods hostage to the pervasive strip search of our lives.[171]

She dates the phenomenon back to April 2002 when, after a series of unexpected spikes across the USA in the googling of the same question about an obscure TV character from the 1970s ('what was Carol Brady's maiden name?'), a Google analyst realised that this was a question posed by the host of *Who Wants to Be a Millionaire?* at forty-eight minutes past each hour as the show aired at the same time in each successive time zone as far as Hawaii.

It wasn't just the accuracy of the data, it was the ability to predict its use that struck Google's executives. They began to see that the data they dismissed as 'behavioural surplus' was not actually surplus at all: it was actually key to their vast future wealth and power.

From their Nest home control system to rifling through our email correspondence, Google is now dedicated to watching our actions and, if possible, the thoughts we express. They do so not to improve their service to customers – we are not customers, because we do not pay them, and are not regarded as such, Zuboff argues – but to make us the subjects and the objects of research using our own data to profit from us. To do so by leaching 'on every aspect of human experience,' she says. And all somehow in the language and rhetoric of liberation and connectedness.

This is linked and parallel to the story of tickbox, since it borrows similar rhetoric – economic liberation – to reassure us that it is simply the replacement of bureaucracy by automation. And it seems to work: even *The Times* defended the 'machines of loving grace' revealed to be watching over us by the documentary maker Adam Curtis in 2011.

The phrase was taken from a poem by the hippy novelist Richard Brautigan, written in 1967, and highly influential in those circles that eventually capitalised on the internet.[172] Curtis's documentary series looked at the strange interconnected stories of those who had shaped the world, and who believed the optimistic idea that human beings would be ruled by such machines and were, perhaps, merely reproducible machines themselves.

Curtis was a real pioneer in this area, his explorations ranging from the ideas of novelist Ayn Rand, via Alan Greenspan, to the doctrine that everything can reach a self-correcting ideal if it is just left alone, watched over by these 'machines of loving grace'. But the idea was misinterpreted as if it was somehow a by-product of the philosophy of localism.[173]

It is almost the exact opposite. The hands-off approach described by Curtis was more like Woodstock meets Milton Friedman. In practice, it is precisely what New Labour believed to apply in most areas of life and tried to organise; the loving machines watched over in turn by McKinsey consultants and provided by a range of IT consultants, hard men who did well out of the New Labour years.

Localism does not mean laissez-faire. Nor does it mean doing nothing. It means doing a great deal, but doing it locally where it is more likely to work. It doesn't mean hands off; it means a great deal of hands on. It means shaping the world, but in a more effective way than is possible with tickbox.

There is also a sense that 'surveillance capitalism' as described by Zuboff is the more sophisticated, private-sector side of tickbox, and vice versa: tickbox is in some sense the public-sector version of surveillance capitalism. When they join up, as they have done in China, then we need to seriously start to worry. That is what I take the new Chinese system of 'social credit' to represent.[174] The system was announced in 2014 and will fully launch in 2020, but many Chinese people have already been refused permission to travel by plane or fly, or given a slow internet connection, because their social credit is too low. The formula remains a closely guarded secret, as it is with Facebook and Google, but you can lose or gain points according to how many computer games you buy and other kinds of anti-social behaviour.

Tickbox would then be the Big Sibling who follows you home at night and sits watching you in your front room. I don't want it.

Civil Exchange

Caroline Slocock is determined to make a difference and reverse the direction of travel. She knows this can't be done in the old way, by central diktat. She is therefore the moving spirit behind a semi-formal group of leaders, in business and public policy, who meet regularly for dinner to discuss how to spread the importance of creativity and flexibility and human connection inside their organisations. She believes that, if these ideas spread, we will once again be able to take back some control over the way the world works.

The group is known as Civil Exchange, and was formed with Steve Wyler, then director of the think tank Locality.[175] The idea is that local 'cells' will form among people who are in a position to lead the change. Their manifesto is built around a series of propositions:

- Prevention is better than cure.
- Building on strengths is better than focusing on weaknesses.
- Relationships are better than impersonal transactions.
- Collaboration is better than competition.
- Mass participation is better than centralised power.
- Local is better than national.
- Principles are better than targets.
- Changing ourselves is better than demanding change from others.

These are all true, but they are assertions which sometimes run ahead of the tickbox evidence. Some of them would run into difficulty with tickbox if that was the only basis for decision-making. Luckily, it isn't.

They all recognise in rather different ways that – as Caroline Slocock puts it – 'to deliver profound change for people, we need to work outside silos'. They also recognise that those key institutions that provide broad benefit – social infrastructure like playgrounds, parks, children's centres or lunch clubs – have been 'quietly lost because they were not captured by the target numbers, because they were off the radar in what they were trying to deliver'. The next chapter looks at what we might be able to do to turn back this drift of human life into machines, but Slocock and colleagues are among many who are also working away below the data radar to keep things human, especially in public services.

I should put my cards on the table too. Personally, I am more comfortable without borders, when people retain the freedom and language to break out of the box, to wriggle their way out of the definitions and tickboxes that limit them.

We are entering a new age, as we do every four decades or so. I am hoping it will be a new 'humanist' age, where humankind can be the measure of all things, diverse and creative, and where our humanity provides a basis for communicating effectively with each other, but – if it does at all – we are going to have to work hard to make that shift happen.

We will need to find a political narrative that can unite right and left. In his study of bureaucracy, *The Utopia of Rules*, the Anglo-American thinker David Graeber talks about bureaucracies as utopias, perhaps draft ones.[176] He seeks in vain for a leftist critique of bureaucracy. But I am not sure he is correct about this – there is a corner of the Green-Liberal left which has always tried to burst out of restrictions on our individuality. The critique applies as much to tickbox, which as we have seen is a kind of utopian bureaucracy without bureaucrats.

But Graeber is perfectly correct about the role that tickbox has played, in its symbolic value, in recent left policy. This has allowed the left to become identified with bureaucracy, form-filling and ticking boxes, because that is the way the welfare system is set up. That was the original Fabian vision that Beatrice and Sidney Webb, the founders of the London School of Economics, built into the way local government works. That is also why so many people on the left have their existence in the world of tickbox, as functionaries in the system of tickboxing, administrators for the giant welfare bureaucracies. The term 'tickbox' is partly a challenge from conservatives, though it is also a challenge to all government, since government is so steeped in it.

The paradox is that, as Graeber says, the system of bureaucratisation (and tickbox) derives from the corporate world and tends to overwhelm all the old informality of the left. And the process is still going on, because how else does a highly centralised government gain purchase on the issues that need solutions? How do we make sure children get the best kind of education? Tick the box that all your teachers have degrees. How do we make sure women play an equally powerful role in the world of work? Tick the box for women on the board. How do we make sure the NHS improves people's health? Tick the box confirming that NICE guidelines have been adhered to.

There is a glimpse here of why policy is so ineffective. Because politicians focus on the favoured symbolic solution, which may or may not have an effect. There are so many other, more effective ways of achieving these objectives which don't involve ticking boxes – but these will not be considered valid, because, well, what about the transparency? How will we know when they have been achieved?

The great socialist and wallpaper designer William Morris noticed this trend over a century ago. 'Men fight and lose the battle,' he wrote in *A Dream of John Ball*.[177] 'And the thing that they fought for will come about in spite of their defeat and, when it comes turns out not to be what they meant, and other men have to fight for what they meant under another name.'

Morris was spot on that this is the real process of political change, though politicians themselves seem to be largely unaware of it. Tickbox embeds the process, as political parties swing from one symbolic gesture to the next. That is one reason why the political world struggles to find levers, beyond the tickable symbolism, that indicate real change. But irritating bureaucracy is not the only reason why we need to push the limits to tickbox back again. We need to do so – to conjure up the ghost of Abraham Lincoln – so that shades of grey, nuance, depth and imagination shall not perish from this earth.

7

Tockbox

We, as we used to take ourselves to be, are to be cultured out, to be replaced by a homogenised creature I can hardly recognise as a human being.

R. D. Laing, *Times Literary Supplement*, 1988

Ludwig Wittgenstein was one of the strangest twentieth-century philosophers, given to delivering long, obsessive diatribes against the discipline to his colleagues before watching cowboy films with his long-suffering friends. The 1920s and 30s saw him slowly demolish his previous philosophy, which had assumed that statements were logical and referred to the concrete world. But the leap of imagination that spurred him on was a conversation he had in 1932 with Italian Marxist economist Piero Sraffa.

'What do you make of this statement?' asked Professor Sraffa, stroking his chin. A very ordinary gesture – but it launched Wittgenstein on a long series of ideas about picture language and the way we actually mean what we say, rather than what the logicians and computer programmers might think we mean.

The ideas led to an unusual argument with computer pioneer Alan Turing about the well-known paradox which might be expressed as: 'All Cretans are liars, as a famous Cretan once told me.'

The so-called Liar's Paradox had famously undermined the

foundations of logical thought and the philosophy of mathematics. But what did it actually mean, Wittgenstein asked. What was in the head of the person who said it? Was it not actually a muddle about words? Really, who but a philosopher would waste any time worrying about it, he asked. Turing countered by suggesting that a mathematical formula which failed to take account of the Liar's Paradox might be used to build a bridge – which would then be in danger of falling down. The jury remains out.

Wittgenstein began to apply his insights about the common-sense approach to logic and scientific method, which he believed was undermining civilisation. He objected to what he called the 'the typical western scientist', driven by a commitment to progress, to 'onwards movement [and to] building ever larger and more complicated structures ... one construction after another, moving on and up, as it were, from one stage to the next'.[178] Science values knowledge, he claimed, only as a means to an end. And 'the spirit in which science is carried on nowadays', he complained, is incompatible with a sense of wonder at nature: 'Man has to awaken to wonder,' he wrote. 'Science is a way of sending him to sleep again.'[179]

Wittgenstein may not have described science very well there. He was echoing William Blake's horror at what he called 'Newton's sleep'. There are actually many scientists who have a sense of wonder about the universe they are studying. But Wittgenstein does seem to me to have tickbox in his sights here, and in this case he is right – it does induce the kind of sleep that comes from what he calls 'our craving for generality'. He describes this as:

Our preoccupation with the method of science. I mean the method of reducing the explanation of natural phenomena to the smallest possible number of primitive natural laws; and, in mathematics, of unifying the treatment of different topics by using a generalization. Philosophers constantly see the method of science before their eyes, and are irresistibly tempted to ask and answer in the way science does. This tendency is the real source of metaphysics, and leads the philosopher into complete darkness. I want to say here that it can never be our job to reduce anything to anything, or to explain anything.[180]

This passage was taken from his mysterious *Blue Book*, in which he wrote his notes on his new philosophy. It marked a break with his *Tractatus Logico-Philosophicus*, which he had only just used as a PhD. thesis and on which he was examined by two of the greatest British philosophers of the day, Bertrand Russell and G. E. Moore. 'Don't worry,' he said as he clapped Moore on the shoulder afterwards. 'I know you will never understand it.'[181]

So perhaps it does not then matter that I am far from certain that Wittgenstein was right that it can never be our job to explain anything, but he has something to say about the way tickbox reduces individual emotions or peculiar phenomena to readily categorisable data. It is impoverishing and it induces a kind of sleep-walking through life, free of nuance or ambiguity or novelty or individuality.

There will always be a place for software and other systems, but those contemporary philosophers who rail against reducing complex human interactions to machine-like algorithms – the American Robert Nozick, for example – are, in this sense, following Wittgenstein's critique of reductionist science.

The Turing Test

Wittgenstein and Turing clashed at a series of Wittgenstein's tutorials in Cambridge. As far as I know, they never met again. But what on earth, you might ask, qualifies me to judge the famous Turing Test, the gold standard for artificial intelligence? I was sceptical – but, I hope, open-minded – about the whole idea for years, as an almost fully paid-up human being. I had poured scorn on the AI enterprise.[182] But then, again, I did write a short biography of Alan Turing himself.[183] And it was Turing, in 1950, who first suggested a mathematical proof that computers would one day assume a kind of humanity.

Public interest in this isn't just down to growing interest in Turing himself. The test he set out is the basis for the controversial idea of 'singularity', the moment when AI comes of age and computers start thinking and learning for themselves. Turing argued that, when you were convinced you couldn't tell a computer and a human being apart during a conversation, then the test would have been passed.

No computer program seemed at all close to passing. So, in 1990, the inventor Hugh Loebner founded the prize which bears his name, a kind of Turing Test lite. This culminates in the top four computer programs talking to the judges individually via a screen for twenty-five minutes each, while each judge simultaneously holds a screen-based conversation with a human being. At the end of each session, the judges have to decide which was which.

Although I felt surprised, I also felt privileged to be asked in 2016 to be one of four judges, and I presented myself fashionably late at Bletchley Park, where (though the prize itself began in Massachusetts) the Loebner Prize/Turing Test has been held in recent years, and where Turing himself helped to crack the Nazi Enigma naval code.[184]

But there was another reason I wanted to be there. The only justification for tickbox, it seems to me, is that it is a work in progress. Okay, the idea of automatic decisions, taken without human influence, is clunky, but there will come a time quite soon when machines can learn to deal with complexity – or so the argument goes. The Turing Test seemed to be one of the best places to see whether robots might soon be able to think as humans do.

So there I was. The other judges included a branding expert, a Sky News technology journalist and a robotics expert who described herself as a 'robot psychiatrist'. I had a moment of nerves a few minutes into the process when my fellow judges made noises to indicate they knew which was which in their conversations, and I was not completely sure about mine (I was in fact engaged with the year's winner, Steve Worswick's Mitsuku program).

In the event, one of the four programs was malfunctioning, spouting stuff about not understanding the letter 'a'. That left three, and it became clear to me pretty quickly that it was the sheer perfection of the robots' answers – perfectly spelled and grammatical – that gave them away. The real humans demonstrated their authenticity by their imperfections, their second thoughts, their hesitations and their mistypings.

One program reflected back my own mistakes – I wrote 'tecah;' instead of 'teach' – which was clever but, equally, was not quite human either. Why would you do that, except to make a point? Nor in the end was the program we all judged the best, which required a strategy for avoiding questions it couldn't answer. When I asked which part of San Francisco it came from, the robot replied: 'Why don't we talk about that later?' But then, arguably, my question wasn't really fair either – it would have been like asking how many sandwiches were left in the computer room from where the competitors operated their machines (I asked that too, and was told later that it was 'borderline sneaky').

We judges needed strategies too. I asked about loving and hating the same person at the same time, an idea I thought might be alien to robots. I also told the old cracker joke about why French people have only one egg at breakfast (answer: because one is *un oeuf*).

One of the robots told me the joke about Tiny the Newt (why is it called Tiny? Because it's my newt). I asked why it was funny. It sidestepped the question.

The programs we talked to were huge achievements. Their non-sequiturs and rapid changes of subject certainly seemed human in a Pinteresque way. But in the end, they were trying to trick us into thinking they were human rather than communicating on an equal basis.

So the experience convinced me that while artificial intelligence is speeding ahead in its abilities, it will not be producing humanoid, thinking robots any time soon. This is partly because the kind of clear unambiguous thinking the AI researchers are striving for is not actually human at all. Human abilities are different, and are vital to making relationships, and therefore organisations, work effectively. It isn't the infallibility of people that makes them human, after all. Quite the reverse; it is their sheer fallibility – their ability to make mistakes, be quirky, make relationships, love and care. It is more unnerving, not more reassuring, to be phoned by a robot that is nearly human than it is to be phoned by an obvious machine.

It may be that computers will be able to do all that one day, but I noticed that I had built some kind of rapport with all four human beings I talked to, even via a screen, but not with any of the robots, though we had talked just as much.

I also felt I had been given some insight into why AI researchers are so keen on their given task – because of an exasperation with human beings, so illogical, so contradictory, so biased. In fact, that seems to have been one of Turing's motivations in developing the idea of his test in the first place. As a gay man, he believed that computers would in the fullness of time be able to do anything human beings could do, yet without discriminating illogically against men who sleep with men.

Oddly enough, the same kind of motivation apparently grips Turing Prize funder Hugh Loebner. He was overwhelmed with criticism after revealing his habit of paying for sex, and seems to regard artificial intelligence as a way out of what he sees as an illogical bias.

Unfortunately for both men, automatic systems using data appear to think along human lines and take decisions along familiar tramlines, because – certainly as far as racial bias is concerned – that is where the data about insurance, bank loans or criminal recidivism seems to take us. Because the computers assume that previous patterns will always apply.

Enough of experts?

The lesson I took from my experience as a Turing Test judge was not that we will never be able to interact with computers – because we already do, and they talk back to us – but that they will not be able to think or communicate in a human way for a long time, and that they may never do.

Neither would we really want them to be human. We want to interact with flawed, peculiar humans with depth, rather than with the kind of shiny, one-dimensional, unambiguous language which machines are good at. And when it comes to kissing them, then really – whatever the prophets of robot sex being 'better than the real thing' might say – I would suggest that flawless kissing is hardly worth the effort.[185] It is like kissing a moving dummy. Try falling in love with your laptop, if you don't believe me ...

The experience of judging the Turing Test was fascinating and I wouldn't willingly have missed it, but I would not want to deal with an organisation which had been so scripted and 'programmed' and managed by a tickbox app. Given that this is clearly the direction of travel in our contemporary world, we need to decide whether there might be a better way. How, in short, do we think our way out of tickbox to a world where it reverses itself? That is the question I shall try to answer in this chapter. Not so much how do we escape from tickbox, but how might we foster its opposite? How do we get to *tockbox*?

First of all, we have to remember why we cling, not just to tickbox, but to the bureaucracy that underpins it and which it is attempting to replace. It may not work very effectively, but there is a purpose behind it. It is designed to manage people and organisations from a distant centre, with a minimum of human intervention. And within that objective, it is designed to reassure, to make sure that the endeavour is transparent or safe, that it lives up to its social obligations – that the right people are employed, that someone has made sure the cladding is safe or that the education or medical skills are up to scratch. Or, more usually, to provide an official imprimatur on this reassurance, even when it is completely hollow.

As we have seen, if this is the purpose of tickbox, it fails to achieve it. We may be reassured – though we are increasingly immune – but we are not actually any safer. We still have terrorist attacks since airline staff started ticking their boxes to reassure them that we have packed our bags ourselves. Child abuse has still occurred since the whole edifice of tickbox safeguarding (criminal record checks and so on) was put in place in 2002. But we *feel* safer. A little bit safer.

You might argue that, because we feel safer, we are a little less vigilant. But we were not actually very vigilant before.

One of the fundamental problems with tickbox is that it seems to offer reassurance, but it is based on virtual systems or numbers which have been designed to replace real trust. So the reassurance seems empty, either because we no longer trust the figures, or the politicians who wield them, or we see through the symbolic gesture they are supposed to represent.

Now, I can't pretend I know what Michael Gove meant during the debate in the run-up to the Brexit referendum, when he claimed that people had 'had enough of experts'.[186] He was roundly condemned by most thoughtful people after this remark. But I did feel that he had articulated an important idea, and I have wondered since – perhaps we distrust these 'experts' because so many of them have become so compromised by the tramline processes of tickbox that they are really just experts in the status quo. They are not, in fact, experts in what-if questions because their knowledge of context is so narrow. And perhaps none more so than qualified economists answering questions about a different kind of world.

Whether or not this was what Gove meant, I believe it to be true. Professional expertise is now so narrowly defined, so compromised by tickbox, that it might explain why experts' views are so often wrong. Either way, we have to make up our own minds.

I know it is received wisdom that, these days, we don't trust the senior figures in society who rule us or control us or wield the authority to do so. I am not convinced we ever did. But my parents' generation did seem to trust the leaders of local institutions – the schoolteachers or doctors they knew – unless there was some reason not to.

It would be a deeply conservative prescription that we should simply go back to trusting such individuals. How can we, given that our headteachers owe us only the allegiance that tickbox allows them, and our doctors are so constrained by their real 'owners', the big American healthcare providers or UK outsourcing specialists, who in turn owe their allegiance to distant shareholders or imperial bosses? That kind of set-up almost rules out personal trust in a professional, however transparent the individual. That is the main reason we can't go back: we have opened Pandora's box and it isn't clear how to close it again. However much we may want to trust them, professionals will not be trustworthy until the management of schools and healthcare is brought a good deal closer to us than it currently is.

So the first policy proposal I make to reduce the influence of tickbox is a radical scaling down of our institutions and corporations.

For the reasons I set out in Chapter 5, the evidence seems to suggest that small businesses are more innovative, imaginative and flexible than big ones. The same is almost self-evidently so in the public sector, where big organisations are run according to the dictates of tickbox far more than human-scale organisations. Of course, the Ofsted reports and ratings provide us with important information about our schools, but we can find out a good deal more by getting to know the teachers and senior staff – and better still, by getting alongside them and helping to run the schools.

In the same way, we might find out some important information from the Care Quality Commission about the doctors and surgeons, the institutions and care homes that treat or look after us. But to get the full picture, we need the practices and hospitals to be small enough for us to sum up the individuals in charge eye to eye, and face to face. We need to be able to know the senior staff of the local institutions we deal with, and they need to have the time to know us. Having formal information without its informal counterpart makes us one-eyed and one-dimensional. It is like telling the time when we have lost our intuitive ability to feel time going by. We need both to check each against the other. We need the rigidity of figures and the fluidity of intuition to navigate the world effectively. 'Of clouds and clocks', as the philosopher Karl Popper put it.[187] We need both to test the other, but tickbox only recognises one of them.

The implications of this are pretty clear. We need to interact with institutions that are, wherever possible, small enough for us to know the people in charge. And to *have* people in charge – there is no point in pretending that most modern bank managers are real, because banks have no human managers. Or that the headteachers, so constrained and cash-strapped, have much in common with the plenipotentiary headteachers of a generation or so back. Their wills have been sapped and taken over by the demands of tickbox. Tickbox flows in their veins.

I am not claiming the shift is all bad. There may be good reasons why these professionals have lost their absolute powers. What I am suggesting is that we may also have lost something vital under tickbox: the relationships with the professionals who serve us. We need to find ways – and this will be hard – that we can do some kind of deal: we will be less cynical and suspicious of professionals, if they will unbend enough for us to trust them.

There is also, as we have seen, another side to the argument – that big remains beautiful because small organisations are more expensive to run. But when you factor in the diseconomies of scale, the inflexibilities, the failure to allow for human relationships, the picture is far less clear. It is certainly a great deal more expensive to do things at scale. But those who designed the tickbox system were blind to that, so the system is too.

So there is the first and most critical element in *tockbox*: make our institutions small enough for us to know who treats us, or know the headteacher responsible for our children's education. So that they have to take account of our needs and, maybe, even talk to us occasionally.

That means we need to do some reorganisation of our biggest institutions, just as they turned Stantonbury Campus in Milton Keynes – one of the largest schools in the UK – into five mini-schools on the same site, but still sharing the same theatre and other facilities.[188] We need to turn the process of mergers into reverse, to divide our schools into units of no more than a thousand pupils – still perhaps linked to other schools with ties of affiliation. We need smaller hospitals than the monsters we have created. We need to slit open the bellies of the big banks, as if they were the wolf from 'Little Red Riding Hood', and let the human-scale banks out again. We also need to make sure than no company has more than 10 per cent of the UK market in its sector, which is in fact more than the Office of Fair Trading says is the minimum before market distortions set in.

There will be complaints that these demergers will be expensive, and they will cost money. But as I have argued throughout, the distortions of tickbox are themselves hugely expensive. We need to give our institutions the wriggle room they need to bypass tickbox if they can.

The counter-argument to this is that people don't have time to forge a relationship with officials. That may be so, and the tickbox system is a result. But at least they would be available to us if we wanted.

Tickbox underpins the idea of economies of scale, which will exist somewhere or other – though finding them is as difficult as pinning down the Easter Bunny. It appears to allow huge institutions to be controlled by a handful of people who look at the figures and simply steer occasionally. It prefers scale over intimacy because it believes that narrow data is better than broad knowledge. Therein lies its great mistake.

The same is true in the corporate world. There is already a head of steam building behind a political project in the USA to go ahead with a new generation of anti-monopolistic corporate break-ups. This has found some traction in continental Europe, where competition commissioner Margrethe Vestager has been forging ahead against the powerful American tech companies.[189] But the idea appears to be completely alien in UK establishment circles, which are still wedded to the primacy of economies of scale.

This is one reason why there is a tickbox blindness about the poor customer service provided by most companies that rely on huge database systems to provide them. There are a handful of exceptions, Amazon being one of them, though as an online retailer, it causes local economic damage instead.

Either way, we urgently need our institutions to be more human in scale. If we can make them so, they will also be considerably more effective and therefore less expensive. But this will by itself not be enough to push back the tentacles of tickbox.

The human factor

I would probably go further than Caroline Slocock, because the problem is not just the inappropriate adoption of business practices by the public sector. Tickbox fails to work effectively in the private sector too. But she was right that this was the policy context for tickbox, and Slocock's team at her think tank Civil Exchange set out their antidote. I particularly focus on one of their suggestions here – that 'relationships are better than impersonal transactions'.

This is not just a pious hope. It is also a prediction of the future of public services, because of the growing realisation that our current service providers are legacy systems made up of everything that it seemed possible to measure in 1998, concreted into an automated tickbox machinery, so that the system narrows what it is possible to achieve. They are machines for spreading costs everywhere else. The future services don't yet exist, but they will require a human-scale reboot to provide some flexibility.

There are clearly less optimistic scenarios, in which the data monopolists Google and Amazon run off with all the prizes, and end up – as Columbus and Cabot attempted to achieve in the 1490s, taking a commission from every trade with China – taking a slice of every transaction. We can't uninvent big data – nor should we – but we do need to remember what it can and can't do.

It can't, for example, measure the most important elements of life, love, health and so on. It can't provide judgement or justification for its implications, or offer ethical understanding or a clear view of what causes what – it can only observe, as David Hume found, that events seem to happen together. It can't escape from the prejudices hidden away in existing data about who is at risk of criminality or debt default. It can, and constantly does, lead us right up the garden path, or – in the case of people too trusting of their sat-nav data – into the river or the path of an oncoming train.

All those extra elements require a human mind if they are to be achieved. When the chess grand master Gary Kasparov was beaten by the IBM computer Deep Blue, it was an opportunity to reassess human skills (in fact, he won the first tournament but lost the second; IBM refused a third). Okay, we can't beat computers at a whole range of tasks (including chess), but we can make relationships, assess what causes what, imagine new possibilities, gather, use and assess informal knowledge. And these abilities are pretty vital too.

So that is the second policy prescription if we are to row back tickbox: recognise and embed the human factor into our institutions, aware that most will fail unless we do so.[190] This requires us to look not just at the way that successful enterprises of all kinds seem to have some kind of human personality behind them, but also at the human needs that the tickbox data seems unable to recognise – joy, humour, green space, hope, friendship, feeling useful, and all those other elements that tickbox can't comprehend because they have no hard data attached.

The third prescription is to rescue knowledge from the

narrowness of tickbox, which in practice means rescuing universities from the dead hand of technocracy.

Universities are supposed to be the shining beacons of knowledge and its development. But over the past generation, they have become hollowed out by an absurd tickbox system called the Research Excellence Framework (REF), which ranks universities according to how much, and where, their faculties have published. There are fascinating disputes about this – if you have something to say in economic history, for example, where should you publish? Economic history is frowned on by mainstream economics departments, and only a couple of mainstream journals are available, which – because they refer to each other too much – have been excised by the gods of REF auditing.[191] This is how one medical researcher put the problem of perverse metrics about 'impact', which often just means counting the number of citations an article gains:

> The apparent endemicity of bad research behaviour is alarming. We aid and abet the worst behaviours. Our acquiescence to the impact factor fuels an unhealthy competition to win a place in a select few journals. Journals are not the only miscreants. Universities are in a perpetual struggle for money and talent, endpoints that foster reductive metrics, such as high-impact publication. National assessment procedures, such as the Research Excellence Framework, incentivise bad practices. And individual scientists, including their most senior leaders, do little to alter a research culture that occasionally veers close to misconduct.[192]

As so often with tickbox, the system seems simple but very rapidly becomes fiendishly complex. All too often, the experts are not so much experts in the broad sweep of their subject but in the narrow confines of whatever tickbox system controls it. Of course we are fed up with that kind of expert. Who wouldn't be? They are peddling conventional knowhow that poses as expertise, but which is actually the tramlined knowledge of the inner workings of a particular tickbox system, which has above all else at its heart a terror of major change.

Again, I can't tell if Michael Gove had this in mind, or whether he was just lashing out under questioning. But if his remark carried a glimmer of recognition for many people, and I believe it did, this may be why.

The fourth area of policy change is to look at social infrastructure as the key to prevention of crime, ill-health, dropping out of school and so on. As Caroline Slocock says, the technocratic mindset – the tickbox approach – has what she calls a blind spot about this. When people live in green areas with parks and trees and lots of local organisations, she says, it is naturally preventive. Yet policy-makers seem to take little notice, preferring to tick off people's needs separately – as if people with depression have nothing to do with people who need childcare, for example, and as if the absence of trees and grass from new housing developments were somehow irrelevant (East Croydon's brand new dark satanic towers spring to mind, looming over the station with hardly a blade of grass between them, and still less a tree).

We have become used to policy-makers implying that somehow the lack of trust or of community institutions – even the lack of grass – are the fault of people who live in poorer areas, but I suspect it is the other way around. When such things exist, people trust each other more and begin to support each other, yet somehow our policy-makers seem to consider that these elements are important only for the better off. I can think of no other explanation why poor people's parks and allotments are sold for development while rich people's parks are protected. It is tempting to think that this is because trust and the need for nature are intangible, and therefore difficult to measure.

The fifth proposition is the importance of concentrating on people's strengths – on what they can *do* instead of what they *need*. The obsession with needs is understandable, but it has also rendered people's needs their only assets, so it is hardly surprising that the system tends to burnish those needs. People's needs are how they assert themselves – not that those needs are not present, of course. The alternative has been dubbed rather awkwardly 'co-production'; it involves concentrating instead much more on people's abilities, and in particular on their ability to care.[193]

If you want to see how this works in practice and at some scale, go to Frome, Somerset, where the doctors' surgery has controversially recruited over 1100 locals as volunteer 'community connectors' whose task is to chat to people, to point them in the direction of people like themselves and generally listen. The lesson of Frome is that if you dump the data analysis about which patients should be prioritised, and you put relationships, not process, at the heart of what you do, you can reduce emergency admissions to hospital by 16 per cent. Which is all the more impressive given that emergency admissions have risen across the county as a whole over the same three years by nearly a third.

I believe these elements will form the basis of the future, because *tockbox* is more effective than the kind of reductionism that tickbox represents. And the disappointment about tickbox in practice – the growing awareness of the gap between appearance and reality – may be enough to make it happen.

Human or algorithm?

As if in confirmation, I recently discovered a recent contribution to the debate in the *New Yorker* by Amazon's healthcare chief Atul Gawande, the champion of checklists. He describes what happens in hospitals when the system takes charge, exhausting the doctors with its demands for information they know perfectly well they can safely ignore. It takes no account of their years of know-how, which is why over 40 per cent of American doctors complain about depression.

Three years after his own hospital was computerised, he said he had 'come to feel that a system that promised to increase my mastery over my work has, instead, increased my work's mastery over me. I'm not the only one.'[194]

He found that the old doctors' handwritten handover notes worked; now, they tend to cut and paste great screeds of stuff which no longer allow their colleagues to grasp the essentials. The Berkeley University psychologist Christina Maslach defined 'burn-out' as a combination of three feelings: 'emotional exhaustion, depersonalization (a cynical, instrumental attitude toward others), and a sense of personal ineffectiveness', wrote Gawande. We can probably all recognise them as symptoms of capture by tickbox.

Gawande's conclusion looks remarkably like mine:

Many fear that the advance of technology will replace us all with robots. Yet in fields like health care the more imminent prospect is that it will make us all behave like robots. And the people we serve need something more than either robots or robot-like people can provide. They need human enterprises that can adapt to change.

Gawande is right again. If, out of a misplaced need to control what people do, we use IT or algorithms or robots in places where we should be using human skills, then the result is inevitable: people will limit their own undoubted genius so that they become more like algorithms themselves. They will also limit their ability to meet the needs of customers or clients in ways which will usually be bad both for the clients and for the community as a whole.

That is a tragedy, and an unnecessary one. We are no longer an empire and we know that empires are not a good way of managing people, because of the sheer inefficiency and the worse ineffectiveness of governing from the centre. The policy response has to be to break out of this imperial mindset and to radically devolve responsibility down to a more human scale, where people know the individual professionals they have to deal with.

That would not *replace* inspection regimes, but it would provide another dimension to test their findings. You need relationships and human skills to test the findings of any inspection regime, as well as vice versa. Of clouds and clocks again. You need both to guarantee human freedom, so we need them to be in some kind of balance, said Popper. It is the same with accountability, which effectively rules out automated management of the tickbox variety.

R. D. Laing and tickbox psychiatry

Which leaves us with our very human rage at the sheer destructive stupidity of tickbox, as it nags away at us and at the way we are treated. If they are just counting people so they can drive them from place to place 'as graziers do their cattle ... let them brand us at once,' said the parliamentary hero William Thornton MP, as he led the opposition to the first planned UK census in 1753.[195] 'While they treat us like oxen and sheep, let them not insult us with the name of men.'

Something of that same anger grows within us every time we are branded and categorised. Our exasperation stems from the disaffection so many of us feel, both at the tickbox gap between rhetoric and reality, and at the way we are treated by the services we use, public and private. If a sense of reciprocity is at the heart of the human experience, as anthropologists like Polly Wiessner say it is, then the way it is constantly betrayed by the organisations which promise us so much is reason in itself to explain this constant background feeling of fury.[196]

Of course, physical or verbal assaults on NHS staff are unforgiveable. But equally, I don't remember that a generation ago there were warning signs on every NHS counter. Perhaps because we are the first generation to be quite so nudged, prodded and tickboxed – and for the good of the administration, not for our own. Why is everyone so angry these days, I get asked from time to time. This is the answer I give.

One of those sent nearly insane by an early version of tickbox was the radical psychiatrist R. D. Laing. There are those who would question Laing's sanity altogether, but his critique of psychiatric tickbox was compelling. Psychiatry is a peculiar case, because on the face of it, it is hard to justify its techniques or underlying beliefs by counting things, or looking at them under a microscope. One reason why Laing remains a hero, and it is what he continued to fight until his death, is that he understood that the dodgy foundations on which conventional psychiatry is built demand an ever closer embrace of tickbox.

For Laing, every patient stood for their own individual case. The existential view of the psyche meant that a patient's actions might seem perfectly logical, their behaviour sane from their own point of view. And that would not be a delusion but a vital clue in the process of recovery. 'The standard psychiatric patient is a function of the standard psychiatrist, and the standard psychiatric hospital,' wrote Laing, and the implication of the existential approach to madness is that everyone's breakdown is going to be different. There is no standard. If you think there is one, you will be pretty useless to your patients, or pretty brutal to them.[197]

The idea of the non-existence of standard patients was a phrase of Laing's from 1956, but it carried a resonance in his work right through to the end. Because, above all else, it was standardisation that Laing fought against. Every profession has groupthink which renders outsiders somehow as victims, whether the professionals are journalists, architects or investment bankers – and certainly psychiatrists.

The last few decades have seen the opening up of some of those professions, either painfully in the case of tabloid journalists, or more gently with the community architecture movement. Psychiatrists have tended to escape the scrutiny of the outside world. It transpired a few years ago that the psychiatrists in charge of a particularly disastrous case in south London had organised an unauthorised system which prevented patients from talking to them directly. Laing would have seen that for what it was – an attempt to raise their status and lower their stress at the expense of their patients' humanity. We have moved on from the days when Laing could find patients given ECT or lobotomised regularly, on the whim of a single doctor, without regard for safety or patient preference, but it wasn't that long ago. And it is only a matter of degree. ECT is still regularly given to people whose medical staff have run out of ideas, despite the dangers.

The problem was the rift between psychiatrists and psychologists, and the purveyors of more holistic talking cures. If you look at people numerically – either as a system of malfunctioning cells and chemicals or as the sum total of their symptoms analysed by a computer – then their personality, Laing said, begins to 'fade from view'. What enraged him until the end of his life in 1989 was the labelling system of the US health insurance system and the way it listed and categorised symptoms – and for its influence on medicine all over the world.

He held in particular contempt the *Diagnostic and Statistical Manual of the American Psychiatric Association*, known at the time as DSM III, the bible of psychiatrists. Scornfully, he would read out passages at conferences, especially in the USA, to show that – using this kind of statistical approach – almost anyone could be treated for almost anything.

This can be true of a range of chronic medical problems which insurance companies, or the NHS, find hard to categorise and therefore to put a price on. But it is particularly true of psychiatric labels, which can't be confirmed by pathologists and which tend to list bundles of symptoms that tend to happen together, then specifying a title and a standard treatment. Take the list of characteristics that define Asperger's syndrome, for example, as listed in the 1991 official criteria. There are six categories, and all six have to be ticked before a diagnosis of Asperger's can be given – but completely different oddities within each category can allow them to be ticked.[198] And if you look closely at the list, you might feel we are absolutely surrounded by people on the autistic spectrum. 'Imposition of routines and interests', for example. Or 'lack of desire to interact with peers'. Or 'clumsiness', which will describe many of us. 'Formal, pedantic language', 'peculiar stiff gaze', or 'absorbing interest more rote than meaning'? These describe most of the current cabinet, and certainly many psychiatrists.

Therein lies the problem. Modern society – and, particularly, the people who rule us – demonstrates many traits of Asperger's, yet we only somehow see them in children. Perhaps that is why bizarre statistics arise like the ones in Illinois, which saw autism cases rise by 62,000 per cent in the 1990s.

This approach has peculiar side-effects, and is the very reverse of the objective, evidence-based foundations it is supposed to rest on. It means that bundles of particular symptoms are often interpreted according to what is trending – which is often a sign of what the drugs companies are pushing at the time. Hence the invention of depression, now a widespread chronic condition, which barely existed as a psychiatric concern before 1980. (In the 1970s, the symptom of choice wasn't depression, it was hypertension.)

Here lies the danger of standardising psychiatry. This is what Laing wrote in 1986 in the *Times Literary Supplement*:

> What DSM III seems to be is a comprehensive compendium of thoughts, feelings, experiences, unusual experiences, impulses, actions, conduct, which are deemed undesirable, and should be put a stop to, in our culture. It is so all-inclusive that most items of what all the world over at all times and places were deemed to be ordinary manifestations of ordinary human minds, speech and conduct, are ruled out. We, as we used to take ourselves to be, are to be cultured out, to be replaced by a homogenised creature I can hardly recognise as a human being.[199]

DSM purports to be a useful categorisation for psychiatrists, but is actually about pricing for insurance companies. Its first incarnation, DSM I, dates back to 1952; my friend the clinical psychologist Craig Newnes tells me that it included 112 diagnoses. DSM IIIR had 292, which was an attempt to diagnose everyone. We have now reached the giddy heights of DSM V, with 365 different diagnoses.

Something of Laing's anger is now everywhere, throughout society, and it begs the question: what can we do about tickbox ourselves, without having to wait for the politicians and policymakers, who – given that they have the most to change and the most to lose – may be the last to understand the problem?

So, for the sake of argument, here is my own twelve-step

programme to face down tickbox in our own lives. It won't be easy, and we will have to forgive ourselves for our collective failure to follow it all the time. We can also console ourselves that the more we can manage it, the less tickbox can cling onto our lives.

1. **Refuse to provide feedback on a scale**

   I came out of the public toilets at Victoria Station to see two little girls playing with the feedback machine (two faces on buttons, one happy and one sad). They were having great fun, and I commend them for it – and wonder what the serious data analysts made of it. So, yes, by all means provide feedback, but not by responding to set questions where the answers can be manipulated. Or by collaborating or colluding with punitive personnel policies. Ironically, this will not make us popular people, either with managers or staff – the managers will not be able to understand it; the staff will resent this failure to provide the five-star ratings they crave. Push-button feedback outside railway lavatories is just the same – it simply has a scale of two – but somebody's performance is measured in this way. I suppose, in the same way, that Pavlov's dogs would have resented the silencing of the little bell that made them drool in anticipation. The alternative is, as a matter of habit, always to give people a 5, as suggested in a recent article called 'Please don't rate your waitress 4/5'.[200] This is almost as effective but somehow, to me, smacks of compromise.

2. **Shun the institutions that come top of the league tables**

   I talked some years ago to one of the inventors of the public service choice system in the UK – an American economist – who was frustrated that people were not simply opting for the safest and best hospitals according to his data. He had tried to persuade the government to send patients automatically to the best hospital. This would have been disastrous because it would have led to hospitals choosing us, rather than us choosing them, in the same way that schools do in London. But it was one of the clues I was given about the problems with tickbox, as if any one measure would suit everyone – and as if the measures were accurate in the first place. I have anecdotal evidence that people are beginning to shun the top institutions of their own accord. They tend to be suspicious of five-star ratings, which carry no conviction about struggle or effort. It is just too shiny and fake – what choice worthy of the name has never had to deal with any difficulties? I am particularly suspicious of the schools that come top of the league tables, afraid that they have got there by excising anything creative from the curriculum and shuffling off responsibility for their more difficult pupils. Like the great outsourcing specialists, they have been spreading costs through the rest of the system, and providing a worse service, primarily to make themselves look good. Don't underestimate what a subversive thing this is to do to tickbox.

3. **Refuse to use robots at checkouts. Or anywhere else**
Difficult, this one. Especially when you are in WH Smith, for example, and there is a long queue at the human checkout and some free machines. Normally, I agree to be beckoned over on condition that they use the machine for me, but I have to admit that makes me feel a bit helpless (which I may be, but not in that way). On the other hand, the experience of checkout machines is usually unpleasant and often frustrating, especially for some reason in the post office. But I could imagine myself and others taking a pledge to put the phone down when I am called by a robot. If it is really

important, I feel sure my bank will find another way to contact me. In any case, nearly every time I have been called by a machine in recent months, it has claimed to be from the BT or Microsoft engineering department, and is therefore a scam. Luckily for us, the automated pollsters that are so ubiquitous in the USA have yet to cross the Atlantic. It has been ten years since I heard the story from a failed Democrat would-be Congressman complaining that his opponent had programmed his own polling robot to ask who the victim was voting for – when they said his name, the machine replied: 'Why are you voting for him? He's a jerk!'

4. **Start a local campaign for real institutions and real knowledge**

In my experience, local community liaison committees tend to be either pushovers or to become hideous caricatures, standing on their dignity. For me there is another way, which means being friendly and assertive at the same time. You need to take St Augustine's advice about being as wise as serpents and as harmless as doves – apparently harmless, at least. Otherwise you may find you are on, for example, a tenant management committee – as they found after the fire in Grenfell Tower, in London – designed to insulate the real managers from the tenants and to close down communication between the two sides. But there is always more leverage you can bring to local housing associations, surgeries, schools and community centres, and on local councillors, at local level, to make sure you know what KPIs govern the institutions you deal with, to start conversations about them and any automated elements they use. Don't let the managers be in any doubt that they must also be accountable to you as a human being, and to your colleagues and friends.

5. **Get to know the people who run your local organisations**

   I needed to meet the new headteacher of my children's secondary school before taking the decision to send them there. I have always regretted my failure to follow up on that initial meeting so that at least he would know who I was. I could then have taken up with him the peculiar incident during the Year 8 parents' evening, when it became clear that one of my son's teachers had no idea who he was. Of course, getting to know people in official positions might be a deeply and occasionally unpleasantly intrusive exercise if everyone were to do it. I think you have to assume that they won't. But it dovetails with step 4: if your local headteacher and their senior staff, or the manager of the local group practice, have no relationship with you as a service user or parent – as tickbox would prefer – then they will listen solely to the deeply intrusive demands of tickbox, rather than the subtle ones coming from the people who rely on their institution. Human relationships are, in this respect, the antidote to the power of tickbox. Such relationships will also help you to interpret the acres of reports from regulators and figures that live untouched on government websites – which is really all we have in the way of accountability or transparency. This injunction is one to make it human, and to keep it so.

6. **Refuse to categorise yourself on feedback or monitoring forms**

   I don't think there is really any injunction to tell the truth to most queries from Facebook and others about my age. I do find it strange every year when my Facebook 'friends' wish me happy birthday on the wrong date. But I must admit I have some qualms about monitoring questions. Would this mean scuppering all the monitoring about race and gender?

Well, it might do, so the question is whether accurate monitoring for the generation of statistics plays a more useful role than actually tackling racism or sexism more directly. I also feel I have unnecessarily narrowed myself if I put myself down as 'white British' again. In the same way, I long to be able to avoid the 'Mr' box and to insist that I should be called 'Professor' or 'the Rt Rev' or something equally misleading like 'Admiral'. Don't worry: I won't do that. But I will continue to tick the Don't Know box when it comes to gender (even if I do know).

7. **Hold our ruling politicians to account**
The last politician I can remember resigning the day after a failure they were nominally responsible for was Nick Clegg in 2015. Before that, I may have to reach back to Lord Carrington as Foreign Secretary after the invasion of the Falklands in 1982. There was a time when cabinet ministers responsible for disasters or cock-ups resigned honourably and were praised for it. These days, they manage to cling to office, insulated by the arm's-length organisation that is responsible for the day-to-day management of prisons or the NHS, itself also insulated by a series of contracts and sub-contracts down to the poor scapegoat who will be held responsible. Of course it makes sense to find out what went wrong, but – now that the era of privatisation and outsourcing is drawing to a penniless close – it will require grassroots action to make sure ministers go back to quietly shuffling themselves off when something goes wrong.

8. **Shop locally and at small shops**
There is no surer way to undermine your local economy than by shopping in a chain store, where they collect all the money

that night and send it away to Hertfordshire (in the case of Tesco), or Luxembourg or Dublin (in the case of Amazon). If you spend money with big corporates, then you are supporting tickbox. So I have no qualms about this one. In fact, it will have the added benefit of being the best thing you can do to make the economy more effective. Locally owned shops and businesses are more friendly, more flexible and a good deal better value for money than the big ones. In a sense, every pound we spend is one either for or against tickbox. Spend your money with the big stores or companies and you vote for tickbox; spend it with their hard-pressed local rivals and you vote to end its rule.

9. **Unwire yourself as far as possible from the big data corporates**

   I mean, of course, Amazon, Facebook and Google – and I might also add Apple and Visa. I am fully aware how difficult this can be. Visa is now impossible to avoid, though it raises prices for smaller businesses by top-slicing every transaction. Amazon is difficult to avoid if you are selling things: since they have more than 85 per cent of the ebook market, if you publish ebooks then you have no choice at all but to sell on their platform. But you *can* stop buying from them where at all possible. I am also completely aware that it may not be easy to detach yourself from Google and the other tentacles of the surveillance economy, but I am certainly trying to do so.

10. **Invest your money in social enterprises, community share issues and small banks**

   This is a work in progress as far as I am concerned. It is difficult to shift your emails or bank accounts, even when the bank branches have closed. But the more we can do so, the more we can foster a little more tockbox. There is the old joke, of course, about putting your money in a small bank by putting it in a big bank that runs into difficulties, but it carries within it a grain of truth: the safest place for our money is certainly not a big bank – we know how dodgy they can be – but a smaller bank where there are regulations against speculation and clear rules about their beneficiaries. Like the *sparkassen* in Germany. If you invest in smaller institutions, it can give a perfectly respectable return, and can underpin a future with a different and less technocratic ethic at its heart.

11. **Hold your own *schrapsessies* with colleagues**

That is the name the new movement in the healthcare sector in the Netherlands has given to the 'scrap sessions' they hold at work to identify regulations, targets, tickbox rules it would be possible to get rid of completely. The idea emerged in 2018 from the Dutch think tank (Ont) Regel de Zorg, but the movement now has a head of steam behind it, and the backing of ministers. It is high time we spread it more enthusiastically over here.

12. **Name the beast**

The word *tickbox* has confused many people who have asked me what I was writing about. At first they think they have misheard and ask me to repeat it. Some then will nod sagely and change the subject; some admit they have no idea what I am talking about. But the beast needs a name, and tickbox is as good as any. Moreover, nothing will happen to change our current direction – and the power that tickbox has gathered to itself – unless people talk about it as an important issue. So if you enjoyed reading this book, perhaps you might consider leaving it lying around, or starting a discussion on the topic ...

The critical fifth

Before we finish, it is worth addressing one objection to the idea that tickbox is where the *one-eyed man is king*. By implication, I mean then that tickbox is – at least according to the famous saying of Erasmus – the country of the blind. I have made that case in most of the preceding chapters.

But it does raise the question – how did such an inadequate, partially blind system grow to have such immense power and influence? There is only really one answer – that tickbox appeals, subtly humours and deludes the ultra-wealthy and the very powerful. That is as good a reason as any other why it needs to go. But let's spell out the more urgent reasons: it has infected and stupidified the official mind and, by doing so, undermined the ability of humanity to act on the world.

The twelve-step programme I have laid out above may seem to entail small shifts, and it may not always be possible to undertake them. They are certainly not easy, yet they are so subversive for those who now manage the world that, if only a fifth of us or so were truly to put them into practice, the world would inevitably change.

That 'fifth' is of course is a numerical target without evidence or justification in the real world, and it is just the kind of tickbox irritant that I have condemned throughout this book. Even so, I believe it to be true.

Acknowledgements

It has been nearly two decades since I began thinking about measurement, and I am enormously grateful for all the help and inspiration I have received in that time as I inched my way to a point of view – especially from my colleagues at the New Economics Foundation, Radix and New Weather.

Two people in particular have helped me with the thinking behind this book, and have given me absolutely invaluable advice. One is Bernie Rochford, whose story appears in Chapter 4; the other is Susan Holliday, whose story is not told here, but whose thinking and writing in the field of psychotherapy has been very influential for me, and hopefully will soon be much more widely known.

I would also like to thank the following people for reading chapters or talking through elements of the book: Samira Ben Omar, Jonathan Calder, Katrina Dunbar, Ian Fitzpatrick, Alice Garner, Penny Godwin, Professor Charles Goodhart, Sara Hamilton, Nikki Hobbs, Judith Hodge, Ben Ludford, Lindsay Mackie, Ed Mayo, Aisha Munro-Collins, Craig Newnes, Michal Siewniak, Andrew Simms, Bob Thust, Kate Vick, Jo Wildy, Alison Young, Joe Zammit-Lucia, and many others. And also the staff at the London Library and the Bentley Historical Library at the University of Michigan, for their unfailing good humour and help.

As always, I owe a huge debt of gratitude to my agent Julian Alexander and my editor Richard Beswick for their wisdom, support and help shaping this book. Finally, but not least, is the huge support I get every day from Sarah, Robin and William, intellectually as well as emotionally. So many of the ideas in this book originally came from them – a bit like Winston Churchill, I feel all I have had to do is to formulate it into a kind of roar. I hope it sounds a little like that ...

Notes

1 Little Boxes

1   Richard Adams, 'Military bureaucracy'. *Military Review*, Jan.–Feb. 2017, https://www.armyupress.army.mil/Journals/Military-Review/English-Edition-Archives/January-February-2017/ART-004/
2   C. P. Snow, *Public Affairs*, New York: Scribner, 1971, 195.
3   http://news.bbc.co.uk/1/hi/uk/6656411.stm
4   See my discussion of this in David Boyle, *The Tyranny of Numbers*, London: HarperCollins, 2001, 51–3.
5   See my approach to this in David Boyle, *The Human Element*, Abingdon: Earthscan, 2011, 91.
6   Bob Carter et al., '"All they lack is a chain": lean and the new performance management in the British civil service', *Public Money and Management* 31:2 (2011).
7   See for example the *Independent*, 25 May 2016, https://www.independent.co.uk/news/uk/home-news/hmrc-blunders-mean-32-million-people-may-have-paid-wrong-tax-a7047546.html
8   Conversation with Samira Ben Omar.
9   *Guardian*, 31 May 2018, https://www.theguardian.com/uk-news/2018/may/31/vital-immigration-papers-lost-by-uk-home-office
10 *Guardian*, 29 June 2018, https://www.theguardian.com/uk-

news/2018/jun/29/mps-condemn-home-office-over-detained-windrush-pair

11   https://www.bbc.co.uk/news/uk-43795077

12   Joint Committee on Human Rights, *Windrush Generation Detention*, London: House of Commons and House of Lords, 2018, 22.

13   *Guardian*, 25 December 2017, https://www.theguardian.com/uk-news/2017/dec/25/asylum-offices-constant-state-crisis-say-whistleblowers-home-office

14   *Computing*, 25 September 2018, https://www.computing.co.uk/ctg/news/3029300/how-the-home-office-moved-immigration-services-to-the-cloud

15   *The Register*, 24 April 2018, https://www.theregister.co.uk/2017/04/28/what_now_for_the_home_office/

16   Independent Chief Inspector of Borders and Immigration, *An inspection of the Home Office's mechanisms for learning from immigration litigation, April–July 2017*, London, 2017, https://assets.publishing.service.gov.uk/government/uploads/system/uploads/attachment_data/file/677560/An_inspection_of_the_Home_Office_s_mechanisms_for_learning_from_litigation.pdf

17   Jeremy Bentham, *Proposal for a New and Less Expensive mode of Employing and Reforming Convicts*, London, 1798; quoted in R. Evans, *The Fabrication of Virtue: English prison architecture*, Cambridge, 1982, 195.

18   *Guardian*, 1 March 2017, https://www.theguardian.com/uk-news/2017/mar/01/britain-one-of-worst-places-western-europe-asylum-seekers

19   Bryan Appleyard, *The Brain is Wider Than the Sky: Why simple solutions don't work in a complex world*, London: Weidenfeld and Nicolson, 2011, 100.

20   Jonathan Vanian, 'Unmasking AI's bias problem', *Fortune*, 1 July 2018.

21   See https://www.innovationinpractice.com/innovation_in_practice/2014/02/thinking-outside-the-box-a-misguided-idea.html

22   *Daily Telegraph*, 18 June 2009, https://www.telegraph.co.uk/news/uknews/5811333/Discrimination-against-northerners-to-be-banned-under-Harriet-Harman-plans.html

23   *Daily Telegraph*, 21 September 2011.

24 Vince Cable, leader's speech, 21 September 2018, https://www.libdems.org.uk/conference-autumn-18-vince-cable-speech-in-full

25 *Guardian*, 12 September 2017, https://www.theguardian.com/commentisfree/2017/sep/12/fetish-tickbox-targets-teachers-educators-schools

26 https://www.telegraph.co.uk/news/uknews/law-and-order/8571187/Chiefs-war-on-jobsworth-police.html

27 BBC News, 7 September 2012, https://www.bbc.co.uk/news/health-20545055

28 Atul Gawande, *The Checklist Manifesto*, London: Profile, 2010.

29 Gawande, *The Checklist Manifesto*, 32ff.

30 Gawande, *The Checklist Manifesto*, 160.

31 See https://en.todoist.com/. Millions are said to use to-do lists: https://blog.hubspot.com/marketing/best-to-do-list-apps-tools

32 Or so the conversation went according to Pete Seeger, who I talked to about it once.

2 Towards a History of Tickbox

33 Martha Banta, *Taylored Lives: Narrative productions in the age of Taylor, Veblen, and Ford*, Chicago: University of Chicago Press, 1993, 93.

34 Peter Drucker, *The Practice of Management*, London: Routledge, 2007, 242.

35 E. P. Thompson, 'Time, work-discipline, and industrial capitalism', Past & Present 38, December 1967.

36 Frederick Winslow Taylor, *The Principles of Scientific Management*, London: Routledge, 2004, 52.

37 Quoted in *Advanced Management Journal* (1936) 1:2, March.

38 Quoted in Garet Garrett, *The Wild Wheel*, New York: Ludwig von Mises Institute, 1952, 140.

39 Taylor, *The Principles of Scientific Management*, 9f.

40 Lloyd Zimpel, *Man Against Work*, New York: Eerdmans, 1974, 123.

41 US Commission on Industrial Relations, 'Congressional Series Set', US Government Printing Office, 1916, 889

42   V. I. Lenin, 'Scientific Management and the dictatorship of the proletariat', Speech, June 1919.

43   John Ralston Saul, *The Doubter's Companion*, New York: Simon and Schuster, 2012, 280.

44   Frank Gilbreth and Ernestine Gilbreth Carey, *Cheaper by the Dozen*, London: Heinemann, 1948.

45   Yevgeny Zamyatin, *We*, trans. Clarence Brown, London: Penguin Classics, 1993.

46   Harry Braverman, *Labor and Monopoly Capital: The degradation of work in the twentieth century*, 25th anniversary edition, New York: Monthly Review Press, 1998.

47   Joseph Tainter, *The Collapse of Complex Societies*, Cambridge: CUP, 1998.

48   I calculated this for my book *The Human Element*, 73. Tainter did the same in his 1988 book and claimed there were 33,000 Admiralty officials administering the navy by 1967; see 107.

49   Baron de Grimm and Diderot, *Correspondance, Littéraire, Philosphique et Critique*, 1753–69, 1813 edn, Vol. 4, 146. Quoted in Martin Albrow, *Bureaucracy*, London: Pall Mall Press, 1970, 16.

50   Wilhelm von Humboldt (1792), *The Limits of State Action*, 1792.

51   Quoted in Albrow, *Bureaucracy*, 4.

52   Max Weber, *The Protestant Ethic and the Spirit of Capitalism*, 1904.

53   J. A. Schumpeter, *Capitalism, Socialism and Democracy*, 3rd edition, London: Allen and Unwin, 1950, 206.

54   *Guardian*, 8 January 1968.

55   Paul du Gay, *In Praise of Bureaucracy*, London: Sage, 2000.

56   A remark the great man is supposed to have made around 1920. Quoted in du Gay, *In Praise of Bureaucracy*, 61.

57   *Guardian*, 22 June 2017, https://www.theguardian.com/healthcare-network/2017/jun/22/friends-suicide-bureaucracy-cuts-quit-nhs-manager

58   See Duncan McCann and Robbie Werrin, *Who Watches the Workers?* London: New Economics Foundation, 2018.

59   https://www.bostonglobe.com/business/2016/02/18/firms-step-monitoring-employee-activities-work/2l5hoCjsEZWA0bp10BzPrN/story.html

60   James O. McKinsey, *Book-keeping and Accounting*, South-Western, 1921.

61   Quoted in John C. Bogle, *Battle for the Soul of Capitalism*, Yale University Press, 2008, 69.

62   *Independent*, 20 January 2002, https://www.independent.co.uk/news/business/analysis-and-features/the-might-of-the-mckinsey-mob-9215959.html

63   Ethan Rasiel, *The McKinsey Way*, New York: McGraw-Hill, 1999, 9.

64   US Senate, *Occupational Safety and Health Reform and Reinvention Act*, Washington, 1996, https://www.congress.gov/104/crpt/srpt308/CRPT-104srpt308.pdf

65   James Vike, 'The bureaucracy as a battleground: Contentious politics surrounding OSHA 1980–2004', *Politics and Policy* 35:3, 2007.

66   This is a key element in what has been known as Upside Down Management. See Boyle, *The Human Element*, 22–3.

67   See my original calculation in Boyle, *The Human Element*, 94–5.

68   D. Osborne and T. Gaebler, *Reinventing Government*, New York: Addison Wesley Longman, 1992.

69   Michael Hammer and H. S. Stanton, *The Re-engineering Revolution: A handbook*, New York: Harper Business, 1995, 41.

70   *Daily Telegraph*, 29 May 2018, https://www.telegraph.co.uk/politics/2018/05/29/taxman-fails-answer-four-million-calls-year-mps-warn-people/

71   Simon Head, *The New Ruthless Economy: Work and power in the digital age*, New York: Oxford University Press, 2003, 8.

72   Quoted in Head, *The New Ruthless Economy*, 90.

73   See for example Mandy Turnbull, 'A qualitative investigation into the experiences, perceptions, beliefs and self-care management of people with type 2 diabetes', Ph.D. thesis, Salford University, 2015, http://usir.salford.ac.uk/37535/1/Mandy%20Turnbull%20PhD%20Final%20Thesis%202015.pdf

3 The Tickbox Men

74   See Deborah Shapley, *Promise and Power: The life and times of Robert McNamara*, New York, Little Brown, 1993, 539ff.

75   Shapley, *Promise and Power*, 474.

76   Quoted in Shapley, *Promise and Power*, 103.

77   Quoted in Shapley, *Promise and Power*, 99.

78   Quoted in the documentary *The Fog of War* (2003).

79   Quoted in Shapley, Promise and Power, 251.

80   David Kilcullen, *Counterinsurgency*, New York: OUP, 2010.

81   Thomas Ricks, 'Kilcullen (I): Here's what not to measure in a COIN campaign', foreignpolicy.com, 8 February 2010, https://foreignpolicy.com/2010/02/08/kilcullen-i-heres-what-not-to-measure-in-a-coin-campaign/

82   Quoted in Shapley, *Promise and Power*, 374.

83   Quoted in Shapley, *Promise and Power*, 546.

84   Wilfred Burns, *New Towns for Old*, London, 1963, 93–4; Newcastle City Council, *Development Plan Review 1963*, 97.

85   Quoted in Shapley, *Promise and Power*, 394–5.

86   J. Welch, *Jack: Straight from the Gut*, New York: Warner Business Books, 2001.

87   Robert Chambers, *Whose Reality Counts?* London: IT Publications, 1997. See e.g. 49ff.

88   Chambers, *Whose Reality Counts?*, 49.

89   Robert McNamara, Speech to World Bank board, 25 September 1972.

90   Morse and Reimer, 'The experimental chance of a major organisational variable', *Journal of Abnormal Social Psychology* 52 (1956), 120–9.

91   Rensis Likert, *The Human Organisation*, New York: McGraw-Hill, 1967, 29ff.

92   Likert, *The Human Organisation*, 134.

93   Naresh Khatri, Jonathon R. B. Halbesleben, Gregory F. Peroski and Wilbert Meyer, 'The relationship between management philosophy and clinical outcomes', *Health Care Management Review* 32:2, April/June 2007. See also Naresh Khatri et al., 'Medical errors and quality of care: from control to commitment', *California Management Review* 48, Spring 2006.

94   See Rensis Likert and Jane Gibson Likert, *New Ways of Managing Conflict*, New York: McGraw-Hill, 1976.

95   http://www.hrmarketer.com/Hypocrisy_Reviews_Report.pdf

96   F. Warneken and M. Tomasello, 'Extrinsic rewards undermine

altruistic tendencies in 20-month-olds', *Developmental Psychology* 44:6 (2008), 1785–8.

97   https://hbr.org/2017/03/research-how-incentive-pay-affects-employee-engagement-satisfaction-and-trust

98   Jerry Muller, *The Tyranny of Metrics*, Princeton University Press, 2018.

4 Goodhart's Law

99   Charles Goodhart, 'Problems of monetary management: The U.K. experience', in Anthony S. Courakis (ed.), *Inflation, Depression, and Economic Policy in the West*, Rowman & Littlefield, 1981, 111–46.

100 C. Goodhart, 'Problems of monetary management: The U.K. experience', in *Papers in Monetary Economics*, Canberra: Reserve Bank of Australia, 1975.

101 See K. Alec Chrystal and Paul D. Mizen, *Goodhart's Law: Its origins, meaning and implications for monetary policy*, Bank of England, 12 November 2001.

102 *Marilyn Strathern, 'Improving Ratings: Audit in the British University System'*, European Review 5 (1997), 305–21.

103 http://www.smbc-comics.com/index.php?id=3978

104 See for example this and other examples in Boyle, *The Tyranny of Numbers*.

105 Quoted in Boyle, *The Human Element*, 93–4.

106 Read the full story of Swale in Boyle, *The Human Element*, 94–7.

107 Quoted in Simon Caulkin, 'How to be big and beautiful', *The Observer*, 30 January 2005.

108 Seddon first used the 'failure demand' phrase in John Seddon, *I Want You to Cheat*, Bedford: Vanguard, 1992. More on the concept in John Seddon, *Freedom from Command and Control*, Bedford: Vanguard, 2003.

109 See *Inside Housing*, 5 November 2009, https://www.insidehousing.co.uk/insight/insight/re-humanising-housing-17471

110 I wrote about this encounter in 'The pitfalls and perils of payment by results', *Local Economy*, December 2010.

111 G. Sturgess, L. Cumming, J. Dicker et al., *Payment By Outcome: A commissioners' toolkit*, London: 2020 Public Services Trust at the RSA, 2011.

112 Boyle, *The Human Element*, 36–8.

113 See David Boyle and Lindsay Mackie, *The Absent Corporation*, Steyning: New Weather Institute, 2017.

114 *Financial Times*, 22 February 2019, https://www.ft.com/content/32d66096-35e9-11e9-bd3a-8b2a211d90d5

115 This quotation taken from Bernadette Rochford, 'Whistleblower – an HG perspective', *Human Givens Journal*, November 2018. See also https://www.youtube.com/watch?v=yZdZVHjSfKQ

116 Rochford, 'Whistleblower – an HG perspective'.

117 Robert Francis (2014), *Freedom to Speak Up*, London: Department of Health, 54-5.

118 NASUWT, *Creativity and the Arts in the Curriculum*, London, 2017, https://www.nasuwt.org.uk/uploads/assets/uploaded/3535be2c-801c-46cb-b4410810472b52a3.pdf

119 http://michaelrosenblog.blogspot.com/2018/05/education-what-for-where-when-how.html

120 https://www.ted.com/talks/ken_robinson_says_schools_kill_creativity?language=en

121 *Guardian*, 28 October 2018, https://www.theguardian.com/education/2018/oct/23/send-special-educational-needs-children-excluded-from-schools

122 *Guardian*, 6 June 2017, https://www.theguardian.com/education/2017/jun/06/sats-tests-cheating-cramming-primary-school-exam

123 https://www.artsprofessional.co.uk/news/ofsted-refocus-broad-curriculum

124 *Guardian*, 17 January 2019, https://www.theguardian.com/education/2019/jan/17/ofsted-inspections-find-three-steiner-schools-to-be-inadequate

5 The Empty Corporation

125 Boyle and Mackie, *The Absent Corporation*.

126 Boyle and Mackie, *The Absent Corporation*.

127 A. Berger, N. Miller, M. Petersen, R. Rajan, J. Stein, 'Does function follow organizational form? Evidence from the lending practices of large and small banks', *Journal of Financial Economics*, 76:2 (2002); R. Cole, L. Goldberg, L. White, 'Cookie-cutter versus character: The micro structure of small business lending by large and small banks', *Journal of Financial and Quantitative Analysis*, 39:2 (2004).

128 Accenture UK, *New Generation SME Banking*, London, 2011.

129 Banking Taskforce, Appeals process: Annual report, 2012, www. betterbusinessfinance.co.uk/images/uploads/Annual_Report_ Master_2012.pdf

130 Lord Sharkey, Speech in Hansard, House of Lords, 15 October 2013.

131 *Guardian*, 31 July 2018, https://www.theguardian.com/ business/2018/jul/31/fca-to-take-no-action-against-rbs-after- mistreatment-of-small-businesses

132 Trisha Greenhalgh, 'Narrative medicine in an evidence-based world', *BMJ*, 1999, https://www.ncbi.nlm.nih.gov/pmc/articles/ PMC1114786/

133 Greenhalgh, 'Narrative medicine in an evidence-based world'.

134 http://www.mehl-madrona.com/

135 David Boyle, *Cancelled! The strange story of the collapse of Southern Rail*, Steyning: The Real Press, 2016.

136 *Guardian*, 12 January 2017, https://www.theguardian.com/ commentisfree/2017/jan/12/southern-rail-passengers-strike- self-respect

137 Robert Atkinson and Michael Lind, *Big is Beautiful*, Cambridge: MIT Press, 2018, 48.

138 Beth Kowitt, 'The war on big food', *Fortune*, 21 May 2015, http:// fortune.com/2015/05/21/the-war-on-big-food/

139 Bruce Mazurek, 'Debunking the myth of peak farmers market', *Resilience* blog, 3 March 2015, https://www.resilience.org/ stories/2015-03-03/debunking-the-myth-of-peak-farmers-market/

140 Kowitt, 'The war on big food'.

141 R. G. Barker and P. V. Gump, *Big School, Small School: High school*

size and student behaviour, Stanford, CA: Stanford University Press, 1964.

142　The best collection of evidence on small schools is Kathleen Cotton's article 'New small learning communities: Findings from recent literature' (Portland, Oregon: Northwest Regional Educational Laboratory, 2001). There is a more recent American summary by the Chicago Public Schools System at smallschools. cps.k12.il.us/research.html. The equivalent UK information is available from Human Scale Education at www.hse.org.uk.

143　See for example Theodore Sizer, *Places for Learning Places for Joy*, Cambridge, MA: Harvard University Press, 1973.

144　Dale Bassett et al., *A New Force*, London: Reform, 2009.

145　Evidence of the rising costs in big US hospitals is from Martin Gaynor and Carol Proper, 'Competition in health care: Lessons from the United States', *Bulletin of the Centre for Market and Public Organisation*, Spring 2004.

146　Robert Waterman, *The Frontiers of Excellence*, Boston: Nicholas Brealey, 1994.

147　*Nation*, 3 July 1953.

148　There is considerable literature on this, starting with Jane Jacobs, *The Death and Life of Great American Cities*, New York: Vintage, 1961.

149　See Boyle, *The Human Element*, 30.

150　Michael Power, *The Audit Explosion*, London: Demos, 1994, 22f.

151　See Atkinson and Lind, *Big is Beautiful*, 81–93.

152　E. L. Glaeser and W. Kerr, 'The secret to job growth: Think small', *Harvard Business Review*, July 2010.

153　D. A. Fleming and S. J. Goetz, 'Does local firm ownership matter?', *Economic Development Quarterly* 25:3, August 2011, 277–81.

154　W. Edwards Deming, *Out of the Crisis*, Boston: MIT Press, 1982.

6 Tickbox Politics

155　C. Hood, 'Public administration and public policy: Intellectual challenges for the 1990s', *Australian Journal of Public Administration* 48, 1989, 346–58.

156　R. Gregory, 'Accountability, responsibility and corruption:

Managing the public production process', in J. Boston (ed.), *The State Under Contract*, Wellington, New Zealand: Bridget Williams Books, 1995.

157 Caroline Slocock, *People Like Us: Margaret Thatcher and me*, London: Biteback, 2018.

158 The story is told in Robert Hackett, 'Can This 22-year-old Coder Out-Bitcoin Bitcoin', *Fortune*, 1 October 2016.

159 For more on Green and his friends, see Matthew Leising, 'The Ether Thief', Bloomberg, 13 June 2017.

160 Linda Skitka et al., 'Does automation bias decision-making?' *International Journal of Human-Computer Studies*, 51, 1999, 991–1006, http://www.idealibrary.com

161 Hannah Fry, *Hello World: How to be human in the age of the machine*, London: Doubleday, 2018, 16–19.

162 Jay Stanley, *Pitfalls of Artificial Intelligence*, ACLU, 2017; quoted in Fry, *Hello World*, 18.

163 Jonathan Vanian, 'Unmasking AI's bias problem', *Fortune*, 25 June 2018.

164 Fry, *Hello World*, 197–8.

165 *Evening Standard*, 2 October 2018.

166 See for example Chambers, *Whose Reality Counts?*, 49–55.

167 David Boyle, *Scandal: How homosexuality was criminalised*, Steyning: The Real Press, 2015.

168 See for example Afua Hirsch, 'Toppling statues? Here's why Nelson's column should be next', *Guardian*, 22 August 2017.

169 See my book, *Authenticity: Brands, fakes, spin and the lust for real life*, London: HarperCollins, 2003.

170 Shoshana Zuboff, *The Age of Surveillance Capitalism*, London: Profile, 2019.

171 Zuboff, *The Age of Surveillance Capitalism*, 521.

172 More on this in Fred Turner, *From Counterculture to Cyberculture: Stewart Brand, the Whole Earth network, and the rise of digital utopianism*, Chicago: University of Chicago Press, 2008.

173 Rachel Sylvester, 'All hands on the machines of loving grace', *The Times*, 7 June 2011.

174 *The Independent*, 10 April 2018, https://www.independent.co.uk/life-style/gadgets-and-tech/china-social-

credit-system-punishments-rewards-explained-a8297486.html
175 www.civilexchange.org.uk
176 David Graeber, *The Utopia of Rules*, New York: Melville House, 2015, 149ff.
177 William Morris, *A Dream of John Ball*, London: Swan, 1893, 39–40.

7 Tockbox

178 Ludwig Wittgenstein, *Culture and Value*, Oxford: Basil Blackwell, 1970, 7.
179 Wittgenstein, *Culture and Value*, 5.
180 Ludwig Wittgenstein, *Preliminary Studies for the 'Philosophical Investigations', Generally known as The Blue and Brown Books*, Oxford: Blackwell, 1958, 18.
181 Ray Monk, *Ludwig Wittgenstein: The duty of genius*. New York: Free Press, 1990, 271.
182 See Boyle, *Authenticity*, 195f.
183 David Boyle, *Alan Turing: Unlocking the enigma*, London: Endeavour Press, 2014.
184 I describe this in more detail in David Boyle, 'What's the difference between robots and humans? It's my newt', *Guardian*, 22 September 2016.
185 Boyle, *Authenticity*, 186–7.
186 *Financial Times*, 3 June 2016, https://www.ft.com/content/3be49734-29cb-11e6-83e4-abc22d5d108c
187 Karl R. Popper, 'Of clouds and clocks', in *Objective Knowledge*, Oxford: OUP, 1972.
188 Mark Wasserberg, *Human Scale Thinking at the Heart of a Large School*, Bristol: Human Scale Education, 2010, http://www.heppell.net/vertical_groups/media/HumanScaleThinking attheHeartofaLargeSchoolbyMarkWasserberg.pdf
189 See for example www.openmarkets.org
190 This is the subject of my book, *The Human Element*.
191 Alberto Baccini, 'Boycott the journal rankings', INET Economics, 27 July 2017. See also https://www.ineteconomics.org/research/research-papers/performance-

based-incentives-research-evaluation-systems-and-the-trickle-down-of-bad-science

192 Richard Horton, 'Offline: What is medicine's 5 sigma?', *The Lancet*, 385.9976, 2015, 1380.

193 See for example: Edgar Cahn, *The Co-production Imperative*, Washington: Essential Books, 2000.

194 Atul Gawande, 'Why doctors hate computers', *New Yorker*, 12 November 2018.

195 Quoted in Boyle, *The Tyranny of Numbers*, 62–3.

196 Boyle, *The Human Element*, 135–6.

197 Quoted in David Boyle, *Ronald Laing*, Steyning: The Real Press, 2017, 86.

198 David Boyle, 'Autism: naughty children and the syndrome that became an epidemic', *New Statesman*, 6 October 2003.

199 R. D. Laing, 'God and psychiatry', *Times Literary Supplement*, 23 May 1986.

200 https://medium.com/@leftoutside/please-dont-rate-your-waitress-4-5-1f19ef3c09f8

Index

Index

Index

Index